THE JOY OF BEING
S · O · B · E · R

A BOOK FOR RECOVERING ALCOHOLICS–AND THOSE WHO LOVE THEM

J · A · C · K   M · U · M · E · Y

Contemporary Books, Inc.
Chicago

Library of Congress Cataloging in Publication Data

Mumey, Jack.
  The joy of being sober: a book for
recovering alcoholics—and those who love them.

  Includes index.
  1. Alcoholism—Treatment.   2. Temperance.   I. Title.
HV5275.M85   1984   362.2'9286   84-1768
ISBN 0-8092-5433-6
ISBN 0-8092-4997-9 (pbk.)

Copyright © 1984 by Jack Mumey
All rights reserved
Published by Contemporary Books, Inc.
180 North Michigan Avenue, Chicago, Illinois 60601
Manufactured in the United States of America
Library of Congress Catalog Card Number: 84-1768
International Standard Book Number: 0-8092-5433-6 (cloth)
                                    0-8092-4997-9 (paper)

Published simultaneously in Canada by Beaverbooks, Ltd.
195 Allstate Parkway, Valleywood Business Park
Markham, Ontario L3R 4T8 Canada

For my wife, Mary Jo . . .
For my children:
Jackson
Tracey
Dana
Dawn,
You had the courage to turn love into action.

Contents

Preface

This is a guidebook for sobriety; the kind of sobriety that means going through your life with a smile on your face instead of looking like you were the bearer of doom and gloom. A guidebook of any kind is designed to show the paths and the runways that one takes through the brush-tangled wilderness of the unknown. It has been my intention from the beginning of this project to make a strong point; namely, this is not a compendium on the treatment of alcoholism, nor does it pretend to take the place of any kind of treatment, private, public, or individual. Secondly, this is a book that contains *tools* for use in leading a joyous sober life. Like any other tool, if you pick it up and learn to use it, it will help get a job accomplished. If you let it lie there, it will be of no use whatsoever!

This book contains methods that I have used in my own recovery program; it outlines successful methods that I have employed as a therapist with other people recovering from the disease of alcoholism. I know these ideas work because I'm alive to be able to share them with you; there was a time when that right to life was in serious jeopardy because of alcohol abuse.

When you speak of the *Joy of Being Sober,* it is almost in direct opposition to what alcohol has been used for in the past. You *drank* to be joyful; at least that was the *temporary* feeling you got when you used alcohol as a means of relieving the stress, tension, and anxieties of everyday human existence. Now, sober, it is my hope you will discover that there is a *permanent* method to feeling so good about your life, yourself, and all whose lives you touch, through the *absence* of alcohol and a commitment to lifelong recovery in sobriety.

The tools in this book can work; they can lead you to discover other tools and ideas of your own that will help you understand what the difference is between being *dry* and being *sober*. If one such idea contained within these pages helps any person suffering through the very trying times of recovery from this devastating disease, then all the effort will have been repaid ten-thousandfold! Speaking of effort, this book would not have been possible without the tremendous support that the author has received from so many different sources.

Many other therapists and alcohol counselors have touched my life, both professionally and personally, in my own recovery. It would be difficult to try and remember them all, but a few people are singularly outstanding as being persons who never wavered in their encouragement. Tyrone Owens comes to mind as one of those. It was "Ty" who was instrumental in getting so much of my attention focused on the process of crisis intervention. It is Ty who continues to care what happens to me. Dr. Larry Gibson continues to this day as a valued friend and colleague. Significant contributions to my own confidence level have been made by Elizabeth "Liz" Telford, one of my running partners who would regularly infuse ideas for a particular chapter while we jogged many miles, alternately arguing, then agreeing on a point or two.

Continental Air Lines Captain Eugene ''Gene'' Dahlquist, Jerry Keenan, David Scott, Lee Gash, Ben Avery, Ernie Long, and Gene Cooper, all were patient soundingboards for various chapter ideas, comments, and criticism. Ruby Nielsen was never too busy for a word of encouragement. My spiritual advisors Del Wiemers and Dave Peters could never be replaced for their help, love, and support.

My mother, Ruth Printz Mumey, would have loved this book and would have been proud of what it meant to our lives. She never knew about it, having died as the result of a tragic automobile accident.

She did live, however, to see her only son begin the process of recovery, and it was a source of great joy for her. All the more, I know, because she herself was alcoholic and succumbed, partially, due to the ravages the disease had made upon her, preventing her from fully coming back from the accident itself. "Nanna" in death inspired a joy to live — sober.

My wife Mary Jo has spent hours pouring over the galley proofs with me, and as always, has been my staunchest supporter in this project while maintaining that detached perspective that has made her the professional woman she is, having worn her nurse's badge with honor and pride since the day it was first pinned on her. She is a loving partner, for sure!

Each of my children have made their own special contributions. The long-distance calls (collect, or not!) were always filled with "You can do it, Dad!" Their own personal recollections of events and problems of recovery have been invaluable.

My neighbor Mike Bond has given generously of his expertise in his capacity as an alcohol program director specialist.

There cannot be enough said for the contribution to this book made by my friend, colleague, and partner Paul F. Staley. It has been Paul's constant encouragement, ever-present and patient dissecting, level sense of perspective, and strong guidance of the direction of not only our treatment center, but of his dedication to the quality of health care service for recovering persons, that has been a source of inspiration for me. Paul and his wife Sandy never waivered in their belief that the book could and would happen.

Finally, I am most indebted to the memory and words of Sir Winston Churchill, whose particular paragraph from one of his tomes became my own personal whip; a challenge that went with me wherever my typewriter or pad were. He said: "Writing a book was an adventure. To begin with it was a toy . . . then it became a mistress, and then a master, and then a tyrant, and in the last phase, when you are reconciled to your servitude, you kill the monster."

From quiet homes and first beginning,
Out to the undiscovered ends,
There's nothing worth the wear of winning,
But laughter and the love of friends.

Hilaire Bellock

1
The Joy of Recovery

The "New Wave" music assaulted our eardrums, as we were positioned far too close to the mobile sound van and its attendant loudspeakers. I didn't need the music to hype me up, I was already "pumped" to full throttle and was in the cooling-down process that accompanies the conclusion of a race.

My wife and one of my twin daughters had never seen me run before, and I felt a lot of personal pride when I spied them among the cheering group that greets the runners as they head for the "chutes" at the conclusion of the race.

It had been a surprisingly tough race for me, a novice in this business of human body-against-dirt road spectacle played out by several hundred persons that Saturday morning. The hill that hit us right after we had cleared the first mile of the scheduled 3.1 mile (5,000 meter) race course had been advertised as "mild." The hell it was!

Bunches of people were *walking* up that hill, sipping or splashing water from the paper cups handed us as we rounded the bend. I wasn't about to stop running. You run for the sake of *finishing* at a sustained pace, and no hill was going to get me if I could help it.

My running coach, colleague, and friend, Paul (more about him in Chapter 4) had kept reminding me: "Don't pay attention to what the others are doing. Just run your own race, your own speed and stride."

Well, I had done just that, saying over and over to myself, like a child reading the story, *The Little Train That Thought It Could,* "I can make it! I can make it!"

I had made it. Up the hill, around the continuing slight incline that made up the next three-quarters of the course, then back through the mile and a half to the finish line.

Like I said, it had been a tough race for me. My wife and daughter and our house guests, who had also come out at the crack of dawn to see the race, decided to head back to our house to start Saturday morning brunch. I wanted to stay for the awards ceremony. I had never done that before. And besides, I couldn't just run 5,000 meters and then wolf down a big breakfast.

I visited with others waiting in a large circle by the sound van, talking, as always, about the "next one." Racing gets in your blood and you rearrange whole weeks of schedules to make another race somewhere in the state — or the country, for that matter.

The music was cut and the awards ceremony began. Not much to it, really. The announcer began with the first place, then second and third place winners in each category, male and female divisions, starting with the youngest participants.

The sponsor of this particular race was the Adolph Coors Brewing Company, and appropriate trophies of placcques, beer goblets, steins, and ribbons were the prizes.

I stood and applauded with the rest as each win, place, and show runner walked out of the circle and up to the announcer to shake his hand and receive the well-earned trophy.

I remarked to a fellow runner that you can always tell the first-race participants; they're the ones wearing the T-shirt that is part of the entry packet for that day's event. Two races ago I had learned that one doesn't wear even the T-shirt to run the race. You wear the shirt, shorts, or prize shoes only *after* the race as a symbol of having competed and finished. I was wearing my Bill Rodgers racing shirt. The Indian beadwork headband I always wear when running was still nailed to my forehead, and it was getting darned hot. I had managed to remove my "Bone-Fone" radio that I wore during the race. (More on that, too, in Chapter 4.)

The announcer was up to my age category: "Male Division, fifty years old, plus."

"The hell with Plus! I'm just fifty, and who cares for plus?" ran through my mind.

The first-place winner was announced, and he stepped forward to

2

much applause — a fine specimen of a guy who had posted a most respectable time for finish. He received a nice wall placque. And then, my God, they were calling my name for second place!

I walked out of the circle and up to the man handing out the trophies. He shook my hand with a hearty, "Congratulations!" and reached into the trophy box. Out came a beautiful, heavy pilsner-style beer glass, the kind that must hold twenty-four ounces. The logo so familiar around the country, "Coors," was emblazoned in red on the goblet. "Thanks," I mumbled, and walked back to the circle, receiving shouts of "Good race!" and "Congrats!" from several onlookers.

Second place! My time had been no track burner, but it was plenty respectable, and my decision to keep running that hill instead of walking it and then trying for a blaze finish had obviously been right. And then the enormity of what I had just accomplished hit me.

Less than three years ago I had been seated in an alcohol recovery ward of St. Luke's Hospital in Denver, Colorado. There were about forty of us on the ward and "Doc" Larry Gibson had just dropped a bomb on me in front of God and everyone.

"Jack Mumey, where are you?" he queried.

"Here, Doc," I raised my hand, still shaking from recent release out of the De-Tox unit.

"Well, Jack, I've got some bad news for you. We just got your neurological data back from University Hospital. You've suffered severe damage to the right hemisphere of your brain, alcoholic impairment, which is why you haven't been walking straight."

"Good God! What was this madman saying?" I thought.

"The damage is severe . . . you might not ever walk straight again."

The impact on me was devastating. My twenty-five-year-plus career in radio and television was down the tubes. I began to cry right there, in that hospital ward room. How the hell could I have let alcohol do this to me? How could I ever go "on camera" again, read copy, or even take a simple piece of stage blocking and make sure it would work? How could I make a living if that brain damage could not be reversed?

But I have since learned that the disease of alcoholism can be conquered — not cured, but put in total remission. It happened to me, and some of the ways that I have learned to make life abundant and joyous are what this book is all about.

As I crossed the parking lot, heading toward my car, I started a slow jog. Some well-wishers saw the red ribbon pinned to my racing number on my shirt, spied the huge pilsner glass in my right hand, and shouted out, "Hey, way to go!"

I grinned and indulged myself in raising both arms "Rocky"-like above my head and shouted back, "Thanks! . . . It's the joy of recovery!"

They didn't know what I meant, but that didn't matter. I knew. The pilsner glass sits today on our home bar, jammed full of pennies. When it's full, they go to the bank and I start filling it again. It's a small, insignificant award in the great scheme of things. But every day of my life of sobriety as a recovering alcoholic is filled with this same joy of living.

What follows in these chapters can help you live your life full of enthusiasm — being a winner over the disease of alcoholism. These chapters are tools that I lay before you. Pick them up! Use them! They are tried and tested procedures that can help you experience the Joy of Recovery!

2
Changing Your Attitude

"Easy for *you* to say!"

"You don't know how tough it *really* is!"

"Why don't *you* try giving up drinking, and see?"

"What the hell *fun* is there?"

"Is *this* what it's going to be like from now on?"

Well, you get the idea. If I listed all the pitiful mournings that have crossed my desk from recovering alcoholics, or better yet, the ones from the *families* of the recovering person, this could be just a book of excuses.

Instead, what we are going to discuss together in this chapter are three monsters of recovery that seem to prevent a change in attitude, a change that *must* happen to your personality to help cement the years of your recovery. These three monsters can be called:

1. The Pity Pot
2. The Grey Ghost Syndrome
3. The Sackcloth and Ashes Number

Now in a way these monsters are all related, for they describe bad, bad attitudes that prevent you from "rejoicing at the firelight," or realizing that all "you see was . . . and still is . . . yours."

Coming back to the world of the living from the end-of-the-line world of alcoholism does not happen overnight; and quite frankly, no one should expect it to. After all, in most cases, the person afflicted with the disease of alcoholism has spent years perfecting the habits of drunken behavior. We should not, therefore, expect an overnight miracle where suddenly everything is coming up roses! It doesn't happen that way.

What we can do, is recognize that our "stinking thinking" from the use of alcohol does not vanish with the booze itself. I have a close friend who never lets himself forget that the old snake of alcohol is always sleeping, always ready to rise up and strike. Mark does this by keeping a perfectly grotesque ceramic statue of a hooded cobra, complete with red beady eyes, staring at him from the dresser opposite his bed. I've told Mark I think that's a bit bizarre, but it works for him. It keeps his attitude on the right track.

If there is to be a serious attempt to adopt a new attitude, it is necessary to review what it is that we are changing—alcoholic behavior. And alcoholic behavior and consequent attitudes about life in general come from the abuse of the drug, alcohol. The disease of alcoholism knows no barriers of race, color, creed, sex, or age.

Keep in mind that what you have is a *disease,* so classified as early as 1782 by Dr. Benjamin Rush. The American Medical Association recognizes it as such and so should you. There are many definitions of alcoholism, but I like to use two to demonstrate the range of absurdity that can and does surround the disease. Here they are: (1) "Alcoholism is really an outward manifestation of an underlying deep-seated drinking problem," said Dr. Robert Stuckey at a recent Sunday Symposium on alcoholism sponsored by the AMA which I attended. He was, of course, speaking very much tongue-in-cheek, for Dr. Stuckey is a very knowledgeable practitioner in the field of treatment for alcoholics. (2) "Alcoholism is really a Valium deficiency." That one has been used so often I can't even quote the original source. The unfortunate part is that too many psychiatrists treat alcoholism just that way—with Valium, a drug having the same chemical effect as alcohol, equivalent to dried Vodka!

How do we know that alcoholism is a disease? We know it because the definition of disease in worldwide use is that it is diagnosable, treatable, progressive, and fatal; alcoholism is all of these things.

1. **Alcoholism is diagnosable.** Your doctor has been seeing signs that are clear blueprints to alcohol abuse. The fluid and electrolyte balance in you has been disturbed. The cardiovascular functions and

carbohydrate metabolism are probably out of whack. You have an elevated blood pressure, and hypertension is clearly linked to alcoholism. Your doctor has seen trauma from your liver indicating that it is fatty; it is not performing its filtering, cleansing functions like it should. He checks the heart again. Alcohol impairs cardiac performance, and the doctor may have detected sub-acute cardiomyopathy — fatty heart. That's not good, friend.

2. **Alcoholism is treatable.** We cannot cure the disease of alcoholism, but it *can* be treated. You and I and the rest of the millions of Americans afflicted with this disease will die alcoholics, but we can die *sober* alcoholics. Treatment programs throughout the world have been designed and are operating with the success factors necessary to put the disease into remission. So you can know that you can live a fruitful life as a treatable, if not curable, alcoholic.

3. **Alcoholism is progressive.** This characteristic that permits alcoholism to be classified as a disease is, of course, disturbing. It shoots down completely the notion that an alcoholic can quit after one or two drinks. No way! It is the nature of the addiction to alcohol that no untreated alcoholic will get better in handling the drug. It's like the *Crackerjacks* slogan, "The More You Eat, The More You Want!" With alcohol it's "The More You Drink, The More You Drink!" Relevant to this point in the classification of alcoholism as a disease is the fact that it is a *primary* disease; that is, it is not the result of something else that is wrong with you. For example, hypoglycemia (a deficiency of sugar in the blood) is due to alcoholism, not the other way around.

4. **Finally, alcoholism is fatal.** Alcoholism, untreated, unchecked, allowed to run its vicious lifelong course, will kill. It is a *fatal* disease. Once the liver has ceased to perform its cleansing functions, and the heart has been strangled by alcohol, when the anxiety, depression, insomnia and other dysfunctioning of the human body have reached their alcoholic peak, the disease will claim its victim.

Cirrhosis of the liver is the nation's seventh biggest killer. Those who die of cirrhosis die a painful death. Ninety percent of the deaths will be to alcoholics, and *ten percent* of alcoholics will get cirrhosis — sobering thoughts, don't you agree?

So now we've dealt with the enemy, and it is ours. Alcoholism is a disease. We can begin to change our attitudes, and step one is: It's okay to have a disease! That's right. If it's okay to have blonde hair, brown eyes, be a little too short or a little too heavy around the jowls, it's okay to have a disease, a disease that you are in the process of treating.

You are not doomed to a life of mediocrity because of this disease, and you certainly don't have to keep nurturing the attitudes that stop you from enjoying your recovery.

When the doctor who first treated your alcoholism put you into treatment, you should have put the old attitudes into the same treatment. Unfortunately, you probably didn't, so now is the time to start taking action. That brings us back to the three monsters I spoke of earlier: the *Pity Pot,* the *Grey Ghost Syndrome,* and the *Sackcloth and Ashes Number.* Remember, they are all related; they can all be *treated,* even though you may carry them with you for the remainder of your recovery, which means the rest of your life. If you know about them and are willing to talk about them, you can put them into almost permanent remission. I said *almost.* Every once in a while one or the other of these maladies of recovery is going to jump up again, and you will have to be prepared to deal with it.

1. **The Pity Pot.** This is a porcelain, or at the least a cold, heavy metal chamber pot that seems to have the miraculous ability to defy physics and expand to several times its normal size. The more you are sitting on this Pity Pot, the larger the rim grows, and before your very eyes (or bottom) you are falling into this pot instead of sitting on it. It is very difficult to pull yourself back up to where you are just sitting on the rim again. In fact, I think it's nearly impossible!

Here you are. It's a perfectly beautiful summer Saturday, and you are tackling the lawn-mowing job. You pause at the completion of your chore and survey the great job of mowing (*this* time you did the whole job instead of leaving huge patches, like in your drinking days) when your neighbor pops over to borrow some lawn-mower gas. Right there, clutched in the hand not occupied with the empty gas can is, God Forbid, a cold can of beer!

It's the coldest, biggest can of beer you've ever seen. They probably used this very can of beer to make the award-winning television commercial. This can of beer is being held by your helpful neighbor, who probably doesn't know you're recovering (see Chapter 13), and has just got to be the ultimate thirst-quencher! Every rivulet of water on the can is in place. The sun has caught the sparkle of each tiny drop and fixed its brilliance on the label. The *smell* is overwhelming! And you, you poor, pitiful thing, you CAN'T HAVE EVEN ONE GOLDEN DELICIOUS SIP!

Poor, poor, you! The Pity Pot has beckoned! As you reluctantly hand your neighbor your gas can, and watch him take both his can of beer and your can of gas away, the agony has struck. You can't wait to climb on the Pity Pot. Out comes the long face accompanied by the deep sigh and the muttered curse.

"What's the matter, Hon?" says wifey from her vantage point in the geranium bed.

"Nothing, 'dammit!" you growl. "Stop nagging me!"

And into the house you skulk, headed for the Pity Pot. As you climb upon its ever-widening rim, the old support attitudes start in.

"A cold beer always tasted great after mowing the lawn!"

"Boy, there's *nothing* like a cold beer on a hot Saturday!" (This can be reworded to accommodate whichever of the seven days of the week it was that you drank cold beer — probably *all* of them!)

"Why can't I have just *one* cold beer?"

"Hell, I did a good job mowing the lawn. I *deserve* a reward, don't I?"

By this time, you've practically fallen clear in. The only thing that will stop the descent is a change of attitude led by the key trooper, **Verbalization.**

That's right! You *talk* about it, right out there in front of God and your spouse. You learn to *say* what the matter is! Let's rerun the previous dialogue, this time with a change of attitude:

WIFE: "What's the matter, Hon?"

NEW YOU: "I want a cold beer so damn bad I can't stand it!"

WIFE: (Understanding) "I know you do."

NEW YOU: (Starting personal reinforcement) "I never did this good a job mowing when I was drinking, though!"

WIFE: (Picking up the cue) "*Everything* you do now is better, Hon!"

NEW YOU: (Losing it a little) "Yeah, but these hot summer days . . . that's when beer tasted best!

WIFE: (With pain) "You never stopped with one beer!"

NEW YOU: (More re-inforcing the positive) "God, I guess! I never even stopped with one six pack! The lawn looked like hell for weeks!"

WIFE: (Planting a kiss instead of a geranium) "*You* looked like hell for weeks!"

NEW YOU: (Putting the nail to the coffin) "And the hangovers made Sundays twice as bad as Saturdays!"

(Appropriate hugs, warm fuzzies are exchanged.)

Well, that's gotten you off the Pity Pot. You *verbalized* your feelings, shared them with another person so that the anguish over not drinking did not have a chance to internalize itself and become deep-seated resentment at being in the recovery process. This turning off the negative attitudes by talking about the *positive* aspects of not drinking, i.e., "Lawn never looked this good," "*You* never looked this good," "hangovers," all help you climb off the Pity Pot before the rim enlarges and let's you fall in. I suggest to people that are really hung up on how good a cold can or glass of beer looks to try a little picture changing technique I learned from my television director days.

Try this. First, look at the big, cold, can of beer. As you stare at it start a "slow dissolve" of one picture into another. Imagine that label on the beer can is changing to read, "Premium *Blood.*" That's right, blood! Imagine your name in fancy script on that label. That can of beer is not very appetizing now, is it?

Drinking for you means sure death. For the non-alcoholic, that beer is what it's intended to be, a fine thirst-quencher. For you, it means poison. I never could envision what a really gruesome can of poison should look like, so I turned to the "blood" image. It works too. I have clients who have reported back that a pitcherful of draft beer so effectively turned to blood before their minds' eyes that they practically called an end to the affair they were attending by pointing this out to the rest of the assembled guests, all of whom were enjoying their pitchers of beer and *not* recovering!

Well, that may or may not be an extreme. Point is, the imaging and the verbalization process will help you get off the Pity Pot. The other vanguard to this attack is to simply state: "I think I must be on the Pity Pot! I'm feeling kind of sorry for myself!"

Once this is said, you'll find the self-pity begin to disappear. So, you are changing your attitude by learning not to keep things *bottled up* inside. You are changing your attitude by learning to give *sight* and *sound* to your *feelings* and to allow yourself the luxury of saying in a forthright manner the pluses and the minuses of a given situation with the special emphasis on reinforcing the way things are *better* now that you are in the recovery process. You'll always find the Pity Pot is lurking just around your emotional corner, but you can make sure that the rim doesn't get larger and swallow you up!

2. **The Grey Ghost Syndrome.** If you want to walk around like Hamlet's father for the rest of your life, go ahead! I tell my recovering clients to go read the story of *Winnie the Pooh,* paying very close attention to poor old miserable, Eeyore.

"Gosh, Pooh," sighs Eeyore, "it's a blustery day!"

Every day is going to be blustery if you make it one. The idea that because you can't get pie-eyed anymore means that the kicks are all gone out of your life is ridiculous.

The Grey Ghost Syndrome makes me madder than anything else in trying to teach the Joy of Recovery. There are those persons who simply believe that all this world's pleasures revolve around the ability to drink alcohol. Thus, hands shoved firmly into coat pockets, collar turned up against the chill winds of despair, the "Grey Ghost" shuffles through his/her sobriety. What nonsense! Are you trying to tell me that little kid with the shiny red wagon is looped the way she hauls her dolls around the playyard? That young couple walking hand in hand with a *Pepsi* being shared between them are drunk alright — drunk on the joys of just being alive. But the "Grey Ghost" is comfortable with his dark forboding and sullen mood. He's working at becoming a recovering zombie!

"I used to have fun when I was drinking," he mutters.

"What's the use of going to the ball game now?" he intones in deathly-low registers.

"I can't *possibly* enjoy dinner out without booze. I'll be a total *bore,*" says the female Grey Ghost.

Ad infinitum. Ad nauseum.

The Grey Ghost Syndrome strikes most generally after a session on the Pity Pot when nothing has been done to start the attitude-changing process. The Grey Ghost stalks the streets of his/her life now devoid of alcohol, and honestly believes that drinking was fun, and that life can't be fun now without it. Well, drinking was *not* fun! Having to call in sick the "next day" because you have been struck with that ancient malady of drinkers, "Irish Flu," waking up in a strange city, having no idea how you got there — that was *fun?* Facing the threat of divorce because you made one pass too many at your mate's best friend — that was *fun?* Hitting your small defenseless youngsters in a fit of drunken anger is fun? I think not, but there are people who absolutely believe that the only role left for them is that of the Grey Ghost, and you need to be counted among those *absent* from that game! So how do you shed the mantle of the Grey Ghost? Well, it's done with mirrors.

When you believe that there is no fun left for you because you are sober and you feel the image of the Grey Ghost creeping into your being, get yourself quickly in front of a mirror, alone. Look closely. The deep-set eyes that were bleary from abuse of alcohol are now in proper position.

Talk to yourself. Say, "No more sagging jowels, that's good!" Pinch your cheeks and watch the red spring to your touch. Say, "Good! Blood circulation is better."

Peer even closer. Notice that the whites of your eyes are now *white;* that awful pale yellow of liver dysfunction has cleared up. Now move back so you are full-length. Pinch at your waist. You may still have a bulge here and there or your "love handles" may still be in evidence, but you say to your image, "Looking good! I'm losing the weight that alcohol was adding; if I keep it up I'm going to be a size smaller!"

The Grey Ghost will begin to be supplanted by an image staring back at you that's full of confidence. But here's the final kicker. Try to resurrect a picture of yourself taken at a party or family outing during your drinking days. Look at it real hard. Then look again at the image of yourself today, as you are in sobriety.

Say out loud, "I'll *never* look like *that* again!" Say it and mean it. There's no room for the Grey Ghost in your life of recovery. Oh, he'll keep trying to creep back in now and then, but you'll know how to deal with him (or her). I named my Grey Ghost. He's called "Ole Creepy," and whenever I think that he's about to pull a number on me, I whip out a polaroid shot we keep in a drawer downstairs. It's enough to make me cry, seeing how I used to look in my drinking days. It's also enough to banish "Ole Creepy" and his despair from my presence. When a member of my family sees me looking at that picture, he knows that I'm doing battle with the Grey Ghost Syndrome. And I win!

3. **The Sackcloth and Ashes Number.** Finally we treat with not too loving care the last factor involved in changing attitude. The Sackcloth and Ashes Number can really keep you down in the trenches, if you let it. What this means, simply stated, is as follows:

What is done is done! You can't go back and undo all the dismal things that you did while in an alcoholic state. It isn't possible to take back the harsh words, abusive behavior, or other memorabilia of your drinking times. The smashed car fenders, broken romances, unbalanced checkbooks, and just plain no-account checks have all been dealt with one way or another, and nothing you can say or do will change that.

Except one thing. You can tell anyone who will listen that you have said you are sorry, and you've said it for the last time. Alcoholic amnesia, "blackouts" as we call them, are a frequent and distressful malady of alcoholism. What you said and what you did as a practicing drinker are over now, and should be done with.

In a word, it's time to take off your sackcloth and penitential ashes and get on with the business of seeing to it that your life is full of meaning from here on out. You'll not change what happened before sobriety, and the quickest way to change your attitude is to stop flogging yourself and trying to win the Academy Award for "Best Dramatic Performance."

The Fellowship of Alcoholics Anonymous makes an excellent point when it admonishes to "make amends (for past wrongs), except when to do so would injure them (or yourself) or others." The "them" refers to the people whose lives you may have messed up by your alcoholism. I added "yourself" because somewhere you have to be *willing to forgive yourself!*

Admitting all your past sins while under John Barleycorn's influence is good for your recovery, *up to a point.* After that, it becomes simply an easy way out of the business of picking up the pieces of your life and getting on with the important business of joyful recovery.

Therefore, cast off this mantle of ashes. Step out of the sackcloth. Go buy yourself some new duds! I don't care if it's just a baseball cap, an inexpensive blouse, or a new tie. Whatever! Just get some new item of clothing for yourself and promptly dub it your "get-rid-of-my-sackcloth" item.

I chose to take a pair of jeans and cut them off, not very expertly, I'll admit. But it became a symbol for me to have cast off (cut off) the old "sin bag" and start new. I got a little carried away because I got hooked on designer jeans, and they're expensive. That was some of my "stinking thinking" about money values creeping back in, so I needed a little help from my wife to keep from running out and buying forty dollar "name" label jeans and whacking them off. You've constantly got to be on guard against the bad habits of the addictive personality!

So, attitude changing is a key to the secret of enjoying sobriety. You have to use this tool every day of your life. You have to force yourself to take the littlest of things and make big comparisons. When you successfully handle a misunderstanding, you say to yourself, "How would I have handled that when I was drinking?"

When you close a big business deal you say, "Would I have put this together when I was drinking? Would I have made any money?" When you kiss someone goodnight you can say to yourself, "Would I have even been allowed this close, smelling like I must have smelled?" In short, what you *were* was an active, *drinking* alcoholic. What you *are,* now, today, is a recovering, joyful, sober alcoholic. There is a difference. *Vive la difference!* Get off the Pity Pot! Bury the Grey Ghost! Step out of the Sackcloth!

*Well, every one can master a grief
but he that has it.*
Shakespeare
Much Ado About Nothing

3
The Dry Drunk Syndrome

"She talks kinda slurred, but I *know* she isn't drinking!"

"His temper's just as bad as when he was drinking!"

"He stormed around the house all weekend, banging doors and generally making everybody else's life hell!"

"She still doesn't balance the damn checkbook! *That's* the way she acted in her drinking days!"

Sound familiar? Sure it does. For every sentence like these there are hundreds and thousands of others uttered by the family and friends of recovering alcoholics. They have sat with me in group therapy when we go around the room and have everyone talk about a behavior pattern observed from the newly sober person in their life.

Hey! That's you and me acting like that! It's been called the *Dry Drunk Syndrome,* and a simple definition of this malaise is the discomfort experienced by the recovering person when he is no longer drinking. It's intoxication and its related behavior *without drinking alcohol.*

It's a state of mind that makes the recovering person act as if he had never stopped drinking, and indeed can be a serious roadblock to total recovery.

This erratic behavior doesn't go away in a few weeks or months, either. It crops up for some people on a regular basis, just like Christmas. You're going along minding your own business when all of a sudden, Wham!

It generally starts with a domestic argument. The simple things in life that get to us and get blown all out of proportion. I think I first heard Dr. Larry Gibson describe these little annoyances as "mouse turds." And that's what they are. We don't worry so much about the recovering person running up Pike's Peak or swimming the English Channel. What needs to be watched is the great possibility of stumbling over life's little mouse turds.

I do it all the time — stumble over the damn mouse turds. What anybody else can handle in the normal course of his daily life, gets all out of whack with me, and probably with you, too. This is because we have been so involved with alcoholic behavior in the past that caused the *excuses* for abominable behavior that we turn to the same kinds of action to excuse us now, when we're sober. Except the alcohol is gone; all that's left is the *action* of alcoholic behavior. Hence, the door-slamming (particularly rough on storm doors because they tend to close nice and efficient-like no matter how hard they're slammed), name-calling, and general "let's-blame-it-all-on-you" dialogues that go with a Dry Drunk.

A close friend of mine who has been in recovery for more than eleven years, told me of getting mad at his wife recently and throwing her car keys in a snowbank while they were on a skiing trip.

"That's the same damn stunt I pulled the last time I got drunk," he told me. We laughed over it, remembering that I had told him at the time that he had better do something about his "drinking problem." He did, but the old Dry Drunk Syndrome still stalks him on occasion, and goes about laying life's little mouse turds in his path.

The Dry Drunk can occur at anytime, anyplace. It's a convenient method employed by the recovering person to cover his or her actions. If the checkbook *doesn't* balance, maybe not even close, the Dry Drunker can say, "You know how I am with things like this!"

She will go on to explain to an exasperated mate that *she knows* how much she has in her checking account so what the hell difference does it make if the little figures on the damn bank statement agree or not?

Or the guy who says he can handle criticism about the way he does a particular job, then flies off the handle the first time that he gets negative feedback. That's the Dry Drunk Syndrome at work. It is telling us that we still are not taking *responsibility* for our actions, and that was one of the key reasons we were forgiven over and over again when we were drinking. No one wanted to blame the alcoholic for what he or she did because after all, we weren't *responsible* for our actions! That's a great comfort and security blanket for life.

Well, that excuse doesn't belong anymore, and when we feel things piling up on us, the ole Dry Drunk creeps along probably at the same time we're on the Pity Pot, and SOCKO! Another mouse turd lands us in the dust.

As long as the recovering person refuses to accept responsibility for life-actions, the Dry Drunk Syndrome will continue to play an all-too-important part in slowing the real joy of recovery. So what do you do about it?

Well, one thing that seems to work is to inform the rest of the folks who are important to you about this Dry Drunk Syndrome. Ask them to point out such behavior to you when they see it happen. Now I know that can be a dangerous weapon, so let's set some ground rules.

1. The Dry Drunk is not an excuse for *all* irrational behavior. Some folks just have a bad temper and non-drinking didn't change that. Call it what it is. "Don't blame *this* on a Dry Drunk, Charlie! You're just plain pissed off at me because I forgot to get the snow tires put on the car! You've a right to be angry!" Now what *this* does is say, "It's okay to be angry, but let's call it for what it is and not create an excuse (Dry Drunk) for blowing up."

2. It will be absolutely essential to be honest with me at all times. "Honey, I'm feeling like I've been grouchy and maybe a little short today. Have I?" Anything less than the absolute truth will only feed into the Dry Drunk and prolong its agony. *Your* part of this rule is that when you get an honest answer, accept it.

3. Verbalize. When you know you are in a Dry Drunk, for Lord's sake tell someone about it! "George, I didn't mean to snap at you last night. I think I'm in a Dry Drunk and I probably tripped on a mouse turd or two at the office yesterday."

4. Ask for help. If you had a broken arm you certainly would ask the doctor to set it. Same thing is true with this recovery business. Ask for help. "I'm feeling like the whole world's against me. I know it's a Dry Drunk coming on. C'mon, let's go for a walk, can we?" Asking for help is different than asking someone else to tell you what a jackass you've become in the last twenty-four hours. It's also taking the steam out of a full-blown fight because who will fight with anyone who already admits that they are in a foul mood and want help to get back on track?

5. Be willing to *accept* help. It's one thing to say "Help me" and then refuse all meaningful attempts. I have heard clients discuss this problem over and over. Husband (recovering) says he wants help to

get out of the Dry Drunk Syndrome he knows is upon him. Wife suggests a picnic. "Nope."

"How about going for a drive."

"No way. Every damn fool in town drives to the hills on Sunday."

"Let's go to a movie."

"What? Spend ten bucks to have a bunch of house rabbits (kids) running up and down the aisles?"

And so forth. Everything suggested to meet the cry for help finds its way to the discard pile, and life continues to be dull and boring for all concerned. The significant other people in the life of the recovering alcoholic *do* have incredible patience, sometimes bordering on true martyrdom, but even that patient string will run out. You have to be willing to take some risks! Run some rapids! Even if you don't care for the initial suggestion to help you through the Dry Drunk, once you have started out to do *something* it will begin to soften its grip on your mood.

There are some other clues to recognizing the Dry Drunk, and you will probably begin to make a mental list of your own to use as tools to recognize this syndrome.

One clue is the tendency to be grandiose about everything. When you were on the "active" drinking list, there were all those "pie-in-the-sky" plans you would brag about/tell about. The big business deal that was "just around the corner," the "trip abroad" for your next anniversary, or the "step up" the promotional ladder, were all part of your everyday pattern and life-style.

The problem is, those same patterns crop up in the Dry Drunk. They come easily to the surface because they were habit forming just like the rest of your alcoholic behavior. They don't belong in your recovery flight plan, however. The one sure way I use to keep such things in check is to sit down with a legal pad and write down all the things I said I was going to do over the past few years. That goes in one column marked, "Promised."

In an opposing column I list what actually got done. This column is headed, "Delivered." One look at that page nearly always brings my thinking back to earth. That doesn't mean you should stop dreaming; it only means that you need to recognize what is said in alcoholic states of mind can also be repeated in Dry Drunk states of mind. That's when you have to apply the bridle to yourself and start dealing with reality. You do this by compromise.

The "trip abroad" *can* be a family motor trip that has long been delayed. Not long ago a family sat in my office and told me with tears in their eyes that they had had the best time *ever* on a trip to Disneyland. It was the first trip they had ever made as a sober family, and it was a delivered promise that had been made many times before only to be washed away in the tide of booze.

Other recovering persons I know tell me they ask to see their work evaluations after gaining their sobriety. In almost all cases seeing the improved nature of their work habits has been like a promotion. It has been a tonic without gin for them, and honest-to-God promotions come shortly thereafter. They don't have to create false positions; they earn newer respect with their recovery plan.

Another compromise is to turn the "big business deal" into a little, solid victory. Try selling something through the newspaper classified ads. You'll probably make a few bucks and you'll renew your confidence in yourself. It doesn't have to be a big deal to be a successful one. I used a car that everyone told me would never bring what I wanted for it. They were right! But after two weeks of haggling on the phone and showing the damn thing in response to the ad, I got close enough to my price to prove I could still handle a "big deal." *That's* compromise.

Another clue for recognizing the Dry Drunk is when you seem to throw out so many ideas and thoughts in any one conversation that people have a hard time keeping up with what you are trying to say, what point you are trying to make. This "confetti" approach is a sure sign that the old habits are creeping in and that a Dry Drunk is about to set itself upon you. This "confetti" number is the old-drinking-you thinking that you have the answer to everything and that only your opinion counts. It's a hard habit to break, but one way is to say out loud, "Am I making any sense here?" A little laugh after that question gives enough pause to get you an honest answer and allow you time to re-sort your thinking into more orderly patterns. Two or three "confetti" conversations in a row will turn on a warning light that says, "Hold it, Buster; here you go again talking like the great Guru, just like when you were drinking!"

See, for every drunken action there's an equal and opposing sober reaction. All you have to do is *label* your behavior. "My God! That last statement sounded like something I would say if I were still drinking!" Or, "Did that sound like a sober statement? (Small laugh.) Let me run that by again and see if it makes sense."

Above all, you must guard against overreacting to life's mouse turds. It isn't anyone else's fault that you can never drink again. Your anger, frustration, and grief will boil to the surface in a Dry Drunk over and over again unless you are able to identify them. Did I say "Grief?" Yep!

There is a definite grieving process that you will go through on your road to recovery. That's why I have stated that the "Pity Pot," "Grey Ghost," and "Sackcloth and Ashes Number" all tie in. They are all part of the grief that you experience when you lose your best friend. Best friend? Right again! You grieve over the loss of your friend, alcohol. It is every bit as real as the loss of a relative or a job or a mate.

The recovering person will ultimately go through the same steps of the grieving process as if he were involved in a death, and that, of course, is what happens when drinking is buried forever in your life. There are lots of experiences of dealing with recovering alcoholics of both sexes that lead one to believe the grief process of giving up drinking falls generally into these four categories:

1. Denial
2. Anger
3. Blame
4. Acceptance

1. It is human nature to deny that a tragedy has taken place. It always happens to someone else, never to me. Therefore, logic dictates that *I* couldn't be the alcoholic! Heavy drinker . . . sometimes . . . maybe . . . but not a true, dyed-in-the-wool alcoholic! Are you faced with all the facts of alcoholic behavior, such as:

- Needing a drink the morning after.
- Liking to drink by myself.
- Losing time away from the job because of drinking.
- Having loss of memory during and after drinking.
- Waiting for "five o'clock" before taking a drink.
- Knowing my moods change drastically when drinking.

Faced with all these telltale signs of dangerous drinking, I still deny it could happen to me. There are self-evaluation lists that contain fifty to one hundred or more such telltale signs, and the real denier can answer every one of them with a "No." If the answers were "Yes," you see, then the grief process can be started and worked through to help cover the loss.

2. Anger. This is second on the list, because after denial has been faced, there is honest-to-God rage that you carry whatever genetic deficiency helped make your system allergic to the chemical alcohol: "Why can't I drink like everyone else?" "Why does this happen to me?"

"Why can't I be like other people who drink and have a good time?"

This anger is liberally sprinkled with the question, "Why, Why, Why?" The best advice for getting through this stage of the Grief Process is to stop asking "Why" in your anger and get on with the business of "What," "How," and "When." There just is no answer to "Why?" People do what they want to do in life, and seeking justification by asking "Why?" is just spinning your emotional wheels. You can work the grieving step of anger by asking yourself, "What did I do when I was drinking that caused embarrassment for me and my family?" "*How* did I get myself into this financial bind? Wasn't drinking the cause of this trouble?" In this case, your anger is turned toward your alcoholic *behavior* instead of toward yourself or others as human beings.

"When did I lose control over my drinking?" And, "When did my life become unmanageable because of alcohol?"

These are good questions that can help you vent justified anger without the unanswerable "Why?" clouding up the issue. For good measure to help you work the grief process you can add the word "Where?" to this emotive state of anger. "*Where* did I do my drinking, anyway?" "*Where* did the money go I had been saving for a trip?"

And so forth. By getting the anger out in the open about what drinking did *to* you instead of what you may have thought it was doing *for* you, you are helping the grief process work to your benefit.

3. The next step in the grieving over giving up alcohol appears to be "Blame." Since rationale does not permit the alcoholic the luxury of thinking himself to blame, it only becomes natural to assuage the pain by blaming someone else. *This* list of who's to blame is practically endless, but you can count on your spouse, parents, and children being right up there at the top, followed closely by your boss and the company you work for. In group therapy I ask the recovering persons to holler out the "reasons" they drank. It gets quite funny hearing the responses:

"It was Saturday noon."

"It was Sunday noon."

"I didn't get the raise."

"I did get the raise."

"The (insert favorite pro-football team) lost the damn game!"

"The (repeat above) *won* the damn game!"

And so forth.

In a 1947 article in *Nation's Business*, one woman claimed to have been cured of her alcoholism by having her mother-in-law removed from the family home! Get a hundred people in a room handing out blame for their drinking, and you'll get a hundred different responses. So, working through this grief process involves establishing some blame, somewhere. But when you see the ridiculousness of laying the blame anywhere else except where it belongs, you take a step forward in the recovery program upon which you've embarked.

Where *does* the blame lie? I won't pretend to the final all-encompassing answers, but there are some exciting things being done in medical research that cast light down a pretty dark tunnel.

The University of Colorado medical research unit has been in the forefront of a set of such research teams linking hereditary genetics to alcoholism. The work seems to say that alcoholics have some genetic deficiency in their bodies that seems to be passed on from generation to generation with a skip generation being hit harder than others.

Boiled down, this says that if you had an alcoholic parent, your chances to inherit this genetic deficiency were above average. It also means your children could receive it from you and their children from them in even stronger hereditary links.

So do you want to blame someone or something for your having the disease of alcoholism? Makes about as much sense to blame good old mom and dad for your brown eyes or golden hair. Genetic responses are handed out on a plane beyond your and my comprehension. If you were born, and obviously you were, then it looks like a good possibility that you could have received the alcoholic traits along with the rest of the family similarities and frailties. But why *blame* someone? Just accept them as part of the way you were made up.

Blaming yourself for what happened in the past is definitely out. You had very little to do with your alcoholism in all probability, and the best action you took was in going into treatment and/or the fellowship of AA to wean you from alcohol.

4. Finally, in working through the grief process as part of the Dry Drunk Syndrome you end up with the fourth element of grief, acceptance. Alcohol will never again be a part of your life. Accept it. For you to drink even one-half glass of wine, or one beer, or an ounce and one-half of whiskey will put you right back where you were no matter how many years you have been sober.

It's a *fact* of the disease. *Accept* it. It may take a matter of hours, days, or weeks, but the recovering person who tries to be that one alcoholic in the world who can take just one more drink and control it is on the road to returning to complete drunkenness. Whatever that genetic deficiency is that makes us alcoholic in the first place and is in our system, it *never* leaves us. That's why the recovering person of thirty-five or forty years duration is just as afraid to put that axiom to the test, "An alcoholic is just one drink away from the next drunk," as a newly recovering person. He *knows*, and you must *accept* and *know* that it is true.

One of the best ways to help you through the grief process and the knowledge that your grief is coming upon you in Dry Drunks is by *making a new sacrifice.* Dr. Blair Carlson, of the Denver Presbyterian-St. Luke's Hospital Alcoholism Recovery Unit, has a great plan that he passes along for strengthening the recovering person. Carlson encourages his patients to visit the de-tox wards of the hospitals on holidays such as Christmas and Easter. When you see the poor devils who are just beginning their road to recovery, it strengthens your acceptance of the fact that yes, you *are* an alcoholic, but YES, you can get on the recovery train and ride it the rest of your life.

People who have been on a Dry Drunk for several days have told me of making a hospital visit and finding their attitude brightening up and their grief over not being able to ever drink again, put to a final rest. (More on this in Chapter 13, "Carrying the Message.")

Each Christmas I make this personal sacrifice myself. It's a way of giving up some time with my family to spend an hour with a suffering alcoholic, and by so doing I am able to arrest any Dry Drunk that I may have felt creeping around.

Grief and the Dry Drunk Syndrome are so tied in that many times hard confrontation with yourself is necessary to snap out of the doldrums. Ask yourself: "Have I allowed myself the freedom for *alcohol to be dead* in my life?" (Grief Process.) "Have I been acting like this because I'm really *afraid to grow* and get on with the joy of recovery?" (Dry Drunk.)

Finally, I invented a system which for lack of a better name I call "Carpet Squares." This system is really a self-appraisal game that I have successfully used with clients in helping them deal with the Dry Drunk. Imagine yourself standing in front of a full-length mirror in which those self-adhesive carpet squares have been used to cover the entire surface of the mirror.

Now, you may begin to "remove" any square you like from the mirror. "Aha!" An elbow appears! Next, select any other square, exposing part of your body. You keep pulling those squares off, one by one, until the only carpet square left is the one covering the reflection of your face. Now comes the test. Ask yourself: "If I remove this last square will *I like* what I see? Will *I* be willing to look at what others have been looking at for days (or hours) since this (Dry Drunk) began?"

Clients have described their actions in imagining themselves picking off that last square and then quickly shoving it back in place before they had to look at themselves. But it helped them realize that they had been in a Dry Drunk and needed to get out of it in a hurry.

This "Carpet Squares" thing came to me when I was laying a large basement floor of those squares for a friend. It had been a rough day, and I was not only on the "Pity Pot" but generally in the doldrums because things had not gone right with this whole little remodeling job. The carpet was one of those pattern things with lines running through it. I had been so busy trying to get the job done that I hadn't paid much attention to how the last few squares had been put down.

When I realized that I had screwed up the flow of the pattern I had to start backtracking and removing some of the squares. The surface I had been covering was an old vinyl tile floor and it was reflective enough that you could see a faint image. There I was swearing up a storm because I had to redo work that I should have done right the first time. "I probably would have done the damn thing right if I was still drinking!" I said out loud. (Combination Pity Pot-Dry Drunk.)

I continued pulling up the squares, quite a number of them as a matter of fact, because I made the mistake in pattern some good yardage behind me. Finally, scowling to beat hell, I jerked up the last square of the mistake. Staring back at me from the reflective surface was this mean-looking son-of-a-bitch who, instead of being grateful that he could even perform this task, was bitching about it!

One look at myself made me realize that *that* was how I looked to other people, and therefore I was making *them* suffer for my actions. That's exactly what I had done as an "active" alcoholic! The realization of this snapped me out of my mood, and I wrote a small note to myself on my scratch pad in the toolbox. The note just said, "Carpet Squares."

If you have the guts to pull off that last carpet square and really look at yourself, it will be ego deflating, and that's what you want, to be taken down a peg or two off of the "high" you were getting from being on this Dry Drunk. You will be clear of mind enough to make some alternate choices in the way you behave, and you will be using the Grief Process in reverse. You will be allowing yourself the *freedom* to *live* life to the fullest!

Recently a woman in the early stages of her recovery refused in the game playing with her therapy group, to remove that last square and see herself as she was appearing to the rest of us. She dropped the group, her recovery program, and went back to drinking. For that unfortunate the Acceptance stage of her Grief process, acceptance that she was a recovering *alcoholic,* was just too great a square for her to lift off the mirror. Rather than face it, she dropped out of her program for recovery and will once again be caught in the alcoholic undertow.

The Grief over giving up alcohol is very real, and the family of the recovering person needs to understand that. It's up to you, though, to have enough fortitude to use the tools you have learned to work with through the stages of this process. By working through with them everytime they crop up, you will learn to recognize the telltale signs that let you know you might be heading for a Dry Drunk.

One other note of caution about the Dry Drunk. I don't know of anyone in recovery who thinks that these drunks are behind them, even after many years of sobriety. Treat them like some immunization program that requires a "booster" shot every so often.

Remember though, this is a mental "shot." Stay out of the bars, Buster! Watch out for those mouse turds, Missy!

The wise, for cure, on exercise depend;
God never made his work for man to mend.

Chesteron
Epistle to John Dryden

4
The Joy of Exercise
(Go For It!)

"D'ya mean to tell me that riding my ten-speed will make me not want to drink?"

"I didn't like exercise when I was drinking. Why the hell would I want to do it when I'm sober?"

The group of hospital patients was fairly hostile that afternoon as I gave one of my weekly lectures on the "Joy of Recovery." The hostility was perfectly understandable. Here's a healthy person talking to them about what life can be like in recovery, and they are still trying to begin the grief process over giving up alcohol. I answered the young man who posed the first question.

"No, riding your ten-speed bike isn't going to keep you from wanting to drink," I agreed. "What it *will* do, is help you discharge the built up adrenalin and nervous energy that accompanies these periods of stress and tension related to your recovery."

And that's what *this* chapter is all about. Learning how to help control the body systems that are undergoing biological adjustments associated with your giving up alcohol. Answering the second question asked in that hospital lecture is one I have to do constantly.

"Nobody said you *would* like to exercise. But it's something you're going to have to do if you want to maintain your sobriety and build a strong road to recovery. And you may learn to *like* exercise."

The thing here is, what *kind* of exercise, and how much of it, done under what circumstances, and for how long a period of time? Well, that's what we'll explore together in these next few pages. First we need some basic medical facts, which don't require an advanced medical degree to understand. Some people think, mistakenly, that exercise makes you feel better because you get "more blood to the brain." Well, the truth is that the flow of blood to your brain is fairly constant, so exercise does not affect *that* much one way or the other. However, doctors believe that exercise possibly can drain certain chemicals, such as adrenalin, that accumulate in the brain. These chemicals affect our moods, and when substances like adrenalin are metabolized during exercise, then we are stimulated; we feel better!

If you have been sitting in your favorite easy chair in front of the tube all day, you have been building up nervous tension — stress. Exercise helps to remove that stress. I can remember when the only exercise I got on a given day was getting up to go across the room and refill my glass with scotch; sometimes even *that* was too much!

Another myth about exercise is the one that says you have to hit it for hours at a time to "really do you any good." The U.S. Department of Health and Human Services confirms that usually as little as 15–30 minutes of vigorous exercise three times a week will help the average individual have a healthier heart, eliminate excess weight, and tone up sagging muscles. Another benefit is you'll *sleep* better. Now that doesn't sound like a heck of a lot of time to devote to your recovery program, does it?

Everyone is calorie conscious; drinking should have brought that fact home to you when you recognized the pounds piling up as quick as the "dead soldier" beer and bourbon bottles.

You were adding 100 calories with every little ounce and a half of scotch you drank; with every can of beer, including at least ninety for the so-called "light" beers. Now if you were a pretty good drinker, seven of those ounce-and-a-half scotch's per day added 1,000 *extra* calories to your daily caloric intake. But who ever poured you just one and a half ounces, pray tell? Even the stingiest of bartenders, who is forced to use an automatic shot dispenser, is prone to sweeten your drink, more so if you have been a regular, good customer.

It's not unrealistic to think that you were adding closer to 1,500 or 2,000 *extra* calories to the ol' bod. And that's just from the booze! We haven't even added the nine potato chips (100 calories), the one ounce of cheese nibblies (100 calories), or the two *plain* cookies (100 calories) that were consumed along with the alcohol!

Do you concede, then, that there is a need to recover from excess caloric binges, too?

"Yeah, but the more I exercise the more I'll eat!" cries the unbeliever. Not so. As physical activity increases there is not necessarily a parallel increase in the amount of food you put away. If your exercise program is combined with a calories reduction from the food you eat, then you have the right combination.

Do this: cut 200 (more or less) calories a day from your food rations. One of those cheaper calorie-counter books at most grocery store checkout counters will let you carry your "What-I-can-and-cannot-eat" list right with you in pocket or purse. Two hundred calories from what your normal caloric intake should be isn't all that much. Now, add another 300 calories in physical activities every day and *Voila!* You are losing 500 big ones from your daily diet, and reducing a lot of tension along with a lot of waistline.

Of course, just like all the ads say, "Before starting this (or any other diet) consult your doctor." The stronger a physical program you are going to undertake, the more important it is for you to have the complete approval from your physician. Before I got very serious about my running program, I took one of those stress tests that have you on a treadmill while you're hooked up like an octopus in tennies. If you shop around, you should find that a treadmill test which measures your heart's tolerance levels to strain, can be had for under $150.

Some will run as little as $50 or $75, which will include the consulting session, the treadmill run itself and, of course, the diagnostic results and recommendations. Look around. Many hospitals in an effort to be more involved in community fitness programs offer these kinds of services and many of them will sponsor walk-a-thons, "fun-runs," bike-a-thons, and the like.

What kinds of physical exercise are best for the recovering person? Hey! I'm not about to dictate to you! I chose running because my colleague, Paul Staley, got me started with a sensible, organized program with built-in rewards that I never thought possible. More on that in a minute. But let's look at forms of exercise other than running or jogging that might strike your fancy. They all take *effort,* remember, and they all contribute to helping you on the recovery road. Further, you burn up calories, so what could be better? Remember, all of these activities are based on what it takes to get rid of 100 calories. If you think they come off easily you're wrong! It requires a good deal of effort to work off just 100 calories, so it's obviously a good idea to combine calorie cutting with an exercise program.

Like to swim? Do it! If you swim 400 yards in nine minutes (that's 45 yards per minute), you've said goodbye to 100 calories. Here's some more: 14 minutes of tennis or 22 minutes of bowling will drop 100 big ones for you. Twenty minutes of golf (however, the time you spend waiting on the foursome ahead of you doesn't count), or 10 minutes of downhill skiing will also chalk off 100 calories. And remember, the cardiovascular improvement is much more important than calories.

"Isn't there something less, ah, strenuous?" you ask, sheepishly.

Sure there is. Do you like gardening or just lying in bed and watching the sun come up? Then this is for you. Messing around out there in the tomatoes or nasturtium beds for twenty minutes, with all that stooping over, clawing, and scratching at the soil, will earn you 100 calories off for your efforts. If you stay in bed for one hour and twenty minutes, in a reclining position, you also burn up 100.

However, this is designed to get you back in the swing of *enjoying* life, and so I'm not personally very big on the lying-in-bed routine. You probably did enough of that in your drinking days, and not by choice! There are other, necessary daily chores that also burn up the calories, and you have to do these things anyhow. For example, washing, showering, and shaving all use up 100 calories when you spend a half hour at it!

If you enjoy the incredible feeling of just being able to walk out of doors and savor the world in which we live, then for goodness sakes, do it! When you walk for twenty minutes for just 1,500 yards at a nice, comfortable 2.6 miles per hour, you are losing unsightly calories, 100 for each of those 1,500 yards. If you walk at a normal, but as I said "brisk" pace, you probably are doing two and one-half to three miles per hour.

For me, having a definite goal is necessary, and the Joy of Exercise is in meeting those goals. For around $12 you can buy a nifty little device called a pedometer. The one my oldest daughter gave me for my birthday hangs as close to the "center of the body" as possible. You adjust the stride lever on the side to the length of your own personal stride as you measure it from the tip of the toe of one foot to the heel of the opposite foot. As you walk, you'll hear a little "click-click," and the needle on the dial begins to click off the distance. You'd be surprised how far you walk in just an hour's time.

The list of exercises is pretty long, and I've just given you a few that I know work for other recovering alcoholics. One of the best ones that intrigues me is the new craze for "Jazzercise" or "Dancercise." It is enormous fun and does a lot in toning up many muscles in the body; muscles you didn't think you even had! Neighborhood shopping centers are attracting these kinds of dance studios by the hundreds, and men and women (albeit probably more women than men) can whip into their leotards and tights and be just a few minutes away from a tough but profitable workout.

Now, to running, the national craze that has so many people hooked, me included. I'm no Jim Fixx, nor Bill Rodgers, and never want to be. But personal goal setting in running has helped my own Joy of Recovery program, and it can work for you. I had never even thought of running. In fact, my wife, Mary Jo, reminded me not long ago that I got pretty heated over wondering what fun "those dumb runners" were having. It was *boring,* boring! That's what I thought.

When Paul got ahold of me he started me on a "walk-run" program that we have since incorporated in our treatment of persons in recovery in the fairly early stages of their program. What this consists of is to start off and walk for three minutes; run, or rather light jog for just *one* minute, then walk for three more minutes. You continue this cycle for a period of fifteen minutes. That's the way you start. No big deal, but you begin to realize that you can ask more of your heart and lungs than you thought possible.

The first time you actually run a full three minutes, up from that first one minute, you will expect a ribbon to be stretched across your path. But that's only the beginning. When you stop to realize that as a recovering person you are just beginning to treat your body with any kind of respect, then *small* victories become big gainers.

The amount of time you run is as important as how far. A consistent pattern of your walk-run, expanded from fifteen to twenty minutes, then twenty-five to finally thirty, will make you feel terrific! The real joy of this kind of exercise for recovery is that you are *competing only against yourself.* That's the goal. Being better this Saturday morning than you were two days ago; going a little longer than you did the last time; finding your lungs expanding easier, and your legs getting stronger!

When Paul told me that I was ready to run a consistent half-mile without stopping for the walk portion, I was hesitant. So we took to measuring off city blocks, discovering that one city blocks was equal to one-twelfth of a mile. My personal goal was just six blocks, but, oh, they seemed like six miles!

You can average out the time you stay on your walk-run program so you will know when you are ready to expand. I started with the basic thing I've described, running it three times a week; always letting one day of rest come between runs. For the recovering person there are some other basics to accept.

1. You will probably tire more easily than your companions.

2. You will be prone to lose interest in your exercise program if you are doing it alone. This seems to apply to *all* exercise programs. It's just another link in your own resolve not to get too tired, too hungry, or too lonely! When you are working on a program *with* somebody you will be able to share his enthusiasm, and your own small triumphs will seem like Olympic achievements. Starting an exercise program with someone will help insure your staying with it long enough to want to continue on your own.

3. You may find your coordination is off, more so than in your past attempts when "doing things." Perfectly natural that it would be. When you were drinking you were putting muscles to sleep at the same time you were sedating part of your brain, and as we do, there seems to be growing evidence that *both* the right *and* the left hemispheres of the brain are "upset" by hard alcohol use. Thus, motor responses and coordination may be slower.

Bowling, tennis swings, golf putting, even the ability to ride a bicycle are all things that might require extra effort in your recovery. Why is this? Why could it happen?

For one thing, competitive sports of any kind bring a certain amount of inner tension, even though you are playing "for fun." If you're a sports professional, it is even worse. So when you were in your drinking prime some key things were happening for the *benefit* of your sport. You were so relaxed (to a point) with alcohol, that normal muscle-brain coordination came a lot more freely. You were using booze to block out some normal cautions. You reached for harder tennis shots (even if you missed more than you made). You swam further (unburdened by the realization that you could be overdoing it). You hit the ol' "pocket" in your bowling games a lot more because you weren't *thinking* a whole lot.

So now, in recovery, some of the natural "klutziness" you may have been hiding all these months or years with alcohol, emerges, and you look and act awkward. Hey! That's okay! You can probably learn to do something the right way this time.

In learning or polishing up particular skills again, without drinking, the old natural responses to tension return. You're more cautious, restrained in your sport activity than before. You probably won't and don't take the chances you used to when you were drinking; and that's definitely good because now you'll be listening to your body when

32

it sends the clear messages of fatigue that you cheerfully ignored before.

Playing doubles tennis is going to be better for you to start back on the recovery road. *Two* lines of bowling might be the order of the night instead of three. Riding your bicycle *one* mile *every* day may be better for you than trying to hit five, ten, and fifteen miles once or twice a week. Nine holes of golf for awhile is going to help build your discovery of the joy of exercise faster than several eighteen hole games where nothing seems to go right for you. Finally, on the basic list:

4. Reward yourself at small achievements, even if they were things you expected to do well. I keep all the old racing numbers from my races tacked to the study well with the times I finished written on them. *Everybody* entering a race gets a number, but I keep mine to show *progress. Achievement.* Here was something I did that I never dreamed I could in my prime time drinking days!

Heck! You didn't think a thing about keeping piles and piles of bottle caps or "dead soldiers" lying around as a symbol of your ability to put it away with the best of them. Why not some small memento of your exercise program?

I know recovering persons who hang up their bowling score sheets or golf and bridge talley cards; hang them someplace or put them in a private drawer, anywhere where they can be easily accessible to remind you that you are *doing something positive now!*

When the trophies come along, when you and your partner have just nailed down the tennis doubles victory for the season, then all the more reason to share your pride! The Joy of Exercise is that you are coming back in true form to what a life free from the bondage of alcohol can be like.

Whatever form of exercise, whatever kind of program you develop for yourself, it's good to keep in mind two things.

1. Your program must provide *relaxation*. It needs to be done *long* enough and *hard* enough and *frequently* enough to provide honest-to-God relaxation. I found a sure-fire way to make certain that I stay out on the running paths long enough to do me some good. I invested in one of those radios that you wear around your neck. There are a lot of different models, all for under $100, surely under $150. They're great! I wear mine even in the races. It helps me keep my own pace, enjoy nature, and also savor the flavor of competition.

2. Your program should provide *personal* satisfaction. Whatever *havoc* you were wreaking on your body with alcohol, you were basically doing it to yourself. Therefore whatever *joys* you experience in recovery are basically selfish. And that's okay!

It's enough for me to run in *many* three-mile and *some* six-mile races without suffering any hunger pangs to do a twenty-six-mile marathon. For you, just seeing some puny muscles increase in size with exercise can be really rewarding! If you're a female, the sagging skin under your eyes will tighten up a little more each time you engage in good, stimulating exercise of some kind. Isn't that reward for you? You bet!

Personal satisfaction for many recovering persons is being able to *complete* a given task, to be motivated enough to walk a mile (lose 60 calories) or run a two-mile "Fun Run" (wear your T-shirt proudly!). In other words, *finishing* is more important to the recovering person than *winning*. It's more important because when you were drinking too much of your life was built around always starting things and *never* finishing. It doesn't matter in what place you cross the line; what does matter is that you cross it. You will gain *many* personal rewards.

Six to eight weeks of Dancercise ought to show a marked improvement in your body tone, in your endurance. Your whole cardiovascular system will be getting stronger.

Four to six weeks of a controlled running program will see your carotid artery pulse stronger and your breathing more controlled and even than you ever would have imagined. You'll begin to feel cheated at not being able to eat up more than three miles a day when you run!

Doing something positive for your physical well-being is doing a whole lot for your personal self-image. Build body — build image! It works! You don't have to win the Miss Universe contest or the Boston Marathon. It's good enough for your recovery to savor the Joy of Exercise.

Don't lose sight of the fact that one of the reasons you need regular exercise is to discharge that adrenalin we talked about in the beginning of this chapter. You need an outlet to help your body restore itself to a true balance. Without alcohol you are going to regain your appetite which in itself is enough good reason to exercise, just to keep on top of all the extra calories.

If you sit around and allow yourself to get a lot of tension and stress built up, then you are flirting with danger! It will take effort on your part, but then, the whole process of recovery takes more effort than you ever dreamed possible.

Have a definite pattern established for your exercise program. Just as you were in the habit of stopping at the neighborhood pub every day at 5:15 p.m., make it a point to don your exercise gear and hit the workout trail at a regular time and place.

A recovering runner friend of mine was overheard to reply to a question from a skeptic:

"Honestly now, would you ever think about going back to drinking?"

"What? And screw up my running program? Not on your life!" he replied.

That's the Joy of Exercise! Go for it!

Marriage has many pains, but celibacy has no pleasure.

Samuel Johnson

5
Re-Establishing Your Marriage

"I don't even know this man, and I've been married to him for ten years!"

"She treats me like some kind of child—just like one of our kids!"

"I'll tell you one thing; I'll give this marriage about another two months—maybe just two weeks, and then I'm splitting!"

Yep! Sounds all too familiar. Anyone who has gone through the pains of marriage counseling has used or heard the above phrases, or at least ones that are similar. My grandmother had a good old-timey phrase that seemed to work pretty well for premarital advice: "Marry in haste, repent in leisure."

But it's too late now. You're already married and what's probably worse is the fact your marriage may be more on the rocks than the way you ordered your drinks. The reason appears to be almost too simple, yet true. While you were drinking and spending all that good companionship time in bars or maybe even with someone else, your spouse was hoping that you'd see the light and get sober. When that finally happened, the spouse is ready to collect the due bill for all the wasted weeks, months, and years that have been invested in a marriage that wasn't paying many dividends.

After all, booze isn't around anymore so what's to stand in the way of making this relationship really hum?

I'll tell you what stands in the way. You don't know each other, that's what. I mean, so much of your married life has been spent with alcohol in the picture that you suddenly sit face to face and realize, "Who is this guy (lady)? I don't remember him (her) being interested in *that*, before!"

It's always a painful realization when one of our clients sits in the comfort of the therapy room and has to admit that they have never *even had a date* where alcohol wasn't involved. That's just in the dating process, not to mention the years that may have gone by in marriage. So here you both are; one of you now free from alcohol and the other one loaded for bear — probably *your* bare hide! After all, you're sober now, aren't you? What's to prevent things from being rosy from here on out? Well, nothing, really, if you both are ready to start at square one.

Your spouse has been the person who has stood beside and behind you no matter what difficulties your drinking produced. Now, maybe you can start being the kind of mate that has been envisioned by your spouse for all this time. So, lesson one is to acknowledge the debt of gratitude you owe your spouse without giving away all your chips. It's important for your continued fight back from alcohol to build self-respect, and slowly you'll do that if you're willing to share the accomplishment of your sobriety with others, namely your mate. Every time you find a way to say "Thank you," you are helping pat yourself on the back, too.

I've found a simple way to do this every day of my life. We hold hands at the dinner table to return thanks. Doesn't matter if you're religious or not; whether you are Christian, Jew, or agnostic. You *owe* a debt of thanks. I happen to believe in God, so holding my wife's hand I thank God for another day of sobriety. That's all there is to it.

By sharing this debt of gratitude openly with my wife, my God, and anyone else sitting at our table, I keep reinforcing my daily sobriety and strengthening the bonds of our marriage.

I'm also saying, "Hey! Join me (by holding hands), and let's all be grateful together for getting well."

Lesson Two. You and your spouse got *sick* together, so you both need to get *well* together. It's going to be difficult for both of you to try new ways, but it's absolutely essential to keep an open mind. This is particularly true of your spouse. This person did so much "enabling" during your drinking, that's it's going to be difficult to give up that terrible habit.

By enabling we mean the things your spouse did *for* you to enable you to continue drinking and not do for yourself. The spouse is generally considered the classic role model of the enabler, but it applies to all persons who aided and abetted the alcoholic in giving up his/her personal responsibilities in life.

Let's take money as an example of a marriage friction point that requires using some new tools for thinking. Money is a problem in a large majority of marriages even when drinking hasn't been around the house. Add the healthy doses of alcohol to that problem and you really have a mess.

But now that you're sober you want the money and checkbook chores and responsibilities back from spouse. Spouse isn't quite yet ready to entrust you with those things, since he or she remembers the many months of staving off the bill collectors or arguing in vain with the bank about "errors" in your account. How to resolve the dilemma? You install the "Two-Month Plan."

THE TWO-MONTH PLAN

This is a really simple method that declares a kind of moratorium on any discussions about *why* you shouldn't get the checkbook back and concentrates on a specific time period to *prove* your reliability. It's not as degrading as you may think. After all, your alcoholic blackouts following heavy drinking left you unable to account for where your money was or even how you spent it. So why should you be touchy about having to earn your money stripes again with your spouse? With the Two-Month Plan you both agree to let you have at the old checkbook for a period of two months. It takes this long to give you and the bank an even break on handling your account with you at the helm again!

For a period of two months you pay all the bills, write all the checks, and balance the account. It will help you build a little more confidence in yourself to see that you really can do things right again. Your spouse gets to look over the accounts and the checkbook to confirm your work. If everything is in order at the end of two months, you agree to add two more months to the system, then finally two more, making a full six months for you to be at the helm.

The two-month span of time is just about right for you to prove your responsibilities and also extends the trust your spouse has to give without making final judgments. Spouse feels comfortable knowing that not "too much" damage can happen to the family finances in a two-month period.

At the end of the full six months, you switch the roles. You can, and should, look over your spouse's shoulder and watch the action in the checkbook but accept none of the immediate decision processes about what or whom should be paid, and how much. What makes this little trial balloon fly is that it's fun. I have known couples who made a betting game out of seeing who could make the fewest mistakes and then the winner would treat for a dinner out. (I hate those people that *never* make checkbook errors.)

It may sound silly and it certainly requires a lot of bothersome work to put this two-month plan into effect, but it *will* work. You are probably not as ready to jump in and control family finances as you think, and your spouse is probably nowhere near ready to suddenly turn every chore back to you — being still quite "gun shy" about your sobriety and the length of time you've been in recovery.

Heck, I've had clients who couldn't wait to try this two-month plan, and after completing the first stretch decided on their own that they didn't *want* the checkbook back in their control. If husband and wife had not been willing to give the plan a try, they would have continued to just deal with the same angers and frustrations that they had when the husband was drinking. By the way, they still play the game of seeing if there were any checkbook errors, and after toting up, go out for dinner "on the bank."

When you stop to think about your marriage you really may be thinking about how to "make up" for lost time that I spoke of earlier. Why not think instead of starting from scratch? Here are five tools for improving your marriage that I find helpful. I often think these things would have been handy when lots of people I know were in the dating stages; they certainly are fed back to me by our clients as being successful in getting more out of their relationship-in-sobriety. These aren't listed in any strong order of preference but just as I find them comfortable to use in getting other people to start with the program of re-establishing their marriage.

OFF-THE-CROSS EXERCISE

This is certainly not meant to be sacrilegious, so don't get uptight about it. So many marriages never get off a dead start after the drinker has obtained sobriety because the spouse (or significant other) never stops "crucifying" the alcoholic for all the past sins committed. I draw a mental picture for clients in treatment about how their "discussions" with each other start in their living room and gradually work their way out the front door, down the street, and on up the hill to the top of Mount Calvary. There, the alcoholic, who has been forced to carry his or her own cross all the way, is now made to climb up on the cross and hang there until the spouse has thoroughly "crucified" him or her over the not-forgotten past.

It won't work! It just won't work. While it's true that everyone has been hurt and hurt deeply by the actions of the alcoholic, nothing of a lasting nature is to be gained by this constant rehash. You all know how the dialogue goes:

SOBER ONE: "Gee, Myrna looked attractive at the birthday party, didn't she, honey?"

SPOUSE: (Warming up) *"You* sure paid attention to her!"

SOBER ONE: (Feeling it coming on) "What's *that* supposed to mean?"

SPOUSE: "You know very well what it means!" (Here it comes) "That's *exactly* how you used to fawn over *every* woman at *every* party we ever went to!"

SOBER ONE: (Now in full-defense mode) "Wait a minute! *That's* when I was drinking! Gimme a break, will ya?"

And we're off and running. Poor "Sober One" has been innocently dragged up the hill and planted firmly on the cross; he'll stay there, too, unless his spouse is willing to bury the past and get on with the future of their relationship. It's easy to forgive. It's not so easy to forget. Every time you haul out that cross and either climb on it yourself or allow yourself to be put on it, the forgetting will never happen.

So, feel free to invoke the Off-The-Cross Exercise by making direct reference to it. When I see that cross being hauled out in a therapy session, I confront the hauler-outer right away.

"How many times does Charlie need to be put on that cross of yours before he's through paying for his past?" I'll say.

The mere reference to a cross is generally enough to make the couple realize that that is exactly what they are doing to each other without realizing that *alcohol* has been the villain in the piece, and "Charlie" has just been the willing vessel for the alcohol.

You can do it the same way. When you feel that your spouse is hauling out the cross, of if you're the spouse reading this and feel that your recovering person is about to lay some more heavy stuff on you, stop the action. Say, "Hold it! I have the feeling we are about to travel up the hill with the cross again. Is that right?"

It may not stop the action entirely, but it *will* call attention to the fact that the beef is going to be centered around something that happened in the *past* and therefore is better off buried and forgotten. If the recovering person is never to be allowed off that cross, there is very little chance that you both can get on with the business of the future. The hurts of the past won't easily go away, but they can be dealt with in a lot more constructive fashion if you try this exercise.

THE TEN MINUTE DRILL

This is one of the most important and successful tools that I know of for putting some new shine back on a relationship. Everyone must have a clock around the house that can be set. I recommend using that neat little timer on your oven; you know, the one that makes that horrendous buzz when the biscuits are done. Well, most everyone has one of those, but if you don't, get something like that from your local hardware. Whatever device you end up with, it has to make a noise. It has to buzz, squawk, ring, chime, or do *something* that says ten minutes are up.

There are some other ground rules that you need to know before employing the ten minute drill:

1. There can be no radio.
2. There can be no TV.
3. There can be no stereo playing.
4. There can be no kids or crying babies in the room.
5. There can be no pets; dogs or cats that require attention, in the room.
6. No telephone or door answering, if possible.

In other words, there can be *no* distractions of *any* kind during the period of the ten minute drill. Now I know this is hard, but it is *not* impossible. You'll find after a couple of times that you can plan your ten minute drill at such a time when these things are easiest to control. I have had clients who finally settled on a very early Saturday morning time to have their drill in quiet and solitude; and it worked for them, even with an active household.

You may have guessed by now the purpose of the ten minute drill. It is a device to attempt to establish communications between the two of you where *active* listening is involved.

Without all those distractions that are a normal part of your everyday world, you are forced to actually listen to what your mate is saying. This is going to be a whole new experience for you. You have become so lazy in interpersonal communications that you wander around saying, "Have a nice day" and "How was work, dear?" and, "What happened at the office today, hon?" and *never* (well almost never) waiting or caring about the answer. So, the ten minute drill.

You set the oven timer for ten minutes, and then in this noise void you have created, you T-A-L-K. I mean you really, honest-to-God,

TALK. For just ten minutes—that's all. When the buzzer goes off, the rule is, you quit and hold whatever may be brewing until the next ten minute drill. There's the hitch. In all the time I have used this drill with people they report having no desire to quit after ten minutes! They enjoy what's happening to them, and they rush up to reset the buzzer for another ten minutes.

I suggest that if this happens to you on the first go around, that you do hold to a limit of *two* ten minute drills in the same sitting.

The subject matter doesn't really count for the ten minute drill. But a very important point to observe is that if a critical argument or brewing topic is started, and then the buzzer goes off, you both agree to hold the topic for the next drill period. This provides three elements:

1. It says that the discussion is important and probably needs to be continued, and,
2. We are providing an automatic "cooling down" process over the subject, but,
3. The subject is important enough to warrant further discussion.

Some couples I have worked with tell me that when the buzzer goes off they are "really rolling" in a worthwhile exchange, and rather than quit, they advance the timer for thirty minutes and keep going. The basis for sticking to ten minute segments is to provide "safe ground." Either party can retreat admirably and with honor from the discussion field and not feel they have given up all their troops in battle.

I said earlier that the subject matter doesn't really count; the ten minute drill is open to all areas. The way I place a priority on what is to be the subject is to use the old refrigerator door-magnetic pot-holder device. When I think of something that has been bugging me or some topic that never gets satisfactorily explored, I write the subject on a piece of message paper and plunk it on the "fridge door" with the magnet. My wife gets a shot at reading, quite openly, what is on my mind for a discussion and that gives her a chance to think about rejoinders, defenses, explanations, points of view, and counter-attacks that will help us solve the nagging question.

The key to this whole thing is the openness of it all; *that's* what's fun about being sober in the first place. You don't have to go around your life in sneaky-Pete fashion. I think a whole book could be done alone on the various ploys, gambits, and general strategies that recovering couples have told me about in using the ten minute drill. Don't be bashful! If you try one and it works, write my publisher, and he'll nag me into starting a collection of successful ten minute drill episodes.

The really beautiful part of the ten minute drill is that it becomes a habit-forming tool of communication between you and your spouse. The lack of outside distractions makes it some of the most therapeutic time you'll ever spend with each other. Another guideline: Don't be afraid to say, "Let's save that for the ten minute drill, okay?" This has the effect of telling your partner that you recognize this as an important subject, but that the time isn't right for discussion when the subject is first brought up. This is particularly important in any sexual activity and bedroom capers that may be in the works. You'll kill *that* whole number if you suddenly get into something that is better saved for the ten minute drill. More on that in the chapter on sexuality.

A word of caution. Please don't try the ten minute drill while the two of you are driving in the car, on bikes, or motorcycles. The very noise of the machine you are on or in can heighten the intensity of what starts out to be a "quiet little discussion," and the ten minute drill will disintegrate into full-fledged shoutin' and hollerin'! Save it! Put it on ice by saying,

"Good point, hon — sounds like something we should schedule for the ten minute drill." or,

"I'm open to kicking that one around. Let's schedule a ten minute drill. This traffic's already got me uptight!" Your responses will be better than mine; just don't be afraid to couch the point in terms of:

1. Acknowledging that a problem area exists
2. Giving it importance by wanting to put it on your agenda
3. Acknowledging the point that he (she) obviously is bothered enough to bring the subject up in the first place,
                            and,
4. Holding out hope that a solution amicable to both of you can be worked out in the ten minute drill(s).

Try it! You'll like it!

QUALITY TIME

I think it's important to acknowledge right off the bat that my wife hates the expression "Quality Time," and we may have to have a ten minute drill over it. Can't help it! I just don't think there is a better way to describe what seems to be missing between the recovering person and his/her spouse; what is missing most in their attempts to bring renewed joy to their partnership. It's Quality Time; the time where the two of you just plain *enjoy* life *together*.

We should start by describing what Quality Time *isn't*.
Quality time is not:
1. Pushing a grocery cart around a supermarket while your spouse gives an x-ray examination to every label on every shelf.
2. Washing windows.
3. Taking down or putting up storm windows.
4. Putting on or taking off snow tires.
5. Rearranging furniture.

Quality Time *can* be:
1. Redecorating a room together.
2. Looking in new car or used car lots. (Don't go into showrooms unless you are seriously ready to select a new car.)
3. Sharing dinner party preparations.
4. Planting the spring garden.

Well, you get the idea. What is missing is best summed up the way we hear it at the Treatment Center — Fun! What happened to the idea of just taking a walk together in the evening? What happened was you were too loaded with booze to even find the front door or just didn't want to get that far away from the bottle. You can now. What makes taking a walk fun in sobriety is that you explore again the real joy of being together away from pressures (telephones, calendars, etc.). What I suggest is that you set a goal for your walk; something with a reward at the end so that this painfully new experience of being together doesn't make you so uncomfortable that all the joy of the walk is smothered in anxiety. I'll give you a goal: ice cream! There's nothing better than suggesting a walk to your local ice cream parlor (as long as it's located at least twenty minutes away). The reward can be a simple *Dairy Queen* scoop or two or a mammoth sundae of some obnoxious weight-producing sauces. Doesn't matter. It's good for you! If you're one of those folks who can't handle sugar in your diet, then make that walk one to the supermarket (picking the *next* nearest one to your house) and purchase diet or non-sugar ice cream to take home.

Hold hands while walking. Ah, c'mon now, you can do it! Yes you can! Time was when you were so close to each other, people tried to pry you apart just to take your coats and hang them up! What's all this distance, now? There's still a special thrill, whether you're eighteen or eighty to taking your companion's hand and *strolling*. Strolling, not trying to set a speed record, but that wonderful, brisk yet lazy pace where you might even *swing* your hands back and forth a little. Now *that's* Quality Time. It's different from ten minute drill time because nothing of real importance can or should be brought

45

up. What you are doing is just enjoying each other, without pressure.

This is a good time to do some dream planning. You might see a particularly nice garden or patio or sun deck that will enable you to say, "That's what would look nice at our place as soon as we can get to it (afford it)," or, "That's sort of what I would like to do with our front yard this year."

If you live in an apartment, I think it's even more fun because you just might wander past the swimming pools, tennis courts, bike paths, or other recreational places that will beckon to the two of you to try again as a couple. You may have thought your tennis game was hotshot when you were drinking, but you'll find you might really enjoy the doubles game with your spouse, now that there is a better than even chance you can return the ball!

If you're not a swimmer, you still could lie around the pool and read while your spouse takes a few laps. The bike paths you pass on your walk to the ice cream reward or even walking on the paths themselves might just spur you to try biking again.

You don't have to run out and buy $400 worth of *Raleighs* or *Moto-bacanes* either. If you live near a city park there might be a bike rental concession. If you are a grandparent, be bold and ask your grandkids to let you borrow their bikes for a weekend. They've probably grown tired of them anyway or have abandoned old-fashioned balloon-tire or three-speed models for the high-powered jobbies with fifteen gears. You don't need that for Quality Time riding.

There's a beautiful old hymn that says something about, "In the rustling grass I can hear Him pass. . . ." I like that, and it has absolutely nothing to do with religious beliefs. It means to me that the joy of being sober can be realized over and over again when my mate and I walk across lush park grounds, hand in hand; I feel good about the world, about her, about myself!

Quality Time, like all other times and exercises that I'm telling you about, needs to be planned. The Sunday drive, now that gas prices no longer seem to be an issue, is still a great chance for the two of you to get together. Notice I said the *two* of you. See, this is different than you piling three kids, grandma, the family pets, and maybe even a neighborhood kid or two into the station wagon and preparing to enjoy yourself! Forget it! Won't happen! There's too much confusion, noise, chaos, and the makings of World War III, to be ever classified as Quality Time.

The *two* of you. Does it sound strange? A little scary, perhaps? Does the thought of buying a couple of symphony tickets (even though you're

46

not a lover of classical music) terrify you? It shouldn't. Most symphony orchestra programs contain program material for everyone. Give it a shot! Tie in a late supper after the concert — *that's* Quality Time. What about taking in a sporting event together? Now here we come to some real diverse opinion. A lot of spouses don't like or maybe understand a particular sport. I'm no expert on any of them, but I'll give you a couple of examples of how you can turn a sporting event into Quality Time instead of a drudging chore and fight-ensuing mess. Let's start with football.

The mistake in trying to make a football game a Quality Time event is that you (either sex) probably know more about the game than your spouse. I know females that can tell me more about football than I even care to know, so don't think I'm saying that it's only men who know the game or appreciate it. When I see a couple starting off for a game I always ask, "Is this what you *both* decided to do?"

The squirm or non-reply by one or the other usually indicates it was his (her) idea. That's bad, because Quality Time should not be spent just satisfying one person's needs. So, before you spend a bundle on a pro game or even a nearby college game, here's a Quality Time tool. Go back to high school. That's right, high school. You'll see some really outstanding football, at a fraction of the cost of either a college or pro game, and the really big bonus is: You can LEAVE at a decent interval and not feel bad about it. Suppose you have made a deal with your spouse who doesn't particularly care about football to go, say, for just one half of the game. That's *your* end of the deal. *You* come with me—*I'll* leave when you want to. In the meantime, you can feel pretty comfortable about explaining certain parts of the game your companion may not understand.

Unless it's your kid playing in the game, the local high school games are just ideal to get somebody enthusiastic about sharing this sport with you. The playing time is quicker; the action is more on fast-pace, and the formations for the most part are easier to see and understand. I know of a couple that tried this Quality Time tool and after two weeks you couldn't have dragged *either* of them away at half time. You see, they had discovered the power of just being with each other. They had no one they knew playing in the game, and they were experimenting with this tool because I had insisted they just give it a try. *Now,* they tell me they are trying for a pro game or two, and they are both becoming pretty hooked on watching the games on television. Point to be made here is they are *doing it together* instead of what was happening when sobriety wasn't in the picture.

You can apply this principle of give and take with any sport. *You give* a little; your *spouse gives* a little, and neither of you has had to make a whole hog commitment to go "off the deep end" about the sport.

I don't like skiing, but you could drop my roommate off on the top of Pike's Peak and she'd have a ball making her way down. So, I am happy that she does that; I can be happy going with her to the mountains and while she does her thing I can hole up with some fine recreational reading or creative sleeping. Then, we have dinner out together. The whole experience is Quality Time for us both.

Bowling is far superior, to say, tennis as a sport for you two to share time with each other. The skill levels are not so far apart on the bowling lanes as they can be on the tennis courts.

If you join a bowling league, I recommend you get on different teams in the same league. The competition then is not reduced to you against your mate, but rather your team against the other. You'll end up bowling against each other several times during the season, but neither of you has to feel that you are out to prove which one of you is better.

There are so many other obvious Quality Time experiences that you can savor; you just need to make the effort and not make a big deal out of it. Part of the joy of your sobriety is that everything no longer has to be the big production number that it once was. If it rains on the day you were going to have a picnic in the country, then forget it! The rain, I mean, not the picnic. Throw the red and white checker cloth on the floor in the living room, put on a little Streisand, Bernstein, or Dan Fogleberg and have the picnic!

There's one other Quality Time event that's really close to my heart, and maybe it'll strike a responsive chord with you, too. I call it "Travel-Teasing." We haven't been able to afford a trip of a very extensive nature, but more fun can be had by getting travel brochures and maps, sitting down on the floor (I'm big on floor sitting, you notice), and spreading the stuff out on the coffee table. We have had more fun planning trips back East, or even looking at Europe, Mexico, and Hawaii that way. It's cheap Quality Time spent in partial dreaming about what might happen, and also sharing what experiences we remember when we did make certain small trips together.

I have a friend in the travel agency business and I don't mind imposing on him one bit for new brochures and travel stuff to help with my "Travel-Teasing." The fact that he is a recovering alcoholic makes it all the more enjoyable. We both profit; if I ever *do* go to Europe or Hawaii, he'll get the business.

THE LAUGHING PLACES

Joel Chandler Harris had the right idea when he had Uncle Remus tell about the Laughing Places. You need them, too, as you struggle to re-establish your marriage. It's been way too long since you and your companion really had a good belly laugh; one that was not brought on by alcohol or the old "life of the party" devices. What I'm talking about here is the ability you must have to laugh at yourself and, more importantly, at each other, without hurt feelings. So often in the past the alcoholic has made someone else the butt of his/her jokes, and it wasn't funny—it just plain hurt! Now, you can each have the freedom to laugh at and with each other by using the Laughing Place device.

You might have observed something about your mate that is really striking you as funny. You've started to snicker and your spouse is beginning to say, "What's so damned funny?" They are suspicious as they are playing an old tape of how it used to be in the drinking days. You can stop this from turning into a donneybrook if you will just say, "Hey! Let's go to the Laughing Place, okay?" That's the signal that something has struck you funny, and you want to *share* that without hurt feelings.

I know people that have tried this and have literally ended up in hysterics over an event that took place once they had accepted that it was happening in their Laughing Place. Sound silly? Try it! You are automatically removing any personal slings and arrows of outrageous fortune by saying that you think your spouse will find what you are about to say funny also. If he or she doesn't think it's funny, then you took the chance and it didn't get out of hand.

You can grow old just sitting there watching the draperies fade or you can make every minute count that you're together; particularly if you recapture the ability to laugh with each other. I hate to admit this, but one of the best laughing places I know is in bed. I don't know why but that seems to be a place that lends itself to recalling and sharing some outrageous incident that can regale you with laughter. The obvious danger, of course, is that the bedroom as a laughter place might come back to haunt you in your attempt to keep that hallowed ground for lovemaking. But if that's where you are comfortable as your Laughing Place, then go for it!

A word of caution to the Significant Other about going to the Laughing Place when it involves a remembered drinking incident. What *you* can now laugh easily about when you remember a drinking episode where your mate made a jackass out of himself to the delight of others, may still be a painful experience for your sober friend.

Often, it takes many months and sometimes a period of a year or more before the sober person can see the humor in a situation that involved his/her drinking. You are best to approach such an incident with a real understanding with, "Honey, I just thought of something that I started laughing about — it's when you were drinking. Is it okay to take it to the Laughing Place?"

This doesn't mean that you will stifle the guffaw that has been building up inside you, bursting to be released. It simply helps do a little ground breaking so that you are suddenly not the recipient of a hurtful barrage because what was funny about your spouse's drinking is nothing for him to laugh about.

All too often I will hear a spouse complain about his/her necessity to "walk around on eggshells," fearing that everything that might be said will set off a torrent of bad words from the recovering person. It just takes a little time to work *together* on where it's okay to tread, and that's what makes the Laughing Place such a super device to make sure there is no one wearing his or her heart on their sleeve.

WARM FUZZIES

I saved this for the end because I think it has done more to bring couples back together than any other tool that may require a little more skill to use effectively. The Warm Fuzzy is that unsolicited hug, embrace, and just plain stand-up cuddly that is freely exchanged to say, "Hey! I love you and care about you!" You can always tell recovering folks who have been in treatment together, perhaps at a hospital unit. They will unabashedly exchange Warm Fuzzies; no matter that it may be two men or two women. The Warm Fuzzy denotes "We have come through something that almost killed us — and we've done it together!"

I rarely attend an AA meeting without exchanging ten minutes of Warm Fuzzies. I think the biggest risk taken is that the spouse who has not been personally involved in treatment may take offense at seeing his/her special friend clasped in a warm embrace with a member of the opposite sex. So, to counteract this, the two of you should begin practicing the Warm Fuzzy between you and allowing it to happen for both of you.

One of the hardest things I do in therapy is to get a couple who have come from very straight-laced nonaffectionate backgrounds to begin exchanging Warm Fuzzies at the end of a session. They are still angry perhaps, but I try and get them to give one another a Warm Fuzzy so they can leave the session realizing that they are working on their problems together. Boy, there is absolutely nothing like a Warm Fuzzy to make the cares of the day go away! You can use the Warm Fuzzy at any time or place to help get rid of "Old Creepy" (remember your Grey Ghost?), and it sure is a tonic when you have something special to celebrate.

I'm sure you have seen those bumper stickers that say things like "Have you hugged your kid today?" or "Have you hugged your lawyer today?" (I love that one!) Well, it's America's return to the Warm Fuzzy, something that never goes out of style, but often gets set aside in the rush and hassle of everyday living.

My close friend, Ty Owens, is a therapist and Employee Assistance Program Administrator for Burlington Northern Railroad. Ty has done a tremendous number of crisis interventions—those therapy sessions that become encounters to get a reluctant person into treatment for alcohol abuse. He is a giant of a black man, a former football lineman, if that helps you picture his size. I personally call him Kunte Kinte, after the *Roots* hero. Well, let me tell you when you get a Warm Fuzzy from Ty you have been Fuzzied! People will stop and look at the two of us in a hospital corridor or on the street or in a restaurant exchanging a Warm Fuzzy. I don't know what they may think, and I personally don't care! It's a special greeting between friends. I have seen Ty give a Warm Fuzzy to a little slip of an old lady or to a man who is equal to his own bulk. He never extends his hand as in a hand-shake for a greeting. With someone he cares about, you can count on a Warm Fuzzy!

And who cares about you more than your own spouse? Who better to exchange frequent and rewarding Warm Fuzzies with than the special person with whom you share your everyday life?

There is absolutely nothing sexual about the exchange of Warm Fuzzies when they are given between persons who are not married. They really don't have much of a sexual connotation when they are given to your spouse; they're not meant for that. A Warm Fuzzy effort-lessly shared between spouses simply says, "It's good to have you back from the world of the damned!"

My wife has turned into a great Warm Fuzzy giver, and I think it's tremendous. Many times when things have been particularly rough, or when I have barked unusually long, having dropped all my tools of communication, she will ask, "Can I get a Warm Fuzzy?" Gee, whiz! All the punch goes right out of the blistering defense I was about to mount. It (trouble) all just melts away, without words, in that fondness of a few moments of holding one another, without words, without having the necessity or pressure to say anything. Just a Warm Fuzzy, a good cup of coffee, and Thou! Eat your heart out, Omar Khayyam!

6
Re-Establishing Your Credit

Well maybe you'll settle for a banker who looks like a hippopotamus, but chances are when you were in your prime drinking days you had a lot of descriptions for those "no-good S.O.B.s" that wouldn't extend you any more credit. I had a few choice descriptions of bankers myself, basically ranking them right up there with lawyers, insurance men, and the Asian Flu.

Now that sobriety is your way of life, you might find out that those moneylenders and policy writers aren't always wearing the black hats after all. As a matter of fact, they can and do help you in your attempt to get "back on your feet." But, there is a lot of basic mind-set that the recovering person has to go through in order to take advantage of the help that is waiting out there. The first element deals with a complete understanding that it was you doing the drinking; not the banker. Secondly, the banker had taken a chance on you at one time and you violated the trust placed in you when the payments continued to slip more and more in arrears.

Let's recap briefly how alcoholics treat money generally and how they treat their bills in general. Money is good for just one thing: to spend, probably on setting up another round of drinks or making sure there's plenty of booze in the house. There may not be enough of the real essentials of life, but you can damn well count on the fact there will always be enough money for cocktail time.

Because money holds no special significance for the alcoholic outside the areas of spending, he/she becomes very careless with it. As the intensity of drinking picks up so does the disregard for the financial responsibilities of the drinker's life. This seems to be due to a great "Avoidance Syndrome." This particular malady says that if you simply avoid the money problems they will go away. We all know the nonsense that thinking like that is for any mature, clearheaded adult. The stickler, of course, is that no drinker is clearheaded for very long, and the more drinking that's done, the less mature he or she becomes. Still, avoiding money issues only means that the alcoholic delays the inevitable collapse of his or her finances. Like all sick people, the alcoholic turns the blame on the nearest institution that represents money, the bank.

I find bankers to be courteous, helpful, bright, energetic, and underpaid. Of course, the chances are very real that they have always been like that, and it was my changing from alcoholic to sober behavior that made me see them in a new light. *You* need to see them in a new light, too, because everyone needs a good banker; particularly the recovering person.

Think of this: When you treated your bills and hence your creditors before, that is while you were drinking, you just took the persistent bill collection notices and stuffed them further into the desk drawer. That's how they "got paid." Why would anyone want to go through the process of extending *more* credit to anyone who acted with that little regard for the people and companies that gave them credit in the first place?

The answer is: they *don't* want to! But you need credit and you probably need to re-establish a solid banking connection again. I have worked with couples who thought they had hit financial bottom and felt that the alcoholic's abusive manner with their bankers had buried them forever in the pit of poverty and despair. Let's face it; in some cases that may be true, but by and large, bankers, to paraphrase Shaw's character Henry Higgins, "are a marvelous lot." The way you get to know them again is for them to get to know you, the *new* you. This involves a lot of humility on your part, and you are going to have to add one more character trait to your life in ever-increasing terms: *Honesty.*

Here are some basic rules for re-establishing good relations with your bank. I strongly recommend you think about them, talk them over with a close friend or spouse, and then get busy.

1. Find out if the person who was handling your delinquent account

is still with the bank. Contact him or her and ask for a *personal* appointment. If they want to know what for, just say you'd rather visit with them in person, not over the phone.

2. Sitting across from that bank person, come clean with what's happened to your life. Tell them that you have been a victim of the disease of alcoholism. Tell them that you have started on the road to recovery, and be sure and tell them by what means such as a treatment program and/or AA.

3. **Don't ask for anything.** Tell them that you realize you were probably pretty abusive and maybe downright vulgar and hostile in your dealings with the bank.

4. Apologize for past behavior but don't grovel! You were sick and not responsible for many of the things you said and did.

5. Tell the bank that you wish to re-establish credit, even though their past experiences with you may have been disastrous. Remember, the bank stays in business by having customers. They want to have as many people as possible doing business with them so there is a certain amount of hope to be found in thinking, "they (the bank) need *me*, too!"

6. **Don't argue!** You're going to get a certain amount of lecture time from the banker, and I tell our clients who are following these rules to just "buck up and take it." Agree with the fact that you have been irresponsible in the past, but be certain and point out that the nature of the disease of alcoholism tends to push *everything* out of the mind except the seeking for the chemical high that drinking gives.

7. Offer a testimonial letter from your treatment center, your AA sponsor, your attending physician. This letter will simply state that you have undergone treatment, or in the case of your AA sponsor, that you are in regular attendance at meetings and remaining motivated for sobriety.

8. Don't ask for the moon, again! If you need a line of credit from this particular banker, ask for something modest; so you know you can pay it back quickly and on time. I recommend starting out with a simple installment loan of three hundred dollars on some sort of collateral purchase; a small appliance or lawn mower or maybe a gas barbeque grill. The important thing is to *use your bank* for the financing, at least the first time around. By paying on and paying off a small loan on time or better yet, *ahead* of time, you will be on the road to re-establishing a little higher line of credit.

9. Don't overextend. Make sure your banker is willing to help you keep a tighter rein on your spending. Many times the euphoria and

joy of sobriety can trap you into making the same mistakes as before. If you'll use your banker for the financial expertise he/she can offer, you'll find out they can really be a "friend in need, a friend indeed."

10. Get to a bank officer. My philosophy is go right to the top, if you can. Most banks now insist their officers and other directors on the premises sit out in the open where they are accessible. It's good therapy for you to introduce yourself to the bank president; you can count on the fact that if he or she doesn't know you, they will go out of their way to ask the loan officer you were working with about you. That's good for your new image. Your sincere image. The one that says, "Sober, I'm worth something to the bank and to myself. Give me another chance."

These ten rules are not to be set in concrete. They need to be used as the other tools in this book — with modification to your own special circumstances. But they have proven successful for a lot of other folks, so they can work for you.

So far, we have assumed that you have a "banking connection." What if you don't? Where do you find one that will be sympathetic to your miserable past balance sheet? I have three top-drawer "pipelines" for you:

1. Your lawyer
2. Any and all AA groups you have attended
3. Your church or temple

If you don't have a lawyer in addition to not having a banker, then ask your employer for his recommendation for both. Your therapist at treatment, your family, or attending physician are also sources to get you some names of bankers who are accessible and interested in helping. At AA, I have heard many a person ask openly if anyone in the fellowship knows of a banker who will help. Five will get you ten that there is at least one banker *in* the meeting, and he or she will surely talk to you.

The church or temple where you have been attending is such a good source because the minister, priest, or rabbi knows his population and is used to handling such matters on a more regular basis than you would suspect.

Now, let's deal with some specific money areas that are difficult for the recovering person to handle but are a real joy when you know how to conquer them.

THE FINANCIAL STATEMENT

Don't you hate those damn things? They must have been devised by the same group of people that have turned you down for all your pipe-dream money schemes of the past! They scare me; I don't like seeing all those "Assets" and "Liabilities," "Net Worth" and "Total Indebtedness" columns. So, I overcame my fear of financial statements by taking the blanks right back to my banker and asking him to help me fill out the first one. It is time consuming, but once you go through the process, you discover that you are worth more than you thought. What you will discover of even greater importance is that you will know where you stand financially and what sort of "game plan" you need to establish to meet certain financial goals.

I'm not expecting bankers who read this to be overjoyed at the prospect of having all their recovering customers come tearing in with their blank financial statements to be done, but then bankers need to understand that the alcoholic has never dealt with the reality of money before and he/she needs strong support as an aid to the joy of being sober. Even if the financial statement doesn't look as good as you'd hoped, it nevertheless is an essential part of re-establishing your credit, and besides it can work for you. That's right! When you are finished with your statement ask for copies to be made. The bank will generally be glad to provide you with at least one copy of your signed and delivered statement. Then, go to your nearest copy machine and make six more copies. You can use these in applying for credit cards and for establishing other lines of credit with merchants and higher-priced credit checkers such as automobile agencies, furniture stores, realty firms, and so forth. One copy of your financial statement should be filed away for your use in one year's time when you will be required to update it again and resubmit it to your bank. Now don't blame the bank; it's not their rule, but rather the government, both state and federal, that require such statements as a condition of loaning you money.

Even if a financial statement is not required because of the small amount of money you may be seeking, I highly recommend asking for and submitting one anyway as a strong means to re-establishing your credit. Even if the statement is bad, it will show that you are sincere in your efforts to start your money life anew in your sobriety, and you will be pleasantly surprised at how your banker will be able to help you show more legitimate assets than perhaps you even knew you had, making your statement even stronger than you suspected.

If you are buying a house, for example, you are entitled to claim half of the equity or value of the house along with the half of the mortgage burden you must show. However, your equity and your house value have been steadily *rising* while your debt has been *diminishing,* thus improving your figures on the financial statement more than you had expected.

That's just a small tip of the iceberg that your banker will help you uncover. There are dozens of others, each item helping you to restore confidence that maybe you're worth more than you thought, and hence, in *sobriety,* making the bank more interested in taking another chance with you.

I have talked to clients who were terrified to handle a financial statement because they had been through a bankruptcy, probably as a direct result of alcoholism. With the help of a banker friend they filled out a statement showing the bankruptcy but attaching a written statement explaining the nature of the action and the part that alcoholism played. That financial statement was filed away by the bank, protected by the laws of confidentiality, but the *honesty* of the approach helped that couple achieve a series of small loans that eventually led to re-establishing a larger line of credit.

By law in most states a bankruptcy will continue to appear on retail credit bureau reports for ten years. A good, solidly prepared financial statement can be given to the Retail Credit Bureau in your city, and they will take new facts into consideration. Get a personal appointment with your credit bureau and ask to see your file. They must, by law, show it to you, and you, by law, have the right to update and supply additional information which will become part of the credit reporting process. Do it. It's worth it.

Everyone can have a financial statement, even if you are a student still going to college. It's a good way to help cement your sober attitude in the minds of the people who will be asked by you to advance sums of money and credit as you rebuild your new life.

THE CREDIT CARD CRUNCH

These pieces of plastic were a great part of your alcoholic behavior pattern, and they should be viewed equally as part enemy/part friend. You very possibly don't have any credit cards left; they have vanished in the wake of your financial woes brought on by drinking. If you still have one or two, then you already have learned that you need to keep it paid and current. But suppose you want a credit card and just know you can't qualify because of previous bad credit? Well, there is a way! Your local savings and loan is probably the best source to obtain and keep a credit card such as a VISA or Mastercard. By depositing funds in an account, many savings and loans, industrial banks, and similar lending institutions will establish a line of credit for you equal to one-half the amount of funds you have on deposit. You will be issued a card and it will entitle you to draw against your line of credit. It may not be as flexible as a "regular" high-line credit card, but it will enable you to carry around some ready credit. Many banks have similar programs, and they are worth investigating.

If you've had bad credit such as that associated with a bankruptcy, you'll probably not get a national credit card until the bankruptcy is "purged" from your records. It's not that the credit card companies may not be sympathetic to your story, it's just that their computers will almost always "kick out" your application as soon as the bankruptcy code comes from your local retail credit bureau computer.

You can try writing a personal letter to the credit card company and explaining your plight. My best advice is to get your Retail Credit Bureau account as solid as you can, first, because ultimately the credit card company will still "query" that source for the final decision on whether to issue you a card.

For your sobriety, the less plastic you have the better. It might lead you right back into the same bad habits that were associated with your drinking days, and you will find yourself right back in the soup. If you get a credit card or two, handle them with care; share their status of use with your Significant Other so that you are not playing old games again. By all means, pay your credit card bills promptly and make certain you are current with your account on the month that your card is due for renewal. If you mess up again, you will probably have a most difficult time in ever getting anyone to go another round with you!

A simpler form of the extended credit card line is the card that is commonly called the "Check Guarantee" card issued by your particular banking institution. Here again, the financial statement you supply will allow the issuing bank or savings and loan to give you a card that will let you make loans to yourself simply by writing a check for it in any amount up to your established limit. Your payback schedule is handled by the lending institution, and the monthly payments are generally deducted from your checking account, automatically. Periodically you may apply for increases in the amount of credit on your credit line and lo! Voila! You have yourself a credit card!

Talk, talk, talk these money issues over with your banking person.

Don't be afraid to ask, "What do you think? What's *your* advice?" This is diametrically opposed to what you were doing in your alcoholic behavior, and it should help bring you joy to know that asking someone else's opinion is really a worthwhile thing to do.

LET'S TALK ABOUT INSURANCE

I feel strongly about your role as a recovering alcoholic in helping to educate and re-educate some folks about your disease. You're going to have to if you need whole life insurance policies. Now before any insurance people get up in arms while reading this, let me say that I have found many companies to be sympathetic to the problem of the recovering person, but not quite as many who are willing to sell you whole life insurance at standard rates. Here's what I did; you will have a different battle plan and a different method of approaching the situation, but all I can share with you is the tool that I have used and recommended to others who have used it successfully.

First, you need to re-evaluate your insurance position. If, during your drinking days you may have let some policies lapse or if treatment ate up the borrowing power of some policies, you probably have left yourself and your loved ones woefully underinsured.

It's entirely possible that you didn't even have any life insurance, but the depth of your bout with the disease of alcoholism has made you aware of the fatal nature of the disease and the imperative need to be protected with adequate insurance. Age, of course, has a bearing on the scale at which insurance companies rate you, but the really sticky part will come when the medical history is taken for your application.

Like many others, insurance companies have been relatively good about recognizing alcoholism as a treatable disease. What's been a little slower has been the realization that the recovering person needs to get a break for *having done something* about treating the disease. That's the rub. Many companies are happy to insure you for almost any amount, but they want to rate you very high up in the "high risk" scale. This is understandable; after all, like many other diseases, there is no guarantee that alcoholism will remain in remission. That's where you have to do some really hard, honest selling on your own behalf. The following tools can work if you're willing to put in the leg work required and handle the problem in as honest and forthright a manner as possible:

1. Contact the person or agency that has handled any insurance for you in the past. This means even if it has been a person that doesn't

normally handle anything but straight liability policies such as auto and theft, etc. This person or agency will have a referral for you to another person or agency that *does* handle whole life underwriting.

2. Spend telephone time. Tell the person that you are recovering from alcoholism, and what is his or her company's policy as to the rating of recovering persons. You want to ask:

A. Can I get *whole life* coverage?

B. Will I be rated at a standard risk scale?

C. Will I be required to supply past records of treatment?

I think you will find that most agents will be willing to look up company policy but will not know it right off the top of their head. I was fortunate in having my longtime agent and friend get right to work. He was equally honest with me by saying, "I don't know the answers to your questions but I'll get them." Can't ask for more than that.

3. Begin drafting an explanatory letter which will detail your treatment of the disease of alcoholism, the length of your sobriety, and the names and places of medical references that could supply further evidence of your state of recovery. If you are recovering by AA alone, tell them that in the letter and detail your regular and continuing participation in the program. Be prepared to supply a cover letter from your AA sponsor who can attest to your efforts to remain sober. Most sponsors I have known are delighted to be of service in this area.

4. Be prepared to take your case beyond the agent level and contact the issuing company directly, with a cover and supporting letter from the agent you are dealing with. This will require your agent to locate the name of the top person in the insurance company you are seeking to be covered through. Don't hesitate to write to the *president* of the organization. The key is you and your agent will have sorted the companies down to the ones that will be "borderline" in whether they will write insurance for a recovering person at a *reasonable* rate. I guarantee you *will* hear from the top person! In one case, a client told me the company president referred him to another competitor who was able to supply what the client wanted.

5. Make your initial request for insurance at $10,000 or above. Premiums, depending on age, can be high no matter where you are rated, and you don't want to get yourself tied up with something too tough to handle.

6. Secure consent forms from your hospital, treatment center, or doctor that will allow them to release information about you to the inquiring company. Time is of the essence. You want to be prepared

to strike when the iron gets hot. Delays of anything over a few days will possibly lessen your chances to prove that you are serious about your request for help.

7. Ask your friends at any AA meeting how they got *their* insurance. What you will uncover very quickly will be a recovering agent or two who will be delighted to help you and will speed up the entire process for you. Insurance companies are constantly changing and updating rules for coverage, and new companies will crop up that you never even heard of before. Doesn't matter; they will be just as reliable as the others and you can count on the fact that any agent that is recovering will have made a thorough check of alcoholism coverage in his/her own search for policies.

8. Contact any hospital patient representative at a hospital that has an alcoholism recovery unit, even if you did not go through that unit. They will have some knowledge of where you might get the information you seek. Oftentimes a company that pays for the inpatient or outpatient services of treatment will have a direct tie with an underwriting firm, or will be happy to recommend one. *Not all* insurance companies provide full or partial coverage for alcoholism—period! Remember, the company that will cover your medical bills for treatment may or may not have a tie-in with a company that will underwrite life insurance for you, but they are a source that should not be overlooked.

Now all of these steps I have outlined will take time and energy on your part. The reward is, you *will* find a source for standard rated whole life insurance, and it will have been worth the effort. It's just like anything else in your sobriety; you'll discover some real satisfaction to be had from doing responsible chores again. One final note: Many people I work with have reported that after a year or so of having coverage at a certain rate they actually received a *lower* rate from their insurance company.

Dealing with your banker, your lawyer, and your insurance agent can be one of the real joys of your sobriety. What was once painful, hostile, and embarrassing can be turned around into long-lasting friendships with people that you once thought were just "out to get you."

Give them a chance. Show them the new, recovering you, and the chances are very real they will stand among the first line of defenders of you and your new way of life!

Children begin by loving their parents. After a time they judge them. Rarely, if ever, do they forgive them.

Oscar Wilde
A Woman of No Importance, I

7
Where Was I When the Kids Were Growing Up?

"I can't believe my mom actually *hears* what I'm saying!"

"Dad, it's so different . . . I mean you can talk and not blow up at me!"

"God! Where *were* you when I really needed you?"

Good question. Where were you? I mean, it's pretty obvious that some of the people in your life thought you had vanished from the face of the earth because you were never sober enough to be of any help when they needed you. If your drinking was even confined to "just" weekend abuse, the chances are pretty good that it was weekends when kids needed things from you, important things like:

1. Your time
2. Your attention
3. Your love,
   and,
4. Your *rational* judgement for meting out discipline.

That's a pretty good shopping list, and one that was rarely filled due to alcohol's importance in your life. But that's behind you now, and you can get on with the business of learning how to be a parent,

63

or a grandparent, or an aunt or uncle. If you don't have kids of your own, read this chapter anyway and apply the principles to your dealings with any younger people in your life. I often think of the trials and tribulation that besets Hank Ketchum's marvelous cartoon character "Mr. Wilson" in Ketchum's popular "Dennis The Menace." Wilson doesn't have any kids and Dennis lives next door. That's bad enough, for Wilson has to learn to deal with Dennis as if Dennis *were* his own kid. Maybe you are a recovering grandparent and have been told over the years that "We're not bringing little Susan to stay with you anymore, Dad. We can't trust you!" I think I will never forget the pain and the tears that I saw exhibited by a grandmother who, in recovery, was having a very difficult time getting her son and his wife to believe that she was different now, that she was *sober* and deserved a second chance.

"What can I do," she asked. "They don't trust me, I guess because they think I'll go back to drinking when they've left my grandson with me!"

Well trust works both ways. The recovering person has an equal chance at being trusted along with the equal chance that the kids get to be a little different themselves. They haven't always been little dears, you know, and quite frankly a child living in an alcoholic home learns to manipulate the situation.

Kids have always had the knack of knowing which "buttons to push" in order to achieve their personal goals. Parents have helped them find those buttons, and the alcoholic parent has practically given the kids a new set of buttons every day to push!

The children have gone through incredibly embarrassing times because of alcohol abuse in the home. Think about it yourself and apply your own situation as you can recall those instances when heartbreaking events occurred because you were caring more for booze than booties!

How many times have I heard a youngster tell that she will no longer have her friends over for a "slumber" party because she can't count on a parent being sober. That same kid will hook up with a friend who has parents that become her surrogate mom and dad, and it is to them she goes when she needs comfort, advice, and love. This only brings more trouble at her own home when the petty jealousies of her parents demand the youngster bring her needs to *them* because, after all, "We *are* your parents!" The problem with that is when alcohol abuse is in the home, no youngster wants to waste the time to try and talk things over with a drinking parent. They know that whatever is said on a drinking day (night) isn't going to be remembered when the drinking episode is over. So why bother bringing anything up to you?

You've got to change that, and we'll look at some ways that have proven helpful in regaining some lost ground between parents who were drinking and, now sober, their awe-struck kids. "Awe-struck," you say? Yep! Kids are perhaps the first to recognize what a big change has occurred between the drinking and the sober parent. So let's set up some basic tools on the counter and see how to use them.

TAKE THEM ONE AT A TIME

There is just one of you, and maybe a whole slew of kids. Even if there is just one, you probably should use this tool. It means dealing with the kids as complete individuals and not as all the kids lumped together. If you do have just one, then it means that you will deal with him or her alone—no mother, grandmother, little friend from next door, or what have you.

The kids learned a long time ago there is safety in numbers, and boy if they can outnumber you they sure are going to try! How many times has the plaintive cry been raised under your roof that goes, "But *all* the others are doing it!" Or, "You *always* let Mary have one of those when *she* wants them!" See? Safety in numbers. But the joy of your being sober now allows you not to knuckle under to being harrassed by a whole army of offspring. You need to establish the fact that you will deal with each of your children on an *individual* basis. I am the father of twins plus two more. I wouldn't trade any of them for the world, but I sure had to learn to deal with them on this one-on-one basis. It's too easy for any recovering person to want to jump right in and meet every kid's needs all at once. Don't try it! Invoke the "One At A Time" rule and then make it stick. This is equally important even if the issue might be the same for all the kids. You still want to sort the issue in your mind on an individual basis. Your brain is going to need recovery time like the rest of your body; so take everything slow and easy. That's part of the new you; you can dictate a few terms based on *your* comfort level, and make it stick!

ALLOW VENTING

This tool is not going to be easy for you to use, and like the castor oil you may have been forced to swallow as a kid yourself, it may not go down easy. The tool works because it says, "I am giving you (kid) permission to vent your anger at me." Further, "I know you *are* angry (at me) and hurt." It helps you give way to the frustrations your young person has been keeping pent up inside for a long time. *How* you allow this venting is the real key to the use of the tool. So, venting is "okay" when:

1. It's clearly defined as "needing to blow off steam."
2. It's understood that there is hurt present as well as anger.
3. There is an attempt to resolve that hurt.

The now-sober person controls the "interview" (with youngster). And you bring into play another tool you're about to learn.

REVERTING TO "I" STATEMENTS

To get the interview for "venting" started you use the "I" statement. It goes, "I have the feeling that there is something troubling you, Susan. Can you help me with why I'm feeling that way?" This clearly states that you are not asking for anything from the other person except to help you sort out *your* feelings. See, no one has to go on the defensive. You are giving permission for venting to start by expressing a desire to have help with feelings about you and the person to whom you are talking. "Susan" might respond with, "Well, Dad, you might be feeling like something is bugging me, because it is. And what's bugging me is you!"

Control yourself! Remember you are giving permission to vent feelings and simply helping that person get started in a clean manner by using the "I" statement. It's obvious that this tool of the "I" statement is a very important one in making the *Re-Establishing Your Marriage* chapter work. I saved it for here to show you that it can be helpful in *all* interpersonal communications.

Every time you employ the "I" statement you take the monkey off the back of the person with whom you are about to have a dialogue. You give them permission in a roundabout way to unload by helping you define your own uneasy feeling(s). What really happens, of course, is you get a solid clue as to what *is* wrong between you and the other person. Armed with the knowledge of *what's* wrong, you can proceed to:

1. *When* did this feeling occur?
2. *How* do you think it happened?
3. *Where* did it start?
   and,
4. *What* do you (we) want to do about it?

Notice the absence of the word, "Why." Don't ask "Why." "Why" only smacks of despair and the "Oh-woe-is-me" attitude that you had when you were drinking. Stick with the other tools to conduct the dialogue with the other person.

The "I" statement tool should be used in any of these dealings with your youngsters, so keep it in mind as we examine the other basic tools of dealing, soberly, with your children.

DON'T OVERREACT

Boy, is this an easy trap to dig yourself into! When you were drinking it would take days, weeks, or even months to get an opinion or decision out of you. Now, sober, you want to jam all systems to "Go!" and solve all your kid's (and anyone else's) problems in thirty seconds flat. Take some time and stop overreacting. You can't make up for all the mistakes of the past anyway, and the ones you can correct can stand the mellowing of a little time. With your kids they want everything now, anyhow, and your new-found sobriety makes you want to jump right in there instead of asking yourself, "What's *really* going on here and what can I (we) do about it?" By establishing some time frames to the problem with your youngster, you are gaining valuable strategy as to how you both can solve the particular dilemma. I don't mean to make everything sound like a battle or skirmish between you and your children, but I am anxious to have you take time to assess everyone's position and point of view before acting on a matter.

Such questions as, "How much time before this has to be done?" and, "Are we able to put this matter 'on hold' until (tomorrow) so we can see what (mom, sis, etc.) have in mind?" all clearly beg for time, but do the begging in a manner that says we are *not* going to forget about the subject. We are just not going to allow (either of us) to get stampeded into foolish action. Taking a second look before acting helps you analyze the situation without undue pressure. It's also the main reason for not dealing with your kids in "packs," but individually as previously stated. No stampedes. You don't need that in your sober life.

Overreacting also tends to make you spend more money and buy more of everything than you probably should. We'll discuss that in more detail under one of the other tools in this chapter. Suffice it to say right now, that it *can* and *does* happen; you are so anxious to prove your sobriety ("How can I get them to trust me?") that you go overboard, and in too big a hurry. Think of overreacting as pushing the red button on the hotline telephone. Once it's pushed there's very little chance of recalling whatever terror you will unleash by not giving the proper time to contemplation of the effects of whatever actions you take.

BE OKAY WITH CRITICISM

Like other tools of sobriety that bring you joy, you'll find this one a real hummer when you get the hang of it. It's a little masochistic at the beginning, but you'll get used to it. This is particularly true if you and your youngster are willing to *trade* criticisms. It goes like this:

KID: "Mom, I really want to talk to you!" (Notice, talk *to* you, not *with* you.)

MOM: (Using "I" statement) "I'm feeling like there is something *more* to just wanting to talk. Can you help me with that?"

KID: (Boy *can* she!) "Yeah! I think you're smoking too much!"

So, there's the opening gambit. She wants to criticize you, and you are okay to take criticism. In your previous drinking state you might have verbally or physically backhanded the little smart-mouth, but not now. Now, it's okay for the criticism bit as long as there is a quid pro quo to the whole thing.

But being okay will mean that you need to take her criticism, and only then venture to offer a counter criticism. You might say,

"It seems like my smoking upsets you, Kate."

This gives her (Kate) a chance to "unload" about seeing you smoke and to offer a bonafide criticism of the habit. You can very well expect your youngsters to tell you that they "wanted" to say something about it before, but "you wouldn't have listened then." A little not-too-subtle jab at the old drinking days, don't you think?

So you listen to her expound on her theory of being bothered about your excessive smoking, and then you are in a position to trade off for something you'd like changed in her. You could say,

"Kate, I think you're right. It even sounds like (very reflective) you might be willing to help me cut down on my smoking; maybe by cutting down on your piecing between meals." Then the clincher:

"Is *that* what I'm hearing?"

You're gonna love it! When you get the hang of this being okay to take criticism and being okay to offer some in return, *without anger,* you are going to experience some real joy.

Never, but never, use this tool to explain why *you* do something ("I'm *older,* after all"), but rather handle the criticism as a method to bring some more positive interaction between you and your youngster(s) into play. Being okay with criticism is another sign of your healing process and it needs to be encouraged and fostered as a valuable tool in your recovery.

ASK FOR POSITIVE FEEDBACK

This may seem like a variation on the "Warm Fuzzy"; they are quite similar, yet different. The "Warm Fuzzy" is a way to say thank you. "Positive Feedback" is a permission giving device (tool) that you can employ to get your kids to tell you what's *right* with your relationship in addition to what's wrong. If you think this sounds a little like sitting up and begging for strokes and ego soothing, you're right. And there's nothing wrong with that! God knows, everyone has been right in there to help say what has been wrong with you, so why not let everyone have a fair shot at helping you feel good about yourself?

For the kids to be involved in Positive Feedback is a double reward. If they can help define the things that you are doing right (in your relationship with them) then they can be made to feel a part of that right.

"Hey, Kevin, that's really great to hear from you! I think I owe a lot of that change to you, too!" Now for the continuation of the Positive Feedback with,

"Is there any other area (thing) where you see some improvement?"

Who can resist an honest opening like that? The chance to share in some credit for seeing improvement in another person. That's fantastic! The using of Positive Feedback as a tool for your continued recovery is valuable because it helps re-establish the fact that *sober,* you're "Okay"; not being sober means you were *not* "Okay."

Once established, you can use the tool of seeking Positive Feedback as a means of having your kids help you fight all sorts of things — namely the "Dry Drunk" attitude and the "Grey Ghost Syndrome." That's when you need Positive Feedback most; when things seem the blackest and the temptation to relapse to a drinking episode might be the strongest.

If you couple Positive Feedback with the tool of being able to accept criticism, the rewards can be endless in your relationship building with your youngsters. This is a tool of your sobriety that says, "How're *we* doing?" and since you are willing to share the credit, more of it will surely come.

REASSESS CRITICAL SITUATIONS

Oftentimes a decision has been made by you or jointly with you, your spouse and the youngster(s) involved, and that's an end to it. This is not a good idea. It's entirely probable that some new information is available on a certain situation and you should not feel "locked in" to a previous decision. This is too reminiscent of "You *promised!*" and, "You can't change your mind now!" which you used to hear quite frequently during drinking days. Well, you *can* change your mind. You *can* take another look at the situation and by so doing you add another rung to your ladder of credibility. *This* time, you're no pushover. *This* time, folks will have to reckon with a sober mind that reserves the right to change his/her mind without it being a major catastrophe.

When a client says, "It's not worth the battle for me to back off of a decision I've made," then I think of telling them, "Look toward winning the war; that requires doing some battles!" If you become too complacent with not making a reassessment of a situation, you are reverting to the alcoholic habit of *never* making a decision. Use the family situation to call a "Pow-Wow" or conference with a single member of the family to talk about changing an already made decision or at least looking at a new alternative.

This is particularly important when it comes to changes in your financial situation. Maybe you've decided that you can afford to buy a car for your college-bound son. He and you decide and pick out what is safe, classy enough and, at the time, affordable. Let's say that he was going to contribute a certain amount to the purchase or the upkeep of the vehicle. Perhaps he had committed funds for the insurance on the car. You have made a decision, but before you can carry it out, "Sonny" tells you that he has lost his job and that he will be unable to carry out his end of the bargain.

Here, a change in plans is clearly called for. If you have to assume this new cost it may cause undue stress on the family budget and on you, personally. Should you go ahead with the purchase anyhow? No. You need to have the courage to make a new assessment of the situation and arrive at a joint decision that will try to meet both your needs and your son's needs. For you to forge blindly ahead is a return to alcoholic behavior patterns, namely actions without regard to consequences. This is not going to help you in either your continuing sobriety or in your trying to build a trust relationship with your youngster(s).

Being "locked in" to a decision means that everyone still has the ability to push the right guilt buttons with you and get whatever they want, even when new information may have been discovered (the loss of a job) which makes a new decision mandatory.

Keep this tool of reassessment handy because you will want to use it frequently even though it will bring loud wails of protest from the "aggrieved" party(s). Basically, it will remind everyone that a more mature, stable, and concerned parent is back in the family setting—one who realizes no decision, *except* the one to remain sober, is poured in cement. Eventually, your children will respect the right for everyone to change their previous collective decisions because it will force all of you to look at alternatives to reach the given objective.

It also says, "As a family unit we can afford the luxury of being flexible; something that didn't seem to be there when alcohol abuse was a part of our lives."

SETTING LIMITS

It is imperative that you not turn into a "gift/money horse" in your sobriety in order to wipe out the guilt that may be heaped on you for the years of drinking. You're going to be the one to pour on this guilt more than anyone else in your family, but let a kid or two throw some fuel onto that fire and many times you'll find you can't reach for your wallet fast enough. That's definitely *not* the answer. There may be many things you would like to do for and with your children, now that you're sober. However, you can have the effect of making *them* drunk with lavish gifts, money, and attention that too often says, "Look how I'm trying to make up for what I've been (and done) in the past."

Setting limits means you recognize both as an individual in sobriety and as a responsible family member, that you can't buy your way into permanent affection, loyalty, or respect. And, by setting limits you actually increase your chances to help yourself and help your children get themselves into a more complete state of wellness around your recovery.

Letting the "sky's the limit" philosophy into your recovery program means continuing the process of enabling all who are near and dear to you to continue in their own self-centered ways. They, like you, need to be willing to take responsibility for their own actions, and if you are the leader in clearly setting limits on your own actions, they will be forced to set limits on their own habits and perhaps, ruinous ones at that.

Setting limits also refers to the physical you — the one that has to learn to say "no" and be comfortable about it. Many times, the euphoria of new-found sobriety will lead you into a real rat race of trying to keep up with all the plans that others are making for you. The long-postponed fishing trips, picnics, bike rides, and other "buddy" activities with your children can wear you down in a hurry; even if you were not in a state of recovery from alcoholism. The good old precept of not letting yourself get too involved too quickly really holds true.

Self-guilt may dictate overindulgence in parent-kid projects; avoid this by sitting down with the youngster(s) involved and explaining that you are recovering from a disease, and that it will take some time before certain mental and physical energy levels are back up where you can cope with demands.

Setting limits means it's okay for you to say that "enough is enough," no matter what the particular demand. It does not mean that you won't rise to the occasion later; it simply means that you need a breather from many things, including being the grand entertainer or family host.

A good way to set limits is to use the phrase, "I think this outing weekend calls for us setting limits." This puts it right up front at the beginning and opens the door for the youngster(s) to be in on the plans of when things will *end* as well as when things will start. A favorite slogan of AA is "Easy Does It." That's just about the name of the tune, and you need to learn to be comfortable with it.

BE CONSISTENT

Your behavior patterns are going to be in wide variance for quite awhile in sobriety. When you are dealing with the kids, this needs to be reinforced. Drinking allowed you to change your mind and the way you did things about as often as you changed your socks — maybe more so. As you recover, there will be a certain feeling of well-being in knowing that you can do things the same way twice. Now, don't confuse this tool of Being Consistent with the tool of reassessing critical situations, which allows you to change both decisions and promises made.

Your kids need to learn and respect the fact that your sober behavior with them is going to stay that way — sober. All the taunting, harrassing, temper tantrums and the like are not going to make you drink. You are committed to the joy of being sober, and you're going to stay that way. Being consistent in your behavior will help solidify that resolve. If, for example, you have established a rule with your kids that says, "You need to call us if you are going to be later than agreed; and we'll call you if we're going to be late," then be consistent. That rule needs to be held by you for as long as it applies to the situation. Nothing could be worse to your new life than to have your kids see you try something a couple of times and then drop it, just like you did with your alcoholic behavior.

This does not mean that you are glued in forever to a particular action that has become unworkable. When this occurs, it's time for the individual pow-wows and resetting of short-term objectives. It's the general "wishy-washy" attitude that you want to avoid. When Charles Shultz, "Charlie Brown's" creator, has one of the kids saying to good ole Charlie, "That's what I like about you, Charlie Brown. You're so wishy-washy!" he must really be saying that lack of consistency is a regular lovable trait in some people. But that's not for you, because that particular trait was too much a sign that you had been hitting the juice, and you could be counted on to change the policy that seemed to be yesterday's Ten Commandments.

The tool of Being Consistent also gives you a way to share many rewards in the form of "Warm Fuzzies" with your kids. It's a simple tool, really; responsible behavior (from you, kid) gets reward from me. Irresponsible behavior gets you nothing; including me *not* giving in to whatever demands you may make to get your way.

This theory, of course, belongs not to me but to the fine reality therapist Dr. William Glasser. It's the theory that I use in my own therapy work. If you want more details, Glasser's book *Reality Therapy* is a jewel.

The more uncomplicated you make your life of sobriety the more joy there is in being sober. The more consistent you become in all your relationships, the more you solidify the fact that you are a different person — one to be reckoned with, and not just put "on hold" during a family discussion. You should learn to forget hearing the ways your kids would say, "Wait awhile. Dad'll change his mind!" *That's* how you were when drinking. Sober, all who deal with you will have to learn that your behavior patterns will begin to emerge as being ones that everyone can count on. As I said earlier, they (behavior patterns) are going to take some wide swings for awhile, but eventually you will find ways to bring each mode of your behavior into clear focus. This will help you and each person with whom you must deal, whether on a short-term, close-range basis, or on an "away-to-college-hit-'em-on-the-phone" contact.

REINFORCE WHAT WORKS

When you and your kids discover that a new way of communicating has arrived between you, then you use this tool, over and over. You can say such things as, "Hey! Remember how we solved the ski trip problem?" or, "Who can tell me what we did when this came up before?" It works even better when you keep your dialogues on the one-on-one basis I have discussed earlier, because it forces the youngster to search his/her memory banks for the way you solved a problem *together.*

If it worked once, it will work again. That's the philosophy behind the tool, and you can trust it. Each time you bring the reinforcement idea into play then you establish stronger ways that problem solving can occur on a regular basis between you. It's a downright thrill to see the many ways you and your kids can get along for a change, if you are willing to work at it. Both parties have to make a commitment to keep reinforcing what works, and also to have an equal desire to throw out what *didn't* work.

That's why I'll play around with a particular furniture design in my home workshop. When I find something that works, I write it down and pin it on the corkboard in the shop. My "mistake box" of wood reminds me that a lot of trial and error went into building some piece of cabinet work, but once I learn something works, I'll use it over and over.

You can assess and reassess the success of a particular idea that seems to work for you in your everyday dealings with your kids. You'll need to stick with, use, and shout about the ones that work; discard and change what doesn't work. It's a good blueprint for you and your kids to keep "pinned" to your relationship.

FIND NEW ACTIVITIES

This tool is fun, exciting, and therapeutically helpful to everyone involved. So many times I will hear people talk about returning to a particular place like "Disneyland," and not really enjoying it. "What do you think was the reason?" I will ask. The reply can generally be boiled down to, "It just wasn't the same!" And it wasn't. Nothing can really be the same anymore because *you* are different, and three cheers for the difference! So, in an effort to regain family closeness, a revisit to old activities more often than not fails. In sobriety you are looking, acting, and feeling so different about yourself that it's as if the activity shouldn't have been attempted in the first place. Maybe you spent money with reckless abandon then, and now your sobriety causes you to be more prudent.

Maybe you packed everyone off on first class airfare, and now it's better that you all drive, which increases tensions but *does* save money. Maybe the old campground no longer appeals to you because of painful memories. So, you search for a *new* camping place or stay in a cabin for most of the trip.

More than half of the fun of new activities is in the planning, and this is an area where you can have real input for the first time, perhaps. Your kids, particularly, will want to have your views on what can be done that's new and different. The reasons for finding new things to share together is so painful reminders of alcoholic behavior do not mar the enjoyment of the vacation or the activity. What family members may think of as being funny may not be anything but hurtful to you. While it is true that you will eventually have to work out those pains and those griefs, I believe that "togetherness" activities are not the place.

I have had people tell me that they did a simple thing like trip, quite by accident, getting off an airplane jetway. Some family members reminded them that "Gee! Nothing's changed. (Mom's) still tripping over things!" This happened to be in reference to a family trip taken when "Mom" was still drinking daily and the kids in her family had come to accept her clumsiness as part of her drinking. The lady told me that she felt so bad after the *sober* tripping incident that it was several days before she "snapped out" of her depression.

Using the tool of New Activities certainly doesn't mean giving up flying because you tripped a few times. It does mean that you need to face up to the possibilities that old recurrences might crop up that will spoil your good times. If so, then a family conference is necessary to agree that when such things do occur they will be dealt with right away and using the Freedom For Criticism and Warm Fuzzy devices, you will weather them.

Generally, though, it will be more of a challenge to try some altogether different things with your kids. *Then,* if an incident occurs such as I just described, you all are experiencing the thing *together,* sober, and able to treat it as its *own* occurrence and not something laden with grief from the past.

The very idea of sitting down and planning a vacation together can be a real joy. You might split up your vacation times so that each of your kids feels that you are sharing part of your leisure time just with him or her. This isn't as hard as it may seem, and many families in recovery have found their way back to each other by taking shorter, more exclusive trips together.

I learned this firsthand when sickness by one of my twin daughters forced her to fly home from college while the other twin and I had to drive back from Minnesota with all the luggage. We had a blast! It was the first time in many years we had been alone together and came to know a lot about each other over that three-day trip. It wasn't planned that way, but since then I have found this a great way to spend some time with my kids.

I take them singly, maybe just out to lunch or to a game, but alone and with an opportunity to explore some new activity together, such as shopping for a new item of clothing for *me*, for a change! In drinking days, this would not have been possible. In sobriety, it's not only possible but downright fun.

There are dozens and dozens of other tools that you will discover if you search for them. Start with these basic few we have been discussing and make your own modifications. You will find a real sense of satisfaction in knowing that you used these guidelines and they worked. Your kid(s) will be equally stunned to find you are capable of setting a "game plan" and making it work.

The joy of your children, grandchildren, or other young friends of yours is a part of your life, a deep part. You don't have to whip yourself into a moral frenzy trying to answer the question posed by this chapter title. Now that you've faced the fact that you *were* there, at least in body, you've got the rest of your life, sober, to be there in the full *spirit* of what being a parent is all about!

*It is a truth universally acknowl-
edged, that a single man in possession of a good fortune, must be in
want of a wife.*

Jane Austen
Pride and Prejudice

*Behold her, single in the field,
Yon solitary Highland lass!*

Wordsworth

8
The Singles Game
Without Booze

Boy! Have all of us been mean to you! I mean, we have been
wretched! We, those that love you and care about you, have taken away
your best friend! Yes! We helped you take away your bottle; your
best friend. How can you *possibly* meet a member of the opposite sex
now?

In the highlight of your drinking days you had no trouble at all
overcoming that innate shyness, that lack of resolution that was always
a part of you until you downed a belt or two. Now, like the "Cowardly
Lion" of "Oz" fame, you are, indeed, in search of courage. The road is
not a yellow-brick number, either. It's rough! Your main battleground,
the bar, appears to be off limits to you if you want to maintain your
sobriety and still meet some available personnel in the dating battle-
field.

What to do? Where to go? Are you forever doomed to sit in the
gloom of your apartment or condo and watch the dust settle on your

77

coffee table? Do you detour on the way home from work so that the local singles bars will not look like some temptress in your path? Are rock concerts now a thing of your past? No, no, no!

What we will discuss together here is the plight of the sober single and like our other chapters, look at some tools that you can try out to help you find added joy in your sobriety while you find added companionship. And don't say, "What does *he* know — *he's* married!" You're right. But I spend an extraordinary amount of time listening to our clients who, in treatment, are facing the very dilemma of single sobriety that you are. I owe many of these tool developments to them, and because they have worked for others, they can work for you. In my lecture work I always look for an opportunity to find other bases where singles are wrestling with these same problems, and the wealth of material provided by talking to these groups, exchanging experiences, disregarding what doesn't seem to work and amplifying the ones that do, provides the groundwork for this chapter.

Recovery, as I have told you before, is an honest program. I'll level with you. I tried a couple of these ideas myself to see if they worked the way I thought they would and the way that they had been presented to me by others. I thought, by slipping my wedding ring into my pocket I could "pass" at a singles gathering and see what was really going on. It didn't work! The ring has left such an indentation on my ring finger that I spent more of my time denying being recently divorced than it was worth! Finally, I settled on coming clean and telling folks what I was up to — just plain old hard background research. I was and am happily married, but could I stay and observe anyhow?

Thus, I can *honestly* tell you, I have tried every one of these tools myself, and they *do* work. I did not, however, use the "advertising" tool that we'll discuss later on; that appeared to be more of a strain on the honesty than I felt was called for. But I have seen others use it and very effectively, so it's included in my material on the sober single.

Let's begin by asking what you know about yourself as a single person. First, there are almost 18 million of you running around out there according to the 1980 Census. One of every three adults in the United States is single, and about 50 million of you fall within the ages of 20 to 55. So much for the statistics. What they all boil down to anyway is, "Where is the male or female for *me*, in all that jungle?" I am variously told, depending on whether the client is male or female, that the "balance" between available men and women is "all out of whack" in this city (Denver). Maybe. But I've heard it in Dallas, read surveys about New York, Atlanta, San Francisco, etc., and all I've come to in the way of a conclusion is, the people who really *want* to find someone who shares sobriety, *do*. Alaska may be the exception, where females seem to be in very short supply. I made that statement to a friend of mine recently and he replied that he had attended an AA meeting in an Alaskan city and met "all kinds" of single ladies; so take that for statistics. They can work for you or against you, depending on what you want to find.

Most all data seems to indicate a common thread or two about the sober single:

1. They are trying to combat loneliness.
2. Their sobriety has fed their insecurity and underlined their fear of rejection,
   and,
3. They would like to meet *friends* of the opposite sex without the enormous sexual pressures of the past.

Fair enough. You can relate to that, can't you? It doesn't really matter whether your sobriety is brand new or several weeks or months old. You need some friends — some one or two people in your life who are willing to contribute to continuing sobriety by sharing time without making too many demands, particularly in the sexual arena.

With that in mind, let's look at what the missing ingredient appears to be in the plight of the sober single.

BAR COURAGE WITHOUT THE BAR

Boy, howdy! When you were on that bar stool quaffing down a few, you were Superman or Wonder Woman, Robert Redford or Farrah Fawcett. Didn't matter what you were *really* like, you were able to have alcohol mask all the imperfections and highlight just the good stuff! That's okay, but now the missing ingredient of alcohol forces you to the great and harsh realizations of exactly *who* and *what* you are. So you are dealing straight for a change. There are no hidden cards up your sleeve, and it scares you to death.

It shouldn't. Let's see what your goals are for meeting people in bars in the first place; that is what they *were* when you were in your drinker's mode. More than likely you perched yourself on a bar stool to satisfy fairly immediate needs:

1. Sex
2. Not spending the evening alone
3. Not spending your own money

4. Developing a solid "contact" place in your life by being one of the establishment "regulars."

Drinking in that bar gave you courage, albeit false courage. The needs may still be there but as we discussed earlier, they have changed, perhaps to more nearly combat loneliness and fear of rejection. Let's face it. Sober, you will wake up and damn well know *how* and *why* and *who* is beside you in bed (if anyone!). That can be scary because it means you need to put a whole lot more effort into the contact in the first place. You need to use some tools to regain bar courage without the bar atmosphere. Here they are:

1. I accept the way I look.
2. There's a lot more to *me* than just a body.
3. Someone is out there *looking* for someone like me.
4. I'm in charge of my life because I'm sober.
5. I can make choices as easily as being the target of someone else's choice.

With alcohol you didn't *care* about those things much less try to use them as everyday tools to your personal growth in life. Now you are sober and seriously capable of adding another ingredient into your recipe for finding a companion. That ingredient is: "I want to find someone I can *count* on, someone who will be there when I need him (her)."

That shows that you are now ready for some kind of relationship that goes beyond the range of the "one-night stand," which, by all accounts, is a very common occurrence in the alcoholic single's life. So, you can afford to take some time and shop around for places where other singles may be congregating. You have some items on a shopping list of your own, and you are beginning to feel better about yourself. It takes work, though.

You are never going to meet anyone staying at home. You will have to force yourself to venture out into public if you are going to test the new waters of the sober single. Your bar courage can and *must* be carried with you wherever you go in an attempt to meet other people. Consider this about bar courage: When you took a few ounces of alcohol, *two* ounces to be exact, you were sedating part of your brain for a period of one and one-half to four hours. Part of your brain was being put to sleep and that included the part about "good judgment," "tension," "stress," and a lot of other inhibitors that were standing in your way to making contacts with members of the opposite sex. The problem is that when the booze wore off, all the inhibitions that were there in the first place returned and you had to start with more booze to regain this false courage. The realities are that you didn't quit with one drink of two ounces of alcohol, but rather several and even *more* than several. Your bar courage came, was nurtured, and vanished when you left the bar.

As a sober single, you can have your courage with you all the time by recalling that you were not necessarily shy, bashful, awkward, incapable of brilliant conversation or any other inhibiting factor. It was the *alcohol,* combined with the *desire to meet someone* that allowed you to put everything into full swing and "score" with a member of the opposite sex. Well the only thing that's different is you have removed the alcohol. The same basic, effervescent, bubbly and brilliant *you* that has been lurking beneath the surface is *still* lurking there and you only have to release it! So, you can treat your encounters with other potential companions with the same bar courage without being in the bar and without drinking. The reason for this is the belief and *understanding* that alcohol didn't *put* any of those neat qualities about your personality in you, it only removed the *inhibitors* (on a very temporary basis) so you felt "free" to act. You are *still* free to act! You are even more in command because you will be aware of every subtlety in the game playing and every nuance. And isn't that great?

WHERE TO MEET THE OTHER NON-DRINKERS

Now we get down to the nitty-gritty. You can pick up so many books, magazine articles, newspaper stories, and even pamphlets about this singles game that I sometimes feel you could spend most of your single time just *reading* about it and not *doing* anything about it! I don't want to add to that clutter, so what you're going to find on the following pages of this chapter is not a random inventory of meeting places but ones that I have culled (with the aid of many client's experiences) into *workable, manageable* meeting situations. You can and will find a hundred more and if you do, use them. Keep in mind that most places suggested by many others will have drinking as a part of the package and we'll discuss those pitfalls later.

For better or worse (forgive the expression!) here is my list:

1. AA and Al-Anon, Ala-Teen
2. Sports, Exercise Clubs
3. Church, Synagogue
4. Classes
5. Concerts
6. Museums, planetariums, gardens

7. Travel—everyday, long range
8. Office buildings, the elevator
9. Stores, "Mom and Pop," Supermarket
10. Advertising

Now, let's dissect the list and amplify its richness as a meeting ground for the sober single.

AA, AL-ANON

There is no question in my mind that regular attendance at your meetings, whether in town or out of town, will acquaint you with other sober singles faster than any other method. At AA and Al-Anon, Ala-Teen, the game playing has long ago been left at the door and you can get right down to an honest confrontation between the sexes. You already have the biggest hurdle removed; it won't require having to "meet for a couple of drinks sometime" before you can begin to find out whether you would enjoy each other's company for an evening or afternoon or Sunday brunch.

Al-Anon, contrary to some popular notions, *will* contain singles; people whose previous relationships were wrecked by alcohol but who found the companionship, warmth, love, and understanding in an Al-Anon group or two and just continued coming to keep their personal growth program intact and operating on the "go" cycle.

The comfort level at AA, Al-Anon, and Ala-Teen is just as high as you want to make it. There's nothing to be afraid of and you all are there with a very common background. Ala-Teen's *know* how to have a great time being drug and alcohol free. Just ask them! Most of the kids I know in Ala-Teen have more dates and social activities on their calendar than any of them can handle. I can honestly say that I have attended many AA meetings and watched people of all ages find each other. You see them come in as singles and suddenly in a few weeks they show up *together* at a meeting you're attending. An AA therapist friend of mine told me once, "I always start with my sober friends in AA for companionship. There I know I'm starting with most of the ego trips out of the way, and I can look for honest relationships!" She's right on target too, for this lady never seems to lack for friends of the opposite sex.

In the chapter on AA group-finding, we'll talk more about "culling" available-people groups.

Remember, the primary purpose of attendance at any AA meeting is to continue to gain strength in your program of lifelong sobriety. Don't clutter that purpose with other things; the companionship you can find in the groups I've mentioned is centered around your common, number one need — the need to remain sober at all costs! Working the main program and meeting available new people will be one of the bonuses for the sober single.

SPORTS, EXERCISE CLUBS

Americans never do anything half-way and the phenomenon of wanting to get in shape and stay in shape continues to be a very major rage. With this surge toward taking care of ourselves has come a booming new and ever-growing industry: the sporting club-exercise-fitness complex. These places range from storefront shopping center operations to large free-standing buildings. For example, at the World Headquarters of the Manville Corporation a huge fitness complex, including indoor pool, is fully staffed and maintained for employee's benefits; the entire operation is housed right in the building and this is no longer unique. Many such corporations are providing fitness rooms and holistic health programs for their employees. Ones that don't provide their own facilities make arrangements for their employees to use nearby places. Better ways to spend a lunch hour simply haven't come along!

These exercise rooms, racquetball courts, running tracks, and indoor pools are a regular gold mine for meeting people. Again, alcohol-free people are going to feel right at home in places more devoted to building up the body than tearing it down. So what if you don't work for a large corporation that has provided you with a membership or place to do all these things? What about the place where you live? Virtually every townhouse, apartment, or condo development offers "amenities" such as these: pool, tennis, "rec" room, pool or billiards, and now, video games in either arcade or lounge settings.

Those are all just facilities. The *meeting* part comes with your willingness to engage in the activities that are offered. I think the mixed tennis "ladders" where your level of skill is matched with others equally skilled (or in my case, *un*skilled) provides an excellent way to meet people. There is beginning racquetball, aerobic dancing, and "Jazzercise" exercise classes where *many* men and women participate.

You already know how I feel about running. Many clubs and condo organizations will hold regular "Fun Runs" of one or two miles, as well as larger 5K or 10K events. Sign up! You'll meet more single folks than you ever thought existed, and you'll quickly find a lot of folks who would *not* be interested in a beer or two, but rather settle for a great iced tea or Gatorade.

If you're not into much more than a couple of laps in the pool or some easy jogging, that's okay too. Investigate the lounge areas of the athletic club where the video games are. You can hover near one of those, acting as if you never heard of "Pac-Man" or "Asteroids," and the chances are you'll be asked if you want to play a game or two. "Buy you a drink?" can be handled really well in an athletic facility that *does* sell alcoholic beverages by countering, "As long as it's soft" or some such reply. No hassles, no laboring over long excuses about not wanting a beer. After all, you *are* in a setting that's conducive to no smoking, and certainly where consuming alcohol is an amenity for the social drinker, and not a temptation for the recovering alcoholic.

CHURCH, SYNAGOGUE

A larger number of clients told me about the opportunities to meet single people at their church or temple than I had counted on when researching this. The participating in such interchurch activities as choir or adult Sunday school, are supplemented by "Young Adult" groups and teaching within the church or temple such crafts and art-skills that you may possess. A person told me of starting a film club at his church. Everyone brought popcorn, and they used a church popper and a micro-wave to make many bowls of popcorn. Then the whole group watched a "classic" movie, which they rented.

This activity has been made even easier with the advent of video-tapes. Films are available for showing in even very small temple and church activity rooms that contain the necessary player and TV set. This young fellow got his group together by having an announcement printed in the church bulletin. A lot of married couples showed up, but so did a surprising number of available singles of both sexes.

The teaching idea came about when a lady said she decided that it would be fun to share her interest in drawing and sketching with others. She used a church bulletin and flushed out a group of just three who wanted to learn more about the craft. She was a sixth-grade art teacher, so she simply broadened her teaching level to include adults and before long the word had gotten around, and eight to ten *singles* were showing up with their drawing gear to spend a couple of hours on an outing near the church, sketching their little hearts out and meeting new people! This teaching episode naturally leads to:

CLASSES, ACADEMIC AND CRAFT

While the idea of going back to school may not appeal to you as a full-time proposition, you certainly might consider the absolutely wild array of *free* classes that are both educational in the academic sense, and skill building. Community recreational centers offer things like "Ms. Mechanic" for the liberated female that wants to be able to fix her own car, "Beginning Spanish," "Learning Guitar," or "Co-Ed Self Defense." Photography classes for the beginner, and cooking for the male and female gourmet, are very popular.

Again, the common thread of whatever the class is all about is helping the sober single to overcome a big barrier that "bar courage" was needed for previously, namely, "What do *you* like to do?" By the way, I mentioned the "Ms. Mechanic" class because a whale of a lot of men want to either help teach that course or take it themselves!

Going back to a regular campus in your community is always worthwhile. If you're an older single, then the community college or city college is going to offer more people your own age than the local four-year liberal arts institution, where most of its population will be right out of high school graduation.

It has been my experience that many divorced, recovering people turn to the educational field to pick up where they left off or simply to try and expand their lives in other ways, for the future. The opportunities present themselves handily to meet other people with the same goals. I can guarantee that one look around and you will definitely not feel "too old" or "out of place" in a classroom setting again. Use your own confidence pusher and give it a try. I would suggest, however, that you not jump into very heavy full loads of any kind of classes if you are new in your sobriety. You will have a tendency to overload yourself, and the pressure can become so intense as to outweigh the therapeutic values of going to a class and meeting new people.

CONCERTS

Today, when you say "concert" to anyone under the age of thirty, they may be inclined to think in terms of rock groups, "Beach Boy" revivals, and Barry Manilow. But what I'm really advocating as a new and proved meeting ground for singles who are sober is a symphonic concert of some kind. If you live in an area that has an orchestra or chorale group that interests you, then by all means attend. The philosophy here is very simple. If you ask for a single ticket at the box office, they are going to sell you seats where, primarily, they know *other* single requests are most often filled.

If the "seat-mate" turns out to be a dud, you still have the beauty of the concert and the show of support for your orchestra. But, really, the fun is in the intermission times. Here, you mingle quite casually among the pieces of art in the lobby, or you step out for a breath of fresh air. You space yourself far enough away from any cluster of people so that it's obvious you are attending alone. If the concert provides drinks as most of them do, make certain you have a *cola* drink of some kind so that you make it obvious you are not consuming one of the alcoholic beverages, such as white wine or champagne, that may be available.

If you are a sober single male, look for the female that is giving these signs of being alone and not interested in drinking. But even if the other person is drinking, you don't have to! What you want is the chance to meet other people with the same interests as you. Concerts are just dandy places to do that.

Once again the initial "interest barrier" has been already broken. Obviously the person you approach at a concert is interested in that kind of entertainment and you can simply capitalize on his or her presence at the event. ("English horns from off-stage really sparked that movement, didn't they?") Actually, concert-going can open up a whole new world for you if you're really into matching intelligence around musical knowledge. I avoid this game like the plague, but I know singles that really know how to use all the right "lines" and how to sincerely feel comfortable in striking up a conversation with a stranger; use the program for the evening as the basis for entry into learning more about the charmer you have selected!

MUSEUMS

This category of single-sober hunting grounds is as broad as the locale in which you reside or are visiting. Art museums and galleries are fine, but here you really need to know your stuff and I advise using them as a base for meeting other singles only if you feel you can really sustain some knowledge around the subject at hand.

However, a client once used the *unknowledgeable* approach in an art museum and it worked fine for her. She just "played dumb" even though she was and is a very fine artist herself, and was quite familiar with the particular works being displayed. Her decision to let a gentleman think he was helping her understand the exhibit better was some danger to the honesty part of her recovery program. She 'fessed up later in the relationship, and all turned out okay. At the same time she owned up to knowing a good deal more about art than she had let on, she also disclosed her disease of alcoholism to the man. She told me in a therapy session later that it was a calculated risk, but it turned out fine. The friend said he was proud of her decision to be in treatment and glad she owned up to the art business, too. He told her he had suspected *that* one all along because the "dumb" questions she asked weren't dumb at all. "What gave me away?" she asked. "You asked whether that particular painting was the best thing in Picasso's Blue Period. Most people who are not well informed about art don't ask questions about an artist's period, but rather 'what the painting is supposed to mean.' "

Doesn't matter. She struck her bait right in the heart!

Museums of an historical nature are a little better "hunting ground." Natural history, botanic gardens, and western Americana provide a wealth of "small talk" when you are trying to make some impression on a single you have spotted.

A young friend of mine told me that he had met "more ladies than ever" at a botanic garden by just wandering around with a houseplant in his hand and asking, "Excuse me, do you know if this thing will grow without direct sunlight?" He confided in me sometime later that he had more fun doing that than all the times he had spent trying to "drink the girls pretty" at a local bar! Ah, the joy of being sober!

Western museums offer the same kinds of comfort-level openers. "That looks like the wagon hitch my grandmother in Missouri told me about," he says. She replies, "You from Missouri? Funny, I thought you sounded Texan!" Write your own dialogue; you get the picture, don't you?

TRAVEL

Too often the newly sober person thinks about "getting away" and for a long period of time. I don't recommend this, whether you are single or not. The strain and pressures to drink might be stronger away from the safety net of home, so for awhile think of shorter trips and more of them instead of one long haul.

We'll deal with jet travel in the chapter devoted to "Flying Without Drinking" later. For now, just consider that you will have opportunities to meet many people when you fly; your big problem will be to determine their availability, whether they are truly single. I don't have a formula for this except you single girls will find more single male flight stewards than men will find unattached female flight attendants.

If you are going to fly make it a short (under 1,000 miles) trip if you can, and ask for the *middle* seat on the plane. You can count on:

1. Getting asked to change places so "we" can sit together, or,
2. Striking up a nice conversation on *both* sides of you which gives you many options.

Train travel has some pitfalls because any socializing is probably going to happen in the club car, even if you're on the Metroliner where every car is a club car! Watch yourself and always, but *always* keep a visible can of soda pop by you, so as not to even hint that "buying you a drink" means a preface to getting you drunk. The beauty of a train ride is the length of time you spend in just being able to shop around for other singles. Ski trains are super; so are short-haul excursions if you have a camera slung around your neck. If you're a male you can look like you know what speed to shoot, and if you're female you can *prove* you know what you're doing by not *having* to ask.

But my favorite method for the sober single to meet other folks is by bus. More specifically, the bus *stop*. That's right, the bus stop. I began to notice as I drove back and forth to the inner city that almost all the very attractive people, male and female, were waiting for the bus. When a snowstorm allowed me to offer to share my car with some people waiting for a bus, we all started to talk. But I listened a lot, and the three others in the car, two girls and a man, were headed in the same general direction, downtown. The man found out that he and one of the girls worked in the same block, and he invited her to lunch with him.

The two girls who were roommates got out of the car first, because they had other appointments before going to the office. That left the young man and me. "You can let me off here in the next block if that's okay," he said.

"But I thought you worked downtown farther," I replied.

"No," he said. "Actually I work out near where you picked us up. But I learned a couple of months ago that if I were to leave my car and ride the bus I would meet a lot of really nice women, and I do!"

"But you told that girl you work in her building!" I said in my most outrageous manner. "How can you start a relationship with lying?"

"It's not really a lie," he told me. "I *do* work in her building. I work in many of those downtown buildings. I'm a computer sales rep, but our main office is out south where you picked us up!" He went on in the remaining time together to tell me that he was totally tired of the singles bar scene and that he had decided to devote two mornings a week to walking from his office over to the bus stops near several apartment complexes where he had observed attractive ladies waiting.

"Usually, I will ride the bus down with someone I met *waiting* for the bus. I'll make some calls that I have to, then come on back to the office. It beats the bar scene all to hell."

And not one person had to buy a drink in that whole encounter.

YOUR OWN OFFICE

This "Elevator Gambit" has been developed and polished to a fine hone by a middle-aged man in recovery who knew there must be a better way to meet singles than to take a chance on going to a bar. When he was drinking he told me, "I could care less about who was in the building where I worked. When I sobered up I began to notice how many really nice people in my age group were riding the elevator with me. I started sort of by accident saying, 'Floor, please,' to the people on the elevator. It was an automatic elevator but people got a kick out of it. After a couple of mornings of doing this I knew the floor where one particular lady I liked got off. I pulled my same routine and when everyone had gotten off the elevator, I went back to the floor where she had gotten off. I just spotted her right away and walked up and asked her to have lunch with me."

I asked him if that was successful, and he said the lady had told him, "You don't have to buy me lunch. I would meet you for a *drink,* though." Our recovering client jumped right in to tell her, "I don't drink anymore and that's why I can *afford* to take you to lunch!"

It was and is a good example of the sober single putting his program to work, and realizing some more joy of being sober.

There have been several other incidents where sober singles have related to me that they have met more new people in the building where they work just by being sober and being able to talk without "acting like an idiot." A favorite method of meeting new people is to "brown bag" it alone. One girl told me she realized she was stifling her chances of meeting men by always sitting on the building's lunch patio with other people.

"I decided to risk going it alone for awhile to see what would happen. I didn't want to risk losing my girlfriends that I had been lunching with, so I hit on a plan. I brought my lunch but kept it in my oversized purse. When lunchtime came, I 'begged off' saying I had to go uptown. I did just that. I went uptown three blocks to the _____ Building and sat on *their* plaza — alone! Worked like a charm!" she chortled.

See how inventive you can be?

STORES AND MARKETS

The supermarket continues to be the national racetrack of meeting singles if you believe all the literature that's written on this subject, but I've stuck with a better one, I think. Forget the supermarket and hit the "Mom and Pop" operations. Those smaller neighborhood markets and delis beat the big stores and supermarkets all to pieces. You have more time to survey the scene, you can move a lot slower (you have to) through the aisles, and "bumping" is a lot more accidental than when you try that in a large supermarket.

Hang out a lot around the soft drink aisles and avoid the beer aisles. When you see someone you like who's loading their basket with soft drinks, too, you can remark, "Sure is nice to see someone who doesn't need a whole basketful of beer!" If that sounds stuffy to you, I challenge you to try it! You can use your own words, but just try the approach. You'll get some answers like, "Yeah, I hate beer. *Vodka's* my drink!" But more often than you'd suspect, you'll get a positive reinforcement about not wanting to drink! As I say; don't take my word for it. Try it out and enjoy the results for yourself.

ADVERTISING

Finally there's this method of meeting another sober single. I think it has merit but only if you are open and forthright with the ad you place in the "personal" column. You should come right out and declare your new sobriety. You're using a hidden box number or at best, a telephone number, so you are pretty well protected. Be prepared! Some eagle-eye AA folks will pick up on such ads and try to get you to a meeting! And that's great! You'll go some places you may not have known about before. But if you want to try your luck on just a one-to-one basis, then you can stay with answering the mail or the telephone and making your own meeting arrangements. Again, I stress that you need to be open, honest, and forthright in using this meeting method. The ad, typically can read:

> Newly sober and single male (female), age 25, wants to meet person equally free of pressure to drink. I'm just a lot more fun to be with. Interested? Call 555-1234, after 6.

How you handle the inquiries is *your* bag, but you *will* get responses and a lot of them will ask you how you got your sobriety and how long you've had it. You can take those questions as your comfort level so dictates. Basically, the *amount* of time you've had your sobriety is of no importance to anyone else. You can counter such questions by asking the inquirer what makes the length of your sobriety important. You might discover another single (or someone else) who is looking for encouragement and direction toward sobriety themselves, in case they have answered the ad seeking such help.

I feel good about you! Yes, I do! I can see you getting all gussied up and trying some of these new tools to meeting other sober singles or singles who won't put pressure on you to break your sobriety. I see you riding on planes, waiting at bus stops, and pushing elevator buttons. I see you wondering aloud if brush strokes really can be forged, and if Coleus plants need to be "talked to" as much as African Violets.

I see you trying as hard as you can to select the right mustard (and needing help); wondering if you are singing that tenor part too loud (you cute little alto); wondering if you didn't meet him at Weiss's bar mitzvah, see her name on the sign-up sheet for mixed doubles.

Oh, you're doing fine, you are! Of *course* you wonder what this class is *really* going to be like! I hear you asking "How's your program coming along? Want to try a meeting on the West Side with me?" Yes, indeed!

You're single. You're sober. You're leading the good life again!

Continental people have sex life;
the English have hot water bottles.

George Mikes

9
Sexuality and Recovery
(Does recovery take away all my fun in bed?)

"I dunno. She says she's interested, but nothing happens."

"It's just not the same; I can't describe it exactly, but it's almost as if he doesn't care about having sex anymore."

"She used to be dynamite in bed, but now that she's sober, well, it's a real drag!"

So, like the English in the quote above, you "reach for the hot water bottle." Sex is now a drag. You're sober and all that it's gotten you is the feeling that you *have* no feelings, sexual feelings anyhow. Well, maybe this chapter will help you understand first what taking alcohol out of your sex life has done, and what you might need to do to bring a little pizazz back in between the sheets. It's not as gruesome as it may seem in the first light of sobriety. You have undergone some physical changes, and your body is naturally wanting a little time to respond to the new game plan of your nonalcoholic new life. So let's just consider what this game plan is to be on as simple a basis as we can make it.

The first thing you need to understand is the effects that alcohol and other drugs have on sex:

1. Use of alcohol simply removes inhibitions.
2. Both alcohol *and* sex affect the pleasure centers of the brain.
3. Alcohol eventually deadens the senses.
4. Psychological barriers may still remain after stopping use of alcohol.

There are other effects, but those four will do; if you want highly detailed research on this, I refer you to Masters and Johnson, Kinsey, Alex Comfort, and a host of other very knowledgeable researchers who have done the most extensive work in the field.

We do know that the sex drive and the craving for drugs and alcohol seem to come from the same area of the brain, the thalamus. It's encouraging to note that the word "Thalamus" is Greek for "bed" or "bedroom." I love it!

We also know that the human brain is conditioned to equate the feelings of being "high" and sexual pleasures. In fact, researchers have been able to make laboratory tapes that showed brain stimulation to drugs, alcohol, and "natural" highs to be fairly indistinguishable one from another. That's good news. We also have good news for those over the so-called "highly erotic" years. The National Institute on Aging publishes a brochure entitled "Sexuality In Later Life." In that publication the Institute dispels a lot of myths about sex for the "elderly" and further proclaims that "most older people want—and are able to lead—an active satisfying sex life."

The Institute notes another strong point. It says that excessive use of *alcohol* is "probably the most widespread drug-related cause of sexual problems."

If the *use* of alcohol causes extensive problems, then we are now looking at what the *absence* of alcohol is doing to our sex lives and the sex lives of the people with whom we are sharing our recovery.

The statements at the beginning of this chapter are typical of those therapists hear on a daily basis from clients wondering "What's happened?" The answer is pretty plain and simple. In most cases, the absence of drinking in your sex life has opened the closed-off floodgates of anxiety, and all the inhibitions you had managed to block have come back to haunt your every move. Those inhibitions about sex and certain acts of sex were probably there all along, but you had managed to camouflage them with booze. Let's start first with the now-sober female to see how she (you) can find a way back.

Here's the formula again:

Past behavior pattern:

"I have certain inhibitions (fears, taboos) about sex. I take enough alcohol into my system; *lose* fears. Take alcohol away (gain sobriety), and reinsert fears (taboos, inhibitions)."

New formula:

"Since I already had some fears and inhibitions about sex, I obviously had to *learn* them (from others; from "bad" experiences).

*Any*thing I learned, I can *un*learn! Alcohol only *prevented* me from learning."

If you stop to remember, the chances are very real that most of your sexual experiences have involved alcohol in one form or another. This begins with the adolescent fumbling around in the back seat (or front) of the car, right up until the much overrated wedding night. If you have been married to or lived with an alcoholic, then you are pretty used to sex being more of a legalized form of rape and very little more.

Now you begin sober sexual relations and what happens? Nothing, that's what! You have high expectations and they lead to failure; suddenly you are hearing terms like "frigid" and "dysfunctionate" applied to you as you try to pick up where you left off before achieving sobriety.

Well, you are *not* dysfunctionate by nature; you had to learn it. Sex therapists think of "dysfunctionate" as a female who cannot achieve orgasm, and maybe that's just happened to you in sobriety. When you were drinking you may well have experienced *multiple* orgasms, having achieved a state of relaxation of your *fears;* everything was just peachy. Sober, you suddenly become a bundle of nerves and even begin to hate the thought of having sex, because it will most certainly lead to "failure" (no orgasm). This failure to reach orgasm can leave you in a high state of frustration and discouragement.

It's safe to say that most of this failure is caused by you *thinking* failure. Your alcoholic old ways say, "I need a couple of belts to bring this off!" Nonsense! You need a re-evaluation of what the sexual needs of your life are. I believe strongly that they are:

1. The need to *share* with someone.
2. The need to *care* about someone before, during, and after.
3. The need to *trust.*

Sex therapists have determined that 95 percent of a female's orgasmatic dysfunction is mental. If you ever read the story of the *Little Train That Thought It Could,* then you've got the idea. "I think I can, I think I can. I *knew* I could! I *knew* I could!"

There are three other major reasons for female dysfunction, according to specialists in the field. Those reasons are:

1. A low sex drive (lack of libido).
2. Painful intercourse (if it hurts, why do it?).
3. Vaginismus (clamping down of the vaginal walls, making penetration difficult and painful).

It is estimated that more than one quarter of all female alcoholics suffer from vaginismus, an outward "and visible sign of inner and

95

spiritual uptightness" as Dr. Alex Comfort so aptly phrases it.

The same new rules or better yet, suggested tools for new sexual relationships apply to recovering males as well. The need to *share, care,* and *trust.*

Before we discuss these tools in detail, let's examine the major reasons for male dysfunction, again as pretty well agreed on by sex therapists, at least the ones I have been privileged to study under.

There are four primary reasons the sober male (and probably even the still-drinking male) fails to "perform." They are:

1. Premature ejaculation.
2. Ejaculation incompetence (lack of ability to achieve orgasm).
3. Primary impotence.
4. Secondary impotence.

I want to add one that I believe may not have been given as much importance as I believe it to be in the recovering male alcoholic. That is, alcoholic neuritis. Many men I have worked with have reported the lack of "feeling anything." The degenerative process of alcohol on the nervous system causes this, with the prognosis good or at best, guarded, depending upon complete abstinence from alcohol and the extent to which the toxic damage was done by drinking in the first place. It *does* get better, but it can add temporarily to the general feeling of being "unable to perform." Time and the total abstinence from all alcohol increase the restoration of the feeling process.

Now to detail, briefly, what seems to cause the four major reasons for male dysfunctioning. "Premature ejaculation" is probably the most common and prominent problem. A man ejaculates before even beginning to satisfy his partner, and there is nothing but frustration left on her part. This dysfunction sometimes appears to have its roots in a man's experience with prostitutes, where the order from her was to "hurry up and get it over with, honey!" This is a deep-set block and depending upon the age that a man first encounters it, can grow stronger as the use of more and more alcohol sets the block deeper and deeper. The second reason for premature ejaculation may be more easily accepted — the experience a man has as a teenager when the fear of discovery caused him to "get it over with" *without* being told. I once worked with a man who had gone through a number of experiences of having to "bail out" of a girl's bedroom window because they heard her parents returning to the house. It took him a long time and a lot of therapy to remove that sexual block.

"Ejaculation incompetency" is said to be caused primarily by the fear of having a child, coupled with religious or other taboos of a man's upbringing. This is the old belief that almost anything was okay as long as a man didn't ejaculate inside a girl. While drinking, he didn't care; now sober, the old taboos come flooding back and he becomes dysfunctionate.

Number three, "primary impotence" seems to be a little more clinical and oriented in some basic pathology. The use of alcohol and drugs is the number one reason given by the experts as the reason for primary impotence. Disease, such as diabetes, is also a major cause, and treatment can help there. When a man's anxiety gets so high and he develops such an intolerance to that anxiety, he will "fail to perform." Part of that anxiety, a great part as a matter of fact, lies in the pressure put upon the male *to* perform. Other anxieties, many of them very deep-seated, can cause mammoth psychological roadblocks that cause some men to become impotent. Their sobriety only makes them more completely aware of this. Patience, time, and continued understanding by all parties concerned can ease this trauma, and once understood through some pretty heavy-duty psychotherapy by skilled sex therapists, the chances for eliminating this roadblock are favorable.

Finally, sexual deviation from heterosexuality and certain religious upbringings can cause primary impotence. The homosexual and lesbian may perform in complete totality while practicing their sexual preferences with members of the same sex, and be totally dysfunctionate in a heterosexual situation. Understandable. The figures show that less than 50 percent of homosexual or lesbian relationships will survive sobriety, since the absence of alcohol may make one of the two partners very much aware of their homosexual behavior and be unable or unwilling to continue the practice.

Religious upbringing in the stricter faiths can and does influence much of this primary impotence in certain men. Again, the key is that alcohol abuse has smothered these feelings and the guilt that went with them. When the alcohol is "out of the picture," as you have heard me say before, the guilt comes flooding back and *must* be dealt with.

"Secondary impotence" as a major cause of male dysfunction is another name for what it *really* is: the inability to maintain an erection. If it happens more than 25 percent of the time, it's considered to be a dysfunction and not just a "fluke." I want to keep tying all this in to your joy of being sober. This whole chapter up till now has been pretty discouraging, hasn't it? There's not much *joy* in finding out that your sobriety is causing you to wonder if you'll ever again be "great in bed," or even if you'll ever again get "back to basics."

Sure you will. And better than ever!

But sex must now be looked at in the light of the concept of *share, care,* and *trust.* At least those are the tools that I've found to be helpful in dealing with others afflicted with the same problems. If you consider that sexual relations with someone was prompted by, heightened by, and fulfilled by alcohol, it's a pretty dismal relationship to start with. So the recovering one and his/her companion need to start all over and ask themselves, "What do I really *want* from this person and, what am I willing to *give?*"

Before, sex was so much a take-only situation and the hangovers and fights that ensued before, during, and after sexual combat steadily reduced it to just that—combat. So, get out of the war! Make *love!* You do this by sharing, caring, and trusting.

SHARING

It's an overworked word, but I'm using it anyhow because it's a tool of our trade, and I'm comfortable with it. "Sharing" is the concept of doing a form of communication that goes beyond "telling." You "tell" small children *what* to do; you "share" your feelings of love, tenderness, and concern *with* them. I had a client once that got extremely irate with me because he wanted me to "just tell" him something instead of "sharing" it. After a few weeks of therapy I noticed him in group saying, "I want to *share* something with you all." Later I asked him why he didn't just *tell* the group instead of *share.* "Because," he said, and not at all with timidity, "the way I *feel* has to be shared!"

Same thing with your lover. He or she needs to be a part, an integral *part* of the love-making process. That's different than just being the *object* of your sexual desires. This calls for sharing of feelings with someone, wanting to let a very special person know what's going on with you, how you feel at the moment and what you are afraid of, if anything, at the moment. It is the sharing of tenderness—of hopes, fears, triumphs—that leads to *desires.* Strong desires will lead, in all probability, to very rewarding sex. Let me state right here that you will get no technique training from this chapter. *Sharing* is not a technique. It is a *tool* for recovery. It means, "I care so very much about you that I'm anxious to just hold you (for awhile) and have you listen to what's going on with me." By your willingness to share *who* you are, you are expressing your willingness to let sex be a further expression of *what* you are and what you want to continue to be—the place you wish to occupy in your very special person's life.

By using the tool of sharing you are expressing the strong point that your lover is such an integral part of your life (and your recovery), that you could not even think of just "having sex" without it meaning a culmination to the expressions of joy you feel in just being with him or her. It says, "Making love with (not to) you is no longer an act of my selfish gratification." Which leads us naturally to:

CARING

The need to *care* about someone before sex, during sex, and after sex is essential if, in recovery, you are going to make progress toward a lasting sobriety. Before, sexual encounters were just that — a "Wham, Bam! Thank you, Ma'm" kind of thing that only fed your lust and did not meet your emotional needs. The "one-night stand" takes care of the moment but seldom says anything about *caring*.

Sobriety, and the joy of it, means that you have a sincere concern for meeting the needs of your partner as well as your own. Sexual encounters become a matter of "what can we do *for* each other, instead of what will I be able to *do to* you." *Caring* means finding again the meaning to the word "tenderness," being gentle, kind, and concerned for your love partner, instead of the old "hit, grab, feel, and run" games of the past.

You no longer have wine and mixed drinks to ply her with before dinner. You *do* still have soft music, candlelight, dinner out, a small lunch in front of the fire on a rainy Saturday afternoon. In short, you have everything for the elements of good sex without needing the alcohol. Believe it! The best thing you have to offer him or her is a sober you, a person that shows how they care by taking a little extra time *before,* a lot of time *during,* and even more time *after* sex.

The tool of caring, properly used, increases the joy of your sexuality because it says, "You are someone so special to me that when we have spent our physical desires, I still want to be right here with you!" The sadness of hearing a woman tell of the age-old habit of her mate to not even take five minutes to hold her after sexual intercourse, is all too depressing. It doesn't have to be that way; *that's* the way it was when you were drinking and when you only cared to satisfy yourself.

I remember a female client telling me that after her lover had made love to her and then just rolled over and gone to sleep she became furious. "You sonofabitch," she roared. "I just made love with you and you can't stay awake even five minutes to hold me!" Understandable anger. No caring; no sharing. Just taking, and taking, and taking.

So *caring* for someone requires your expression of that feeling *after* the various acts of sexual gratification. You don't have to jump right up and run for the shower! That's old habit patterns creeping in and saying, "there must be something dirty or unclean about this!" Take time and *hold* your mate. The holding, dearly, of one body against the other is such a warm fuzzy that has "Care" written all over it. It says something of the dignity you ascribe to the person you have just shared the ultimate experience with. You are worth everything you think you are! Your sobriety now allows you the freedom to express your feelings of your mate's worth to you, by *caring* for their feelings, their fears, their *needs*. Which leads to:

TRUST

Over and over you want to feel that you can trust the person to whom you have given the gift of your body. In sobriety, this gift becomes even more precious than it ever was in drunkenness. "Can I trust you?" used to mean, "Can I be sure you will be faithful to me?" Now, the word "trust" means, "I want to know that you are with me, beside me, encouraging me, and helping me as never before to remain sober." As a token of that trust, you become willing to share your body with that special person. Does that make sense to you?

So much of your sexual activity before was not a willingness but rather a reward or perhaps just something that "was expected." A "payoff" for an evening out, or what "you had to do" if you went away for a day or two. And there was little or no trust in either the sex or the relationship. The trust lasted as long as the alcohol lasted; that was the sum total of many commitments.

Now, *trust* is earned and not expected. It's given after very careful examination of the other elements of sharing and caring that make up this new triumvirate of your sexuality in recovery. But you need to trust that very special, *special* someone in your life because you are going to be very fragile for quite awhile. Time will help heal the wounds of sexual abuse that were caused by alcohol abuse, but the element of trust will have to be an immediate and ever-building process that doesn't end.

Your word didn't mean very much in alcoholic days; you could not be trusted and therefore you didn't expect much trust from anyone else. But all that's changed, and you *need* to be trusted as much as you need to trust. It, like the other tools, is a mutually sought after and shared experience, and one that you may never have used very much before.

When you practice the use of these tools of *sharing, caring,* and *trust,* the other elements of a satisfying sexual relationship will begin to grow. Recovery, after all, does not mean nor was it ever intended to relegate you to a life of celibacy. It is a state in which new values around your sexuality replace some old very bad habits.

The exploring of one another's sexual needs, and meeting those needs is twice as satisfying in recovery because you *remember* them! You don't have to wake up and wonder who that person is beside you; you *know,* and it was by choice. The sexual fantasies that came pickled in alcohol previously, can now be played out with loving sharing, caring, and trusting in, and with, the person in your bed, or sleeping bag, or whatever!

You certainly have the same capacities for making love as before. Your sex drive may even by considerably greater than it was when you were drinking, because honest feelings have replaced false ones. More than ever this is the time in your recovery program when you can "reach out and touch someone" and make it really count. Sobriety allows you the latitude to *know* the sexual experience. It doesn't have to happen in bed, either. It can be felt riding side by side in a car, or walking hand in hand, or even just sitting side by side watching television. It is a very different feeling than sexual arousal caused by stimulation with alcohol. It is real and lasting and an emotion upon which you can build and rebuild.

Like everything else connected with your sober life, this feeling can be made more secure by sharing the rare moments with others. For couples straining at the bit to "get it on" with the intensity of many other previous experiences I say, "Mellow out! Take it easy!" Savor the joy of your sex by starting over with new guidelines, as we have discussed. If you care about someone, you'll put their needs *ahead* of yours, and by so doing, *your* needs will continue to be met at a stronger rate than you ever thought possible.

If you want to settle for the "hot water bottle," then have it! But not me. Recovery and sobriety are destined to put the fun *back* in bed, and maybe a few other places too!

So God created man in his own image, in the image of God created he him; male and female created he them.

Genesis

If God made us in His image, we have certainly returned the compliment.

Voltaire

10
The Joy of Religion

Saying "Hello" to your God again is not as hard as it may seem at first glance. It's just as easy as the time before when you were drinking and you said, "Goodbye." Who me? Yes, *you!* You did it; you walked away from your God beating your chest and crying up and down the aisles like some modern-day Job, "Why me? Why can't I *drink* like everyone else? Why am *I* different?" We knew whose fault it was, didn't we? It was God's! Sure enough, you were damned with the disease of alcoholism because your God didn't love you quite enough; so you walked away. "Galloped" might have been a better description.

Either way, you got up from your pew seat and walked away. It could have been in the city's finest cathedral or temple. It might have been in that little clapboard-sided church at the far end of the farmland. It might have been at the inner-city storefront church. It doesn't matter. You got up and stumbled out and away from the whole idea that there even *was* a God. But that was the old alcoholic you. Now, there is the sober, joyous person who has timidly tested the waters of wanting to get back into the fellowship of your church or temple and not knowing quite how to do it. It's easy. You walk in.

There is a "shame" you believe in standing in the church parlor or the fellowship room of the temple and having to answer a bunch of questions about "your sickness." I have a friend at church that never could bring himself to talk alcoholism. Instead, he would ask me in great tones of seriousness, "How's your trouble?" It was a long time before I could get him to understand that I didn't have any "trouble"; what I had and still *have* is a disease. What is even more important, I have my church again.

Like you (and me), thousands of other recovering alcoholics have turned to the fellowship of Alcoholics Anonymous and discovered the concept about turning the problem of your drinking over to God, the God of your understanding. For many of them, this has replaced what was the formal experience of their churchgoing, even though AA is *not* a religious, but rather a spiritual experience.

Why not both? There is a real joy on a Sunday morning (or Sabbath Day) in attending a church or temple service, and then going to an AA meeting. It sort of ties up the week at the same time it helps begin the new week, with powerful tools of resolve and hopes for the new, sober you.

What I have discovered is that the comfort level in returning to the church you walked away from is so low, that you actually think that they might not want you back. This reminds me of the guy who wanted to attend a meeting of "Paranoids Anonymous" but no one would tell him where the meetings were! You *do* get paranoid about so many things in recovery that it's easy to see how returning to a church or temple, where you were noticeably abusing alcohol at times normally reserved for worship and praise, could be difficult. So, once again, here are a few tools for your consideration to make the job easier.

BE AGGRESSIVE

This will *not* be an easy tool for you to handle, particularly if you were abusing alcohol just to get over your shyness and to be aggressive, sociable, and comfortable around people in the first place. But it's important for you to be able to show others, as well as yourself, that you no longer need any kind of crutch to exchange greetings and accept well-wishes from your fellow members of the congregation. The key is to remember that it is *they* who are embarrassed to approach you for fear of offending you. It's as if you observe them wanting to find a way to think that you never were gone from them in the first place, even though they knew that alcohol had taken over so much of your life, taken it over so much that you had stopped even coming to church.

So, you have to make it easy for them! Be aggressive and walk up to people you have known in the past and greet *them!* You will instantly find them pleased and happy and no longer gun-shy about you. They will not want to jump right in and ask you about your recovery. They will say things about how much better you look and "how much weight you've lost!" Things like that. But the reason they don't say anything else is because they don't know *what* to say! So, you have to employ the next tool to increase your comfort level:

BE HONEST ABOUT YOURSELF

"Where have I been lately? I have been recovering from a disease," you reply. If you can say it for them, it will make it easier. You can overcome any paranoia by just assuming that rumor has been around long enough about your "drinking problem," so what good will it do to just let it continue to be rumor? Put it to rest with an honest approach to your church friends. Tell them how great it is to be back and how you've missed it all. Tell them about your bout with alcoholism and by helping them overcome their own embarrassment, you receive strength for yourself. You see, they don't talk about it because they don't *know* much about it. So I tell them openly and with the viewpoint that "I feel good about being here (in church), and I'm glad you missed me!"

When you "invade" these little groups of people that are standing around talking, you are giving a clear message that you are "back," and that you are approachable. Approachable? Yes! Have you ever stopped to think how many times your drinking problem has been treated like some kind of leprosy? You know, the old "Careful! It might be contagious!" routine? Your willingness to be open and honest about your disease will accomplish two things; namely, it will make them feel it's "okay" to talk about your past drinking, and it will also make disclosure of the past much easier for you, *every time* you do it. The church and the temple are ideal locations for this kind of disclosure.

Once, I became aware that two ladies in the church parlor were looking at me, then talking to each other and looking at me again. I walked over saying, "My ears are burning! What's up?"

"We were just saying to each other," one of them replied, "how good you look and how *good* it is to see you back in church!" Well! You can't beat that kind of a warm fuzzy, and I never would have known about it if I hadn't been aggressive enough to take the risk and ask the question.

COME TO THE QUIET PLACES

In every church, temple sanctuary, parlor, or "fellowship" hall, is a quiet corner. It is *your* kind of place. It is the place for you to come ahead of the rest of the congregation to have your quiet time with the process of making friends again with the God of your understanding. I like to go alone to the very front of the church, off to the side where I can sit in relative darkness and just think how fortunate, how grateful I am that freedom from alcoholism has helped me find the way back to the church—my church.

This "quiet communion" is a rewarding process for your sobriety. It is here that you can find the kind of peace that proves to you it was *you* who did the "walking out" and not your God. Ten minutes is plenty of time to sit in meditation about all the *joy* that has been associated with your being in this place. You don't dwell on the heartache; that's past. You concentrate on the present relationship that you are enjoying with this unseen God.

This tool of a "Quiet Place" is even fun to search for. It's very much like the "Laughing Place" we spoke of in Chapter 5. It is a *special* place in your church or synagogue that you can call your very own for just a few minutes once a week. Does it take a little extra effort on your part? Sure. Sobriety takes a *lot* of effort, but this is one of those very personal rewards that I feel sorry cannot be enjoyed by the "always-sober" persons! It's not the same for them as it is for you, because it is in your Quiet Place that you can be aware that the *place* (church) itself *never left,* and the Divine Spirit you are talking with is to be found there *just as before.* It's as if you had taken a short trip and have, over and over again, the thrill of realizing that you have come back.

When I see people alone in such a place, I assume they are in some sort of prayer. I don't do that in my Quiet Place. I have a little chat with my God, and I expect Him to listen! And as I leave my Quiet Place steady and upright, I am convinced all over again that He always *did* listen. He was just waiting for me to catch up!

HANDLING COMMUNION OR SACRAMENTAL WINES

I am indebted to many pastors, priests, and rabbis who have shared with me some ways that the recovering person can participate in the meaningful use of wine in the Eucharist of their faith. Alcoholics cannot, of course, handle even that little "thimbleful" that is used in many

Protestant congregations as part of the communion service. But you want to, and *should* participate in the service itself. Here are some ways to tackle the problem:

1. Your pastor, priest, or rabbi will know of your problem. They can insert a dose of straight grape juice or "Kool-Aid" in the tray with the other little cups. No one but the two of you will know the difference.
2. You can use the two fingers of the right hand and gently touch the chalice or "common cup" lightly on the rim; then touch your own lips as you pass the "common cup" on. It's a *very* rewarding gesture!
3. You can take a private communion (use "Kool-Aid" or grape juice).
4. You can substitute a dose of plain, clear water.

This last point (4) requires further explanation. My pastor and I were searching for a new and meaningful method in which the celebration of the communion could be perhaps as symbolically powerful as the use of wine without having to have the wine. It was "Pastor Del" who hit on the idea of inserting a few words around the "Marriage Feast of Cannan" where the miracle of transformation from water to wine is recorded.

We simply used a small thimble of water and Del retold the New Testament story around the water-to-wine episode. He added the words, "Receive this water, in the spirit of the wine which it was to become for all who are believers." It's a beautiful thought and I make use of this in private communion at least twice a year. Somehow it has taken on as much or more meaning than before. It is a simple tool, but I have shared it with a number of recovering people and they have all reported back enthusiastically.

You can handle wine in the temple or synagogue in much the same manner. Your rabbi is anxious that you participate in the service of worship and will assist you in every way possible to do just that. The key of course is to talk it over with your spiritual advisor. You'll be in for a big surprise. You'll head in to that person's study or office thinking you may be the only one in the whole congregation who is recovering. Wrong! He will put your mind quickly at ease by telling you that several others need to have communion or celebration wine handled the same way, and they'll just make provision for one more. It's a good feeling! See, you are *not* alone!

GET INVOLVED

One of the quickest ways for you to say "hello" again is to insert yourself firmly into a church or temple activity; something you have shunned before when you were an active alcoholic. Choir, Sunday school and adult teaching, nursery, camping activities and the like are obvious and logical choices. A word about the "nursery" job. I once had a female client who purposely set out to get the noisy task of running her church nursery when the position became vacant. "What in the world possessed you to tackle *that* job?" a therapy group member asked. The young woman replied, "I wanted those (church) people to see me being trusted with their most precious possession, their babies. I wanted to show them I was a different person!"

It was an effective tool for this woman because she had the courage to take the risk and ask for the job, and because she gained the best reward of all from *getting* the job, namely, a great big dose of self-confidence.

Don't bite off more than you can chew; take it easy and just look around a lot before you jump right in and find the pressures too much for you. If your church or temple has a library you might want to help out there. Most of them that I've seen could use more help than they ever get. The work is quiet, and you can go at your own pace.

Be sure that you don't confuse the task at hand. Bowling *with* the church bowling group is great, but it doesn't replace *giving* some of your time and talent *back* into your congregation. Hospital calling may have always been something you shunned as a very disagreeable task. It *is* in many ways, but as a recovering person you can reap new joy in your sobriety by paying a visit or two to those persons who are *now* less fortunate than you when you were in your sickest times of alcoholism.

Finally, this may sound like heresy, but I would strongly recommend that you be open to visiting some new places of worship, particularly in the comfort and security of knowing that you are just expanding your horizons of sobriety. Take another AA friend or ask to go to another sober person's church or synagogue. The point to all this is to reinforce the knowledge that your sobriety now allows you the richness of knowing that you have many ways and many places in which you can say "Hello" again to your God. Before, alcohol was the limiting barrier to any kind of spiritual relationship you may have had. Now, you are free to express your joy and your new-found gratitude in many ways and in many different places.

You'll feel a new comfort in places of worship that you never found before and when you walk out of a church or synagogue it will be with pride, not anger, blame, or mistrust. *That* was the *old* you!

*Fellowship is heaven, and lack of
fellowship is hell; fellowship is life,
and lack of fellowship is death. . . .*

William Morris

11

The Fellowship Experience: AA Revisited

"You'll never find me at one of *those* meetings!"

"I walked in on one of those AA things and it scared the hell outta me!"

"It's nothing but some dame talkin' about how drunk she used to get!"

"I never spent any time in the 'slammer.' What do I want to hear about *his* jail time for?"

And so it goes. All of the reasons and at least a million others why the fellowship of Alcoholics Anonymous is *not* for you, right? It seems in almost every case history of persons coming into treatment for the disease of alcoholism, they have either already formed an opinion about AA or have adopted someone else's opinion. What it eventually boils down to is the person has had one or two bad experiences; by "bad" I mean visits to AA meetings that were not suited to his or her needs at the moment. Well, we are going to "shop around" a little and see if we can't find the kind of meeting that is just right for you.

Let's begin by understanding that being actively involved in the AA fellowship as a part of your treatment for the recovery from your disease is a dynamite tool. It is a lifelong process that will help to cement your resolve, help to sustain your courage, and continue to forge strong links in the chain of support that is so needed for living a life that is dominated by sobriety.

The friendships you form from the fellowship will be the strongest ones you will have throughout your life. It is these friendships which continue to support the basic philosophy of AA:

"If all the people in this (AA) room with me have stayed sober; if they have found the ways to do it; then I must be able to do it, too!"

What I want to do in this chapter is help you shop for the kind of meeting that best suits you. You wouldn't dream of walking into a store and buying the first suit on the rack, nor is it likely that the very first or even second model of car you see will be the one you buy. Humans like to make choices. You can remind yourself of this every time you try and find your favorite cereal on the store shelves, packed in with what seems like a thousand *other* choices.

So no matter what your previous AA experience has been, let's shop around and look at various kinds of AA meetings. Be aware that these groups are the ones I have used as a shopping list for myself and also for others who are in the recovery process. There's nothing terribly official about the list. AA itself has taught from the beginning that all that is necessary to hold a meeting is two people and a copy of the "Big Book." I've known countless people that have done just that; many of them without even a book to aid them, only the desire to get sober and *stay* sober.

First, my list, not ranked in any order of priority:

1. Closed Discussion
2. Closed Speaker
3. Open Discussion
4. Open Speaker
5. Closed Step
6. Open Step
7. Home Group
8. Special Interest Group
9. Women's Group
10. Gay Group
11. Specific Minorities
12. Young People's Group

CLOSED DISCUSSION

This is my favorite group and the one that I have chosen for my own "Home Group" designation; that is, the group that I try to attend on a regular meeting basis, even if I can't make any other meeting.

The closed discussion group is limited in attendance by only those people who are recovering. There are no spouses or "significant other" persons allowed. The exception to this rule is when a member may have, for example, an out-of-town visitor that he or she specifically wants to be in attendance. The alcoholic can request a "group conscience" vote for permission to have the visitor in attendance. However, the group may still elect, by vote, not to allow a guest.

The meeting is run by a selected chairperson who may or may not have a topic to discuss. If no topic is specified, the chairperson may ask if anyone in the room has a topic they want to bring up, or a specific problem they wish to discuss. If you are new, the chances are you will be greeted with a round of applause; not because you are an alcoholic, but because you have taken the courageous step to come to a meeting. If you don't wish to participate you can politely decline with, "I think I'd rather just listen," or some such phrase.

Everyone who speaks at an AA meeting follows custom by identifying themselves and their problem. For example, "My name is Jack, and I'm an alcoholic." *Now,* we have the problem! So many people will say, "I can't stand up and do that! What if I see somebody there I *know?*"

Boy, I love an opening like that. First of all, you don't have to *stand* up; you can remain seated if you want to. Secondly, if you see someone at an AA meeting that you know, you just assume they are there for the same reason you are.

The topic chosen is then commented on by the speaker who may "pass" to another person he or she knows, or just call on someone at random and ask them to "pass" to someone after speaking. It's *very* casual, very informal. At any AA meeting you may get up and get coffee, even when others are speaking; you may leave the room and go to the restroom. You may leave early although, by tradition, AA meetings of any kind only last one hour.

The closed discussion meeting allows you and your fellow recoverers to "let your hair down" in a way that people who have not been afflicted with the disease may not appreciate.

My home group named "Crossroads" has been so supportive of me and the years of my recovery have been joyous and bright because of the laughter, the tears, the meaningful discussions that have filled my life on the times when I have been in that room. It can be that way for you, too!

There is very little formality in group, mostly traditions, and here are three that are pretty much standard no matter what kind of group you attend. You will be asked to join in repeating the "Serenity Prayer" at the start of every meeting, as you stand. It'll take you less than fifteen seconds to say (in unison, remember):

God grant me the *serenity* to accept the things I cannot change. *Courage* to change the things I can.

And *Wisdom* to know the difference.

Nothing to panic about *there,* is there?

Next, the speaker will either read or will have chosen someone to read from Chapter 5, "How It Works," of the "Big Book." That's it until the end of the meeting.

About five minutes before the meeting is to end you will notice a basket or plate or empty coffee can coming around from person to person. Tradition will allow you to put in a buck to defray costs of the meeting room, coffee, etc., since AA tradition calls for groups to be self-supporting and to "pay their own way." My close friend David taught me years ago to "put something in if you have it. If you *need* it, then take something out!" That's how it works; All for One, and One for All, to borrow from Dumas and the *Three Musketeers.*

When the meeting is over the speaker will ask, "Will those who *care* to, join me in the Lord's Prayer?" This is another tradition, but notice the *choice* is *yours.* More times than I care to remember I have stood saying this prayer side by side with a Jew, an Indian, an Arab, or an Oriental. The choice is always yours.

The closed discussion group is a good one for you to investigate with another sober person who uses the fellowship of AA to gain strength in sobriety.

CLOSED SPEAKER

This kind of meeting is probably the kind that may have turned you "off" about going back to AA because it may center around just one, or at the most three or four persons relating what has become known as a "drunkalogue." It is essential that you understand the very great need for the speaker(s) to be able to relate the horrors of their past active alcoholic life, in order to share with you their profound gratitude at their sobriety. The *closed speaker* meeting may not be for you, but it serves a very great purpose and certainly provides a platform for some absolutely outstanding people to talk with you, people who are famous, or totally unknown to you. All are sharing the common thread of telling their life stories or particular incidents that reflect in its harshest forms the ravages of the disease we all share. The main difference in this kind of meeting is, of course, you do not participate, but rather listen to the speaker(s). Again, only recovering persons may attend a closed speaker meeting. Most clients in treatment that I have worked with find this kind of meeting hard; they can't relate. Again, if you shop around, even among the closed speaker meetings, you can find some that are real dandies.

Call Alcoholics Anonymous in any city in the country and in most cities abroad and the people on duty can direct you to the kind of meeting you want, day or night, seven days a week. When you attend a meeting you like, pick up a local, free directory from the table where other literature is displayed. It will give you day-by-day listings, type by type, of all meetings in your area.

OPEN DISCUSSION

This is another spectacular way to revisit AA and to become involved again with the fellowship. At this type of meeting your "significant other" (spouse, kids, roommate, boss) can attend with you. Nothing they will see or hear will be any different than traditions followed at regular *closed* meetings. The only difference is that the alcoholic shares with others in the room who may or may not be recovering.

I find these groups stimulating and try to attend with my wife or one of my kids. The open discussion meeting allows great amounts of input from husbands, wives, and others that help show your *own* significant other person that they have not been and are not alone either. There is a lot of Al-Anon and Ala-Teen feedback that can enhance a group such as this.

Many times a recovering person can attend with his/her spouse and discover the beginnings of what will turn out to be a crackerjack "couples group." For one evening a week, for example, you and your spouse can make attendance at the open discussion type meeting a regular part of a "Quality Time" experience. It's relaxing, beneficial, and fun!

I use the word "fun" a lot in referring to the fellowship of AA. That's because it *is*. It is not the grim, lecturing "cold fish" kind of thing you may have imagined or been falsely told. *You'll* never know, of course, unless you take the risk! I have rarely been to a meeting of *any* kind where some laughter was not present; and many times I have witnessed outright gales of it, washing over the whole group like some wonderful miraculous spring rain that freshens the mind and the body.

The open discussion group is a built-in "escape hatch," of course, for the ultimate shy person that just can't bring themselves to disclose they are an alcoholic, particularly in front of other people. But many times I have confronted someone who had "hidden out" at an open discussion meeting, and invariably after a few shots at this game playing, they announced that *they* were a recovering person. That's great! It doesn't really matter *how* you get on the boat, as long as you don't stand on the pier and let it leave without you!

OPEN SPEAKER

This is the vehicle most often used for the "celebrity" speaker and state, national, or local conventions where the benefits of what the speaker has to say should be heard by all. It is also a meeting that is ideal for the person who needs and desires the support of friends who have aided in recovery. Bring them to an open speaker's meeting to hear more of what this disease is all about; you'll all be the richer for it.

CLOSED STEP

In this type of meeting, one or more of the Twelve Steps of Alcoholics Anonymous is discussed and commented upon. Again, the clue to what kind of meeting is in the word "closed." It means only you, the recovering person, may attend. This is a marvelous experience for the new person to the fellowship of AA. The people with more sobriety years, months and weeks than you have, help with your understanding of what the particular step means to your sobriety. Other group members share their opinions of what the step has meant to them, and, the most important point of all, how they have *used* it as a tool to their complete recovery program.

Many times this is a meeting that your AA sponsor will want you to attend with him or her. AA is like any other tool that is used to help you maintain lifelong sobriety; it has to be used to be of any value. The closed step meeting is a continuous study program that helps you understand the concepts behind the fellowship, and what has made them work for generations of alcoholics.

If you don't have an AA sponsor, get one. This is a person, usually of the same sex, who has more time in sobriety than you have and who has been that special person who has helped see you through your treatment perhaps; it might just be the person you kept hearing at a particular meeting and liked what he or she had to say. It's a great honor to be asked to be a sponsor, and they will not take it lightly, when you ask.

I have seen a close friend, a member of my "Home Group," proudly display a pearl necklace that gets a new pearl for each one of the new women she sponsors in the fellowship. Ruby wears this necklace with more pride than the Queen wears her diamond tiara!

OPEN STEP

It's obvious that this kind of meeting is similar to the one just outlined except of course it is "open" to alcoholic and non-alcoholics alike. The really great benefit of this kind of meeting is you can share a learning experience with someone you love or care about in a special way. Together, you can learn more about the Twelve Steps and get questions answered. Again, this is a very nonthreatening kind of meeting as most meetings go, and one in which you can truly say, "We got sick together, we can learn and recover together."

The open step meeting has ready-made subject material at hand by its very nature, and there is no pressure to have to come up with a topic. Your "significant other" person can be as involved as he or she desires; both of you can ask as many questions as you like and hopefully be spurred to share experiences of your own around the use of the Twelve Steps.

HOME GROUP

This kind of meeting is not to be confused with the "home group" I mentioned earlier as being that group you consider to be your home base for AA attendance. The home group kind of meeting is just what the name implies. Several of the fellowship, usually no more than twelve or so, gather on alternate weeks at one or another of the member's homes. The meeting is still closed, generally, although I have been in attendance at open home group meetings.

We have clients who have combined the best of both worlds, entertainment and "group work." They meet weekly at one couple's home. They will spend the first part of some time in a group meeting, closed among the recovering persons. The "Significant Others" will meet in another part of the house. Following this meeting, they spend the rest of the night playing cards. It's a great meeting for them, and they have shared with us many times the benefits of their home group.

The same ever-present coffee pot is always on at home group meetings just like at other kinds. Tradition calls for throwing a buck into the pot to reimburse the host for expenses of having the meeting at his or her house. Needless to say, most of these kinds of meetings also seem to magically produce brownies, fudge, or coffee cake and cookies along with the coffee!

The home group kind of meeting is often a favorite for professional men and women whose schedules make this meeting more attractive than one of the larger kinds. The home group meeting is also used many times where illness may prevent a member from attending in a large crowded place, but where the desire to have a meeting is still strong and necessary to continued after-care.

Home group meetings are very often the seedlings that grow into larger meetings of one kind or another as the need for accommodating more persons into the fellowship of AA occurs. A small farm community comes to mind as just such an example of where this happened. As word got around that "there was a meeting," people began asking from neighboring small towns if they could attend. What started out as a home group of five or so became, eventually, a rather well-stocked group of twenty-plus, meeting in the town church one night a week, instead of at a member's home.

SPECIAL INTEREST GROUP

Just as the name implies, this kind of group forms out of the need to want to share recovering experiences as a member of the same kind of interest in life. This is where the "doctors," "lawyers," "pilots," or what have you, may want to get together in fellowship, and because they feel they have some unique problems that will benefit each other more if they remain together. If you are such a professional person, you have only to inquire at any meeting you may attend of a closed discussion or any other kind about the possible existence of a special interest group, and you will find it. The network of AA is so efficient that the word gets around in really expert fashion, due largely to the fellowship wanting to provide *no excuses* as to why someone can't attend a particular meeting! You express a need for a special interest group, and chances are you'll have that need met.

Handicapped persons may, by choice, have a particular place where they are more mobile in attendance. This may start out as a special interest group for them, but can and often does expand to include others outside the special interest. I know of a group of teachers that formed such a special group, and it has been quite successful and is growing in both the frequency and numbers in attendance.

A particular special interest group that is common to many larger communities are the men and women like myself who are both recovering and are also therapists. It is obvious that these men and women have unique needs to be met as both alcohol professionals and "professional" alcoholics, as we like to say about ourselves!

There is almost no limit to the kinds of special interest groups that may be available. Again, if you take the risk and ask around, you'll turn up one or two if you're looking.

WOMEN'S GROUP

I can't say enough about this kind of AA support group even though it's obvious that I can't attend. The comfort level of female alcoholics is considerably increased with participation in a women's group, and often it is the only kind of group where the female will attend on any regular basis. If you are this kind of sober female, then I suggest you can start with such a group and as your comfort level goes up, you can expand your horizons and attend other kinds of meetings.

The advantages of a women's group for those women with small, dependent children are great. Many such groups will have a nursery kind of setting, so that the alcoholic mothers-in-recovery can get group support and still keep an eye on the "little dears." You may wonder why you can't just stay in such a women's group and never try anything else. Well, of course, you can, but remember this is a book about the Joy of Being Sober, and part of your joy comes from personal growth, from learning to meet new people and expanding your personal horizons. Thus, the more you get out of your too-comfortable modes and start a little growing, the more solid will be your joy! Use your women's group as your "home group" if you like, but make yourself venture out into the larger world of different kinds of AA meetings. It's well worth it.

Many women in recovery I know have found their first women's group through their sponsor who takes them to such a group. Before you know it, as the months of your own sobriety build up, you will be asked by some frightened, unsure person, such as you were, to help steer them to a group. Then is when you will most value your women's group and the special fellowship it provides.

GAY GROUP

More and more we are experiencing the opportunity to allow gay men or women to identify themselves not only as members of the homosexual community but as recovering alcoholics who also happen to have a sexual preference different from ours. Thus, the gay group is the ideal setting for AA fellowship. Once again, there are good and not so good kinds of gay group meetings, just like any other kind of meeting. It all depends on the makeup of the core group and on the willingness of the group members to put in the effort for the group to function in as productive a fashion as possible.

Remember that the common ground of the gay group meeting is not really that a person is gay, but rather that the person is an *alcoholic*. The fact that you may enjoy the gay life-style as a matter of personal preference does not submerge the fact of your sobriety being in as much jeopardy as the "straight"-world people.

Again, a phone call to Alcoholics Anonymous, or to a treatment center or hospital can help you find the gay groups in your community or the community that you are visiting. You may find that gay groups will expand and have many different types of AA meetings such as step, speaker, and discussion meetings, open or closed.

The gay group is a most valuable tool for the recovery of the homosexual man or woman, and you will find such groups to be highly supportive of your efforts to continue your life of sobriety.

SPECIFIC MINORITY GROUPS

There is no question but what this kind of group work fills a very large need. We see it working constantly in the many fine black, Hispanic, and Native American groups of our own community of Denver. Minority alcoholism is *still* alcoholism, and sobriety requires support. When members in recovery speak the same native language, then sometimes the understanding of the disease and its effects upon our lives becomes clearer and the resolve to maintain lifelong sobriety is strengthened.

Many minority AA groups will be identified by their names and will be easy to find. Some others may be a mixture of many ethnic backgrounds, and it will not be readily apparent that this may be the minority group you might be seeking. The cardinal rule is: "If in doubt, go to the meeting!" Go to the meeting no matter what, and see if there isn't a person in that group that can direct you to more specific minority meetings.

We have a dynamite group in our area called "Black Rap." It is such a fine meeting that it is openly attended by many people both Anglo and black. See, it's the *quality* of the meeting that makes the difference, and, once again, the common denominator is everyone in the room is a "brother" in the folds of recovery from alcoholism.

YOUNG PEOPLE'S GROUP

This kind of group can be found almost anywhere but is often an outcrop of another kind of meeting where many young people find there are more and more of *them* and want to narrow some fields of interest. It is in such groups that specific problems of non-alcoholic dating and peer-pressure tactics can really be laid on the table and chewed about.

A young adult's group is often formed from a larger, open discussion group, and this new splinter group will grow and become a regular couples group still dealing with the problems of their recovery. It doesn't matter if the couples are married or not; the binding element is the age bracketing that can happen. The problems of the young person in recovery are partially the same and partially unique. Often the seriousness of the disease has not struck home as much to the younger alcoholic as it has to the middle-aged or even older alcoholic. There is some sort of wishful thinking in the young that tends to say, "I've got plenty of time. So *what* if I slip a time or two?" A young people's group will help people like that understand that age doesn't matter. An alcoholic is one drink away from the next drunk!

Again, a young people's group may be expanded to be an open group that will allow the influx of many Ala-Teen people — those particular teenage "significant others" who have suffered from the effects of alcoholic behavior just as much as the active alcoholic. I have witnessed as a guest some fine meetings of this kind. The lively discussions and honest approach to the problems of sobriety were refreshing and very stimulating.

Al-Anon and Ala-Teen people are very special in their own right, and their participation in young people's groups, or any of the AA groups where they are appropriate, is a real plus for the recovering persons.

So that's *my* shopping list for giving AA another shot. As a treatment professional I realize the importance of Alcoholics Anonymous to the total recovery of the person afflicted with the disease. As a tool in combination with treatment I believe it is absolutely unbeatable! AA does not take on the function of professional treatment for alcoholism as its objective; treatment is the responsibility of the treatment centers and hospitals that are better equipped to perform those tasks. But AA is the very powerful tool of after-care that makes it the worldwide success it is.

The fellowship of AA will go with you long after you have left formal treatment and will remain with you as long as you live. It is a whole new and exciting world out there in AA-land. You may have had a bad taste of the AA experience, just like any other thing you may have tried and then passed judgment on without giving it a second chance.

What I hope you will do is pick up some of these tools around AA attendance and try them out. You can be assured that wherever you are in the world, you can "always find a meeting" and that in itself is one of the biggest joys of being sober.

It means that the traveler doesn't have to sit alone in one motel or hotel room after another with "nothing to do." There's a meeting you can attend! You no longer have to think of yourself as being a stranger in a strange town. You see, you have friends; pick up the phone and find a meeting. Need a place to stay temporarily while the local garage rebuilds your car? You'll be amazed at how many offers you'll get for hospitality from a member of the fellowship.

In short, make it high on your list of priorities to revisit an AA meeting. Remember, you already possess an "addictive" personality, so feel free — get "hooked" back into AA!

So munch on, crunch on, take your nuncheon, / breakfast, supper, dinner, luncheon!

Robert Browning
Pied Piper of Hamelin

12
The Joy of
Martini-Less Lunches

Have you seen that television commercial where people "at random" are asked, "What did you have (to eat) today?" No one can remember, except of course the people who are eating the particular brand of cereal being pushed.

Drinking your lunch was a lot like that, wasn't it? Didn't matter a whole lot *where* you ate, or *if* you ate, as long as the martinis kept coming around. If martinis weren't your bag, then feel free to substitute whatever your favorite noontime (libation) imbiber was. Well, there is a real joy to having lunch, sober! Not only do you care what you're ordering, but you can become very choosy about where you want to eat and also with whom you wish to have lunch. Seems fair enough, doesn't it? Consider the proposition that the main idea is to take a midday break and put some sustenance into your body; you remember, vitamins, minerals, all the good things that you need to carry out a full afternoon of work or pleasure.

What you did in your drinking days was to forget about the real reasons for having lunch and get right to the *real* joy of your noontime — drinking. A friend of mine, when ordering a vodka martini used to tell the waitress, "I want you to think of the driest vodka martini

123

this place has ever made — I want mine *drier!*" We laughed then, but now, in sobriety, it's kind of sad, isn't it?

What can happen to you in sobriety is that you begin to make a festive occasion out of going to lunch. You can actually look forward to it for a whole new set of reasons. You can make lunch time an event in your life that can set up your whole day or make what has been a dismal week, something quite brighter.

As a newly sober person, you need some new ground rules about lunch:

1. Pick places where you haven't been during drinking days.
2. Try to pick people who don't drink much, if at all.
3. Be good and hungry (this is no time to diet).
4. Set limits on the time spent at lunch.
5. Set a regular weekly time and place to meet.
6. Have your own transportation, if possible.

NEW PLACES

You are a creature of habit — your past drinking habit. You need to break that habit and the way to do it is to not return to the "scene of the crime." You will have a tendency to spend too much time reminiscing about "how the old days were" and "remember how drunk we got here?" All that belongs in the past. Let it stay there and move on to the present and to the future. Do this by looking around for the places where you have wanted to go with your friends or by yourself, but never did.

There is no point in trying to find a place that doesn't serve alcohol, because they are so rare that they are almost nonexistent. I am, of course, excluding the fast-food operations. I am talking about nice sit-down kinds of establishments that make your lunch an occasion.

A generally good rule to follow is to make sure there is a separate dining room; don't try to grab lunch in the dark confines of a cocktail lounge. If the restaurant you choose serves lunch in the lounge, don't sit there, even if it means waiting for awhile to get a table in the main room.

A really nice bonus right off the bat is that you can afford to eat more. Wow! I mean, do you realize what you spent on just the *booze* tab before? You'll be absolutely amazed at how two people can have a really elegant lunch in a nice place and get out for well under fifteen bucks! There was a time in your life when the bar tab for lunch ran over twenty dollars, so right away you can see that you can afford this nice luxury of eating out more.

That's what makes picking new places so exciting. There's practically no restaurant beyond your financial reach, once the bar bill is out of the picture.

PICK NEW PEOPLE

This sounds a lot harder than it really is. There have been those times when you wanted to have lunch with someone and didn't make the effort because they didn't drink. Of course the way you were drinking then would have made them uncomfortable, but not now. Now you can make up a list of "people I always wanted to have lunch with but was afraid (embarrassed) to ask before!" Just think of that. You avoided taking people to lunch who couldn't or wouldn't keep up with your drinks, so you never had the pleasure of their company. Now, all that can be changed. Again, be honest with yourself and "bite off" only what you can chew, if you'll forgive the pun.

Don't start off with having tables of six for lunch. You can't handle it emotionally and probably not financially either. Which brings up an important point to remember. It is not essential for you to pick up every lunch check. You did that before in your drinking days because it was a way you could keep on ordering more drinks and no one could or would complain.

What happens if your luncheon companion(s) wants to order a drink for themselves? Will you help them over their quandary? Of course. It's *you* who has the alcohol problem, not them. But your friends won't know how you'll react if they want a glass of wine or a martini for themselves. Help them out by saying, "Please feel free to order something from the bar if you like." They're going to say something back to you like, "Doesn't that *bother* you?" You say, honestly, "Sure. Sometimes. But drinking for me means sure and premature death," or answer with whatever you feel comfortable.

The point for you to stress is that alcohol and your life are inextricably intertwined, and you are not about to monkey around with the odds. What I've suggested for you to say is what *I* say; you choose your own words just as long as you get the idea across to your friends that you are *allergic* to the chemical alcohol. *You,* not them!

Your new-found friends at AA are ideal lunch companions, but you don't have to limit yourself to people who don't drink at all. You will be able to handle, say, your spouse, taking a drink before or with lunch. You help yourself out by ordering something to sip along with them. Iced tea is great, or, of course, coffee or de-caf or a soft drink. We'll discuss more specific drinks for the alcoholic in another chapter.

Don't allow yourself to "dawdle" over a pre-lunch drink; get on with it, which brings us to:

BE GOOD AND HUNGRY

Since you are no longer drinking, your food is tasting better to you and yes, you've probably put on a few pounds even though not as much as you did when you were abusing alcohol. What you want to do is really *enjoy* lunch for what it is — good food, good friend(s). If you are not properly hungry, it might be too easy a temptation to dwell over the pre-lunch drink your friend is having. Now is the time to break old habits, and it is *not* necessary to wait for a "second round" for your friend before ordering your lunch. What I do when the cocktail person comes to the table to see if there will be more drinks is say, "I'm ready to order, but maybe my friend wants another." Most times, *most*, not always, my companion will shut off his drinking and order his lunch.

With new friends you have invited for lunch, whose drinking habits may not be known fully to you, I say, "Are you ready to order?" This puts the ball squarely in his court. If he does order another drink and the cocktail person wants to know if I'll have another of whatever I am drinking, I'll say, "No, thanks, I'm ready for you to take my order." This sets a limit, and my companion can pick up on the hint that this is an *eating* lunch. It also helps you:

SET LIMITS ON THE TIME SPENT AT LUNCH

In the beginning, you are going to be a little nervous just sitting without a drink in front of you. So be prepared to set limits. My friends and I who have a regular Wednesday lunch and act crazy together, meet at 11:30. That way we get a table without waiting too long and we are ready to be back at work by 1:00. The secret here is the longer you delay getting started, the longer you will want to spend at the lunch table, and this is too reminiscent of the old habits.

If you have a set lunch hour and can't go as early as I have suggested, then do everything in your power to still set one-and-one-half hours as the maximum time to be at lunch. If you are a "brown bagger" then it's even easier. But use the opportunity for lunch as a way to assert yourself and meet new people. You have a ready-built safety valve when you see another person with his or her sack lunch. You know they are not into drinking for lunch, and you can feel secure right from the start.

It's a good way to help yourself over a rough time or two. If you are worried about going to a restaurant you can set a limit and tell a friend, "I only have an hour for lunch." Then suggest that maybe you can "brown bag" it together. This will be a novel idea for you, even if you are not used to taking a lunch to work. You can make a picnic out of it; an open space and imagination is all that you need. Try it a time or two yourself, until you feel comfortable enough to handle a restaurant situation when liquor is all around you.

Again, whatever you do, make your social contacts in the new world of your sobriety more frequent and less lengthy in nature. More one-hour lunches with new people will do you more good than one big two-hour blowout once a month.

SET A REGULAR WEEKLY TIME AND PLACE

In sobriety you need something fun to look forward to, something that you can count on to bring brightness into your new world. Setting a regular weekly luncheon with one or two friends is a great way to meet this need. I mentioned earlier about "getting crazy" with some sober friends at lunch. We are all recovering people, and we meet every week at a favorite restaurant of ours. No one has to call and confirm; we all know where we are going to be on that special day, and we mark our calendars accordingly. We have been known to get up and sing "Happy Birthday" to friends or acquaintances we see in the place. It doesn't matter whether it's their birthday or not (it never is). We do it just for the sheer joy of it! This weekly lunch is a miniature AA meeting of sorts. We have been joined on many occasions by another recovering person who will have brought a new member of the fellowship with him or her to show them that sobriety is not all "doom and gloom."

This weekly luncheon for us is a very bright spot in our week. It is a tool you can use, too. Midweek is the best time, and a place that can be flexible enough to expand from say, two to six people for lunch is necessary. Other than that, you only need to take the risk and get a weekly gathering of your own going.

It's a positive reinforcement of the fact that the joy of being sober is a constant celebration of *just being alive* and free from the bondage of alcoholism. If a member of the group has a problem or seems down-cast, you can depend on the rest of the group helping cheer him or her up. You'll find more exhilaration in a sober lunch than you ever experienced drinking! If you don't make any other appointment during the week, you will find yourself not wanting to miss this set date with the people who, like you, are constantly reaffirming to themselves that the sober life is the only life for them.

Recently, I overheard another restaurant customer ask a waitress if "those people are drinking or, *what?* They're so happy, they *must* be!" Our waitress stepped in and said, "Those folks are in here every week and not one of them has ever ordered a drink!" We stopped to think about it and realized that in more than two years of lunching at this particular spot, we had never mentioned that we were recovering alcoholics. We never had to. No one has more genuine fun and celebrates the joy of life more than a recovering person. You'll see!

HAVE YOUR OWN TRANSPORTATION IF POSSIBLE

This is important for your comfort level at trying this new drinkless lunch plan. The very nature of your disease has made you restless and oftentimes you may feel "boxed in" and slightly claustrophobic. When that kind of anxiety attack happens, you usually want some form of reassurance that you can get up and leave the place. If you have your own form of transportation — car, bike, or supply of bus tokens — you *can* leave if the pressure gets to be too much. What you want to avoid at all costs is the idea that for you to conquer the anxiety you need a "little drink" to calm your nerves. That's a disaster in the making.

So, have your own way to the meeting. Be independent if possible, and then there will be no excuse for your having to remain at the restaurant in an uncomfortable situation just because you are beholden to someone for a ride.

This uncomfortable feeling of anxiety will pass in time as you get more secure with your sobriety and realize that you can handle all or most all social situations without feeling the pressure to drink. Being open with a friend who says, "It's silly to take *two* cars!" is the best and only way. Inform your friend that you need your own car in case you feel too pressed by the situation. It's no different if you were coming out of the hospital from an operation and not wanting to overdo or tax your strength too much.

You are coming off of a disease that has altered your life and will require time, patience, and honesty to help you heal. Be honest and tell your friend that you're not yet sure how strong you are for this social situation without alcohol. Your friend will help you, if he or she understands that you are *trying* and need whatever securities you can muster, such as your own car, to help you through the trying new times.

It may be using a "crutch," but use it anyway until you build your "CQ," Confidence Quotient.

Having lunch out in the company of someone you really care about, having a business lunch that really means you will talk business, having the taste of your food be real and savored, these are some of the rewards of the martini-less lunches that can and will be a part of your new life of sobriety.

You've heard about the woman who, dreading her husband's pending retirement, said matter-of-factly, "Honey, I married you for better or worse, but *not* for lunch!" Well you can make lunch more than just a break between breakfast and dinner. In sobriety you can make lunch a refreshing experience, not something to be dreaded and not something that you have spent time, trouble, and money in making numb with alcohol.

Bon Appetit!

*Reach out . . . reach out and touch
someone.*

The Bell System

13
The Joy of Carrying
the Message

"Sometimes, I think I could shout it from the rooftops!"

"I look at those people standing around boozing and think, 'That used to be me! Don't they know what they're doing?' "

"Every time I tell someone else about how super it is to be sober, they look kinda funny at me — sooner or later they dig what I'm talking about!"

"My God! *Everyone* tells me how great I look since I've been sober!"

Carrying the message. That's what it's all about. This business of finding the *joy* of being sober is too good to keep. The remarks quoted above have come from people just like you, the newly sober and those with longer time in recovery. They have all learned what is essential to continued happiness and joy in recovery; if you feel *that* good about yourself, then carry the message to someone else!

This is the main work of Alcoholics Anonymous; it is the main theme of the *New Testament* in its urgings to take the Gospel, "Good News," to the whole world.

The big difference for you is the how and where of your journeys — *how* to do it, and *where* to do it. And how to do it without preaching or sounding "holier than thou" when carrying the message.

What is the message? It is basically what this whole book is about.

There is a *joy* in *being sober;* your life can be fuller, more enriching and rewarding than you ever thought possible when you have separated yourself from the bonds of alcohol.

So many people, including yourself at one time, didn't want to break the mold, didn't want to "test the waters" of sobriety because you were convinced that life after booze was no life at all. Now, you know that just the opposite is true. What you thought was "life" before was really a nightmare of drunkenness, hangovers, debt, and disasters of the worst kind in all your interpersonal relationships.

Alcohol for you meant poison to your life. To drink for you was to die, not live. So, you have an obligation of sorts to carry on the message of what sobriety can mean to someone else. Yes, I said "obligation!" The reason for making it so strong is the well-known fact among all who have and *do* carry the message. By telling someone else about alcoholism, you keep *yourself* strong in sobriety. Simple isn't it? Why complicate it when it stands out and slaps you squarely in the face? If sobriety can do this for me, it certainly can do this for you!

HOW TO DO IT

This begins with a complete understanding that *honesty* will always be your best tool. The collection of statements heard at various gatherings by recovering alcoholics who can't deal honestly with their sobriety, is endless. Some of my favorites and those collected from patients and clients include these:

"My doctor thought I ought to take off a few pounds, so I'm not drinking!"

"My blood pressure was getting up there; thought I'd 'lay off' the booze awhile."

"I thought I'd better 'cut down' on my drinking a bit!"

"Well, I've been having a bout with the flu — stuff doesn't taste as good."

(From a pregnant woman): "Thought I'd lay off until after the baby comes!"

"I'm on some kinda antihistamine thing that gives me a reaction when I drink."

(From a Jew): "I never drink during the High Holy Days!"

(From a Catholic): "Gave it up for Lent — do it for good, probably!"

And then my all-time favorite, one which has been used from the first for people who are always on the fence with their sobriety:

"I'm on the wagon!"

What wagon? The *water* wagon, of course. If you're "on the wagon," you're abstaining from alcoholic beverages. But you see how all of these statements skirt the *real* issue? You, as the newly sober person anxious to continually reinforce your sobriety should say:

"I'm a recovering alcoholic." Or, if that's still too tough right at this stage,

"I've discovered that I'm allergic to the chemical alcohol." And that's the truth; no hedging, there! There is something in your genetic makeup both psychologically and pathologically, that makes you unable to assimilate alcohol in your system like "normal" drinkers.

But I prefer that you plunge right in. "I'm recovering!" is generally all that you need to say. Most everyone will understand, and the beautiful part of it is the *reaction* you will get! It's worth the price of admission. Once you have honestly disclosed your disease you will begin to hear most of the statements I just quoted, except now they will be said by people you are talking to as projected plans of action for them! For example,

"Gee, that's great! I'm really proud of you! You know (here it comes!) my doctor thinks maybe I should 'cut down' a little!" Or,

"Really? I never thought you had a drinking problem! Well, I'm giving it up for Lent this year, myself!"

The *How* to help carry the message then is to start, carry on, and end with honesty. You can respond to any of the people you know to have a drinking problem of their own by telling *them* to be honest with themselves.

"I have the disease of alcoholism," you say, "and I'm doing something about it. How about you?"

Well no one is going to jump right up and down and be glad to hear they might have a disease of *any* kind, much less alcoholism. But you can point out to them that if alcohol is becoming a problem in their lives then maybe they need to think about it! *That's* carrying the message.

There is a vast distinction between carrying the message and carrying the drunk. You *can't* carry the drunk; you only have the ability to share with others what your sobriety has done for you. They must take the steps themselves to ask for and seek help, but you are a constant example to the most hard-core drinking friend you know; "it can be done!" is the banner that you carry everywhere you go.

The longer you delay calling your sobriety a direct result of your battle in the *alcoholic* wars, the longer you delay building your own strength and the ability to share that strength, that joy, with others. Go ahead and choke over the words "recovering" and "alcoholic" for awhile if you have to, but spit them out every time you have the chance, every time you are confronted with "Why aren't you drinking?"

You'll be amazed at how much *positive* response you will receive and how many pats on the back you will garner from your honesty, and from your attempts (successful) to do something about your alcoholism! What about the business of using "recovering" as opposed to "recover*ed*?" You can do as you like, but my strong suggestion is to keep using the term "recovering," the present tense. This says two facts about your disease:

1. Recovering is a lifelong process that never ends.
2. You are just one drink away from the next drunk, no matter how long you have been sober.

In more concrete terms, the disease of alcoholism is *treatable* as we have mentioned many times; it is *not* curable.

Using the expression "recovering" indicates to yourself as well as others that you are engaged in a process that will require your attention every hour of your life, but the *message* is, "How worthwhile that is!"

At various AA meetings you may attend you will hear the message being passed to the new people like yourself every time someone introduces him or herself. The message may say, "I'm Peggy and I'm a *grateful* alcoholic!" or, "My name is Jim, and I'm a *sober* alcoholic!" No matter how you hear it, you will always hear the word "alcoholic" in the greeting, even though it may be hard to get out of the mouth of the person saying it. What this does, every time you acknowledge your disease, is own up to the fact that what you are dealing with in your life, for the *rest* of your life, is a *deadly chemical.*

Isn't there a joy in knowing that you are learning how to get on with the business of living *without* that chemical? You bet! So why not just be up front with those you are in contact with when they present the many openings for you to disclose your disease *and* the conquering of it on a day-to-day basis?

If you walked into a room with a mangled arm dangling at your side, sat down at a table, and painfully hauled the obviously broken limb up on the table people would be aghast. "What on earth is the matter with you!" they would cry. "What are you trying to do?" Can you see yourself replying, "Oh, that. It's nothing but a broken arm." The hue and cry from your friends would be overpowering, "Why isn't it in a cast? Aren't you going to *do* something about it!?"

So, the next time you walk into the same room, your arm is in a cast as is proper and necessary to the healing process of the broken bone. Everyone rushes over to you to sign the cast, an expression of their desire for you to get well.

Your disease is not outwardly visible, except when you were manifesting it by the alcoholic behavior patterns of your life. But it's still there, and you *are* treating it just as surely as if it were in a cast. Why not, then, allow your friends to "sign" the cast of your recovery by telling them about it, showing them how they too can enjoy healing a broken body?

Every time you carry the message of your recovering process called "sobriety," you are helping not only those who hear the message but you as the giver. You are applying a little more gauze, tape, and plaster of paris to the break and by so doing are making the healing process stronger.

WHERE TO DO IT

It has been a policy of mine since my own recovering began to spend Christmas Day and New Year's Day at a hospital, visiting either a de-tox ward or just the in-patients who have not been able to go home to their families. These people are suffering from the same disease that is in my body and yours.

It's an idea that was passed on to me by a recovering doctor friend of mine, Blair Carlson, director of the Alcoholism Recovery Unit of St. Luke's Hospital, Denver. Blair follows the practice himself, even though he, like any of us in the field, works with alcoholics twenty-four hours a day.

Spending an hour with people in de-tox or on the ward, reminds you that you have much to be grateful for; you are sober this day and you can offer that same message of encouragement to the poor, sick person that lies there in that hospital bed. That's *where* you go to carry the message!

A client of ours recently found herself doing something that she never thought possible. She spent part of Mother's Day with some strangers in a nursing home, some mothers who were not going to have a visitor from their family on this special day. For our recovering friend it was an act of carrying the message of her new-found sobriety by being able to share her wellness with others who needed contact *with* wellness.

You can do it too! Your church or synagogue has an all too heavy load of hospitalized or otherwise homebound people who would welcome a visit from you. Who are you doing this for? Yourself and them and that's okay to be a little bit selfish as you share your visit with another person.

135

The theory here is sound. By giving your message of sobriety and the joy of being sober to another, you add to your own joy. It's simple and it *does* work.

You don't have to wait for holidays to do this either. Many times I have recommended to people in new recovery to get to a hospital and pay a visit when they feel a "Dry Drunk" coming on. It's great therapy for you and the person you visit in the hospital. It will remind you of how far you have come in your sobriety; at the same time it will remind you of how quickly *you* could be back in that De-Tox ward, in that hospital bed!

Combine a visit with an AA meeting and you won't have to worry too long about your "blues" and depression. Carrying the message and hearing the message are dynamite one-two knockout punches for Dry Drunk Syndrome and Pity-Pot sitting.

Another place that can use your message-bearing efforts are schools, either through organized citywide programs or directly through a local PTA or concerned teacher group. One of the most rewarding experiences you can ever have is to sit in a classroom of junior high, high, or even elementary school kids and answer their very bright questions about the disease of alcoholism. You don't have to be an expert; you can simply share your story of what it's like to be free from alcohol.

This takes guts on your part because it's making a *public* commitment to your lifelong sobriety, but that's what you want, isn't it? You can garner all the invitations to speak to service clubs, women's groups, or other organizations in your hometown. Don't be afraid to take the wraps off your "trouble." Steel yourself to be proud to share your recovering life with others. Somewhere in every audience you speak with is someone who is in trouble with alcohol. You might just be the flicker of hope for that housewife, the lawyer, or teenager that hears you talk "off the cuff" about your recovery.

You will be amazed at the interest from, say, a church group of yours, or the teachers themselves at your local school. What if it's a school where your own kids attend? Do you still make yourself available, say, for a program dealing with alcohol and other drug abuse? The gauge I use is to ask myself: "Did I ever show up at this school in a state of alcohol abuse that embarrassed me or my kids? How do my kids feel about me disclosing to their peer group about my disease?"

Each person has to make these decisions for themselves, but I think its benefits far outweigh the disadvantages. Your alcoholism didn't fool anyone, even though you were convinced that you were fooling *everyone.* Your kids probably took a whole lot of abuse when you showed up half smashed at the school fair or play or cookie sale or what have you.

What a marvelous opportunity for you to reappear, carrying the message that you have found joy in being sober, that your life (and theirs) is so different now that alcohol is no longer a part of the family scene. When a few people in group therapy discussed this means of carrying the message, most found it unthinkable. A few weeks later, two members of the group disclosed they had taken the risk and volunteered to be part of a panel discussion on alcohol abuse at their children's schools. The panel groups were part of a citywide "awareness week" on alcoholism, and the two group members were at quite different schools in different parts of the city.

Their reports back to the therapy group were highly stimulating. Not only the recovering persons found some new friends in recovery (one of them her son's "home room" teacher), but all of the friends of their own children had taken special pains to thank the speakers and express their *pride* in knowing them!

One father told me in an individual therapy session that his son had been so proud of him coming to school and talking to his class that he (the son) had found some new friends; children who had alcohol-abusing parents who were still at active drinking. The kids were glad to hear and to meet another kid who held out visible hope that things could be better—better for them, too! Carry the message, not the drunk, but carry it everywhere you do and to as many lives as you can touch. It will bring you unbridled joy!

Party is the madness of many for the gain of a few.

Jonathan Swift

The sooner every party breaks up the better.

Jane Austen

14
Handling the Cocktail Party

Perhaps the most asked question from a recovering person is "Why can't I drink like everybody else?" We've already discussed that you must stop asking "Why" and move on to more positive strokes of "What" (can I do about it) and "Where" (do I begin).

The second most popular wail and lament appears to be, "How am I ever going to be able to go to a cocktail party again?"

The answer is simple. You just go. But here are some new rules and new tools that are designed to help you find fun at a cocktail party and not spend every moment in sheer agony.

The first thing to understand is cocktail parties are designed for one thing; to consume great quantities of alcoholic beverages. That's the name of the game, and you've been playing it for years. So, let's decide what *you're* going to do *instead* of putting away your share of booze! These are "new rules," so we'll call them that.

NEW RULE #1

The recovering alcoholic *will* make it a point to discuss the exact nature of the purpose of going to this party in the first place; i.e., "Is this really an *important* event for the advancement of my (your) career?" Armed with the appropriate answer, you follow with:

"What happens if we decline the invitation?" Or, if you are operating as a solo number, "What are the consequences to me if I decline?"

Knowing the purpose for attending can often give you the kind of support you will need to set limits on what you can handle at the event. Which leads us to:

NEW RULE #2

The recovering person will stay at a cocktail party for no more than forty-five minutes, give or take ten minutes. *Because:*

Just about everything that's going to happen at a party is going to happen in the first forty-five minutes. You will have made all the bright remarks you're going to make; your friends will have made all the extracurricular passes that will be made; and you will have had most of the numbers worked on you that will happen for the whole night!

That whole action will happen in the first forty-five minutes or so of just about any cocktail party. From that point on, it's just a matter of playing the same old tape over and over with different people moving in and out of the picture, getting progressively more inebriated. So why stay and play old tapes?

You can make a very good appearance and accomplish the purpose of having been there in the first place. But to follow this new rule you have to do some groundwork with whomever is going with you to the affair. If you are the recovering person and you are doing the escorting of someone who is a social drinker, then it requires the same amount of preplanning and agreement, *before* you ever leave your place, headed for the party. That groundwork and agreement is:

"It's necessary that I not stay longer than forty-five minutes at this thing. Is that going to be okay with you? If it isn't, then I probably shouldn't go!"

You then outline the reasoning just the way I have given it to you, with the added emphasis that it is perfectly acceptable and socially proper to *not* overstay at a cocktail party. "Well," you ask, "What if this is a cocktail *hour* that is happening before the banquet (dinner)?"

"Fine," you reply. Can we agree to split the difference then and go for the cocktail hour *thirty* minutes ahead of dinner instead of the full time called for on the invitation?" Thirty minutes is more than enough time for you to see to it that your companion has the option of having one or two cocktails; you don't have to push your stress points quite as long before you are going in for dinner.

I have discovered that I can use up thirty minutes just standing in line to buy my wife a cocktail at one of these things! If it is a "double date" affair and you feel that you are imposing on the other couple by following this new rule, then you have the options:

1. You can explain the pressure points of cocktail parties to them, which, of course, helps your *honesty* program, and,
2. You can agree to meet them there and go into dinner together. (Not a very satisfactory arrangement if this is a "double date") or,
3. You can suggest meeting at your place at the time the cocktail party hour was supposed to start. You can offer your guest the first drink at your house, leave after that one drink, and *still* arrive very fashionably at the cocktail hour in time to offer a second round, if it seems desirable.

All of these option points help *keep you in control* instead of you being the controlled person.

By following New Rule #2 you won't make anyone angry at you for being a "spoil sport," nor will you offend the people who have invited you and yours in the first place. That's because you will bring New Rule #3 into play, which is:

NEW RULE #3

The recovering person will make sure he or she greets the host and hostess or chief "mucka-muck" as soon as he/she can after arrival. That way they will *know* you have been to their party and therefore won't be all bent out of shape when you leave. If you are only staying for forty-five minutes, *other* folks can get pretty snockered by then, and you want to make sure that your appearance was felt *before* everyone gets such a glow on!

A friend who has perfected and honed most of these rules to a fine edge has added a nice touch to New Rule #3. "I make damn sure *everyone* knows I've shown up," he says, " 'cause most of them won't remember in the morning!"

I try to never leave my wife's side and often will hurry her along to greet the party-giver right off the bat, even though it made her (my wife) uncomfortable to do this the first few times we pulled it off.

You may be saying, "What's a few minutes more or less going to matter? I'll get around to the host or hostess eventually!" And that's the very point! By the time you have stopped and chitchatted with everyone *else,* most of your allotted time is up. You hit the party-givers first; a task made considerably easier if they greet you at the door.

This is becoming so difficult, however, as cocktail parties are getting bigger and bigger and making it harder for the host and hostess to stand by the entrance.

So, make a beeline for your benefactors, boss, or whomever is in charge. Thank them for the "lovely invitation"; make quick short small talk if you can, and beat it around for more greeting and *more* greeting! You want folks to be able to say, "Ol' Charlie was *too* there! I *saw* him!"

A newly sober person can make a lot of points for his or her self esteem if thank you notes are utilized as a means of cementing the fact that you *did* attend. The reason for all this emphasis on your being noticed is because many people will not want to include a recovering person on the list for cocktail parties, thinking it will be too "difficult" for you or because "you might start drinking again!" Well, they just don't know you, do they? They don't know that you have joy in being sober and that you don't want to be left out of the fun. And it *is* fun.

I developed a game for myself which I now pass along to you. I imagine what people would look like if I had the power to remove the glasses or beer bottles or cans from their hands! Try it! It's a scream to just see the little knots of two or three people making "party talk," but standing in that peculiar bent over shape, but without the glass in their hands! The ridiculous poses look like so many comic strip characters.

Another trick I recommend to help cement your value at being asked to a party is to tell your host or hostess how nice it is to really "enjoy" their party for a change. You might find yourself being among the minority that can say that honestly to them, especially on "Hangover Sunday."

The host and hostess appreciate hearing that people are enjoying the efforts they have put forth, and an hour or so later they may wonder why they didn't just throw all the booze up for grabs and forget having any kind of a social mixer!

NEW RULE #4

The recovering alcoholic will absolutely *never* pretend that the drink he or she is carrying around is "real!" Boy, this is one of my pet peeves, and I have angered some folks, I'm sure, by calling this dishonesty to their attention as game-playing! You are *not* carrying around an alcoholic drink, so why pretend you are? The whole idea of your sobriety is to break old habits, and walking around with a "Virgin Mary" or a drink that looks like a vodka and tonic but is really just tonic and lime in the *same kind of glass,* is not being fair to yourself, or anyone else, for that matter. (More on this in a few pages.)

Honesty! That's your battle cry from now on. It will be too easy for some well-meaning friend to refill your drinking glass with the real thing, and before you know it you'll be a goner!

Avoid punch bowls like they are filled with bubonic plague! There is always some clown at every party who believes that the punch needs a little "picking up," and the best intentioned plans to have an alcoholic and non-alcoholic punch will go down the tubes when a bottle of gin or vodka is slipped into the "safe" punch!

So what do you drink?

ALTERNATIVE DRINKS

You will find that the very habit of carrying something around in your hand is a hard one to break, and you may have particular trouble in feeling somewhat "naked" without a glass in your hand. You can conquer this habit by switching to coffee at a cocktail party. Now, I know that just may drive you up a tree; here are all the folks doing their best to consume as much liquor as they want, and I'm telling you to walk around with a cup of coffee in your hand!

You don't have to do it every time—just at the beginning if you are a newly sober person; trust me, please! It may feel a little awkward to try and balance a coffee cup and saucer, but I'll let you in on what every recovering person already knows: if you'll ask the bartender or cocktail waitress who is "circulating" the party for coffee in a *mug*, you'll probably get it. Lots of folks like drinking coffee/liqueur combinations, such as coffee and kahlua or brandy, so the party will probably have some of those coffee mugs for just that purpose. But even if you can't have a mug, make the effort to take a cup of coffee or de-caf coffee as your drink. There are two reasons for this. The first is it helps identify that there is a new *you* at this cocktail party, one who no longer has to have alcohol to be part of the scene. Secondly, it will help you explain your sobriety by simply telling inquiring people, "I *choose* coffee as part of my recovery!" "Recovery?" they ask. "Yep," you say, and the door is open. They will say things at the beginning like, "What? You're drinking coffee? What in God's name for?!" You can reply, "I'm allergic to alcohol and so coffee is my drink, now, okay?" The "okay" is to help establish that you mean business and to enlist their support in *not* pushing alcohol on you.

You can't beat iced tea, and fresh mint with a lemon wedge. If it's cold weather, I prefer to switch back to coffee, though, rather than try hot tea, which really *should* be nestled on a saucer. If you like orange

143

juice, try this for a terrific drink. Ask for one-half orange juice topped with sparkling soda. It's not only refreshing, but the sparkling soda makes a delightful "bounce" to the drink. Hang on to your glass, though, as it may be mistaken for an orange blossom or screwdriver, and you don't want that. One way to help make sure that folks know there is a difference in your drink is to ask the barman to put a fresh orange slice on the rim of your glass. Orange blossoms and screwdrivers are rarely dished up this way, so you are showing a different flag at the party, a drink that says, "non-alcoholic."

Perrier mineral water or any of the other "premier" waters are, of course, acceptable and good tasting. I like *Perrier* because I can ask for the bottle to be brought with the drink (no chance for it being mistaken for something else). If there are small tables at the party, I can set the *Perrier* bottle in plain sight and that labels me a "non-drinker." The same goes for tonic (and lime) or plain club soda (and lemon and lime wedges). If you can set the small bottle on the table with your glass, then it's okay — not much danger of it being confused with an alcoholic beverage.

This is a good place to mention a very serious "no-no" for you at any function where liquor is served and you are standing at the bar to get your order. *Never* accept tonic, soda, or plain water that is dispensed from a multiple head "shot-gun." These heads will many times also be switched to dispense gin or vodka along with *7-Up* and the other beverages I mentioned. Don't hesitate to ask for your tonic, *7-Up,* or club soda from a bottle.

Cola drinks don't require any explanation. The old word of caution is, if possible use the "can" rule; either carry the soft drink can and plunk a straw into it, or have the can sitting on the table with you, if possible. All of these drink suggestions lead to:

NEW RULE #5

Always inform your barperson and cocktail waiter or waitress that you are recovering. These people are the best friends you will have at a cocktail party! Even in private home parties, if there is a circulating waiter or waitress, take them aside and ask, "Will you please help me out tonight? I'm recovering!" That's all you have to say. There isn't a bartender or waiter or waitress who won't watch out for you. They approve of your courage and are anxious to help.

Some people I've given this rule to say they feel silly asking "to be taken care of," that is, until they try it once! Then, they report back,

"I've never had a more relaxed evening! I didn't have to worry the entire evening!"

I have observed many bartenders who, when asked to watch out for a recovering person at a party, will tell a waitress, "You come directly to me for this (man's/lady's) drinks!" The same New Rule works with those banquets where the favorite dessert may be "wine sundae" masked under such fancy names as "Virginia Dare Delight" or what have you.

Get your waitress's attention, and when she comes over by your place simply tell her, "I'm recovering. Is there some other desert I can have or maybe *plain* ice cream?"

So you may think this is going to cause a big stir; well it isn't! See, other folks have been drinking, probably a lot. They are wrapped up in their own conversations and won't even notice the little bit of talk you have with a waiter or waitress. The same goes for any embarrassment you may feel about standing at the bar and telling the bartender not to give you your soft drink from the "shot-gun." He or she will know instantly that you are a recovering person if you simply say, "May I please have a (*Coke*) and not from the gun dispenser!"

Many bartenders will automatically respond with, "You don't have to worry. This is strictly for soft drinks!" or something like that.

If there are people around you when it's your turn to order, again you must remember that they have been, or are, intaking alcohol, and they don't much care what anyone else orders except themselves. *Plus,* you'll be surprised at how softly you can give instructions to a bartender and be heard. The very change of voice level alerts them to listen, and you can give your order in a perfectly normal tone of voice. It's the people who are drinking alcohol that continue to raise their decibels, in direct proportion usually to the amount of drinking they are doing!

I once gave this as an assignment to a therapy group: go to a crowded function and "elbow" your way to the bar. Try the New Rule #5 of informing the bartender of your recovery. Tell him in a normal voice.

Four people reported great success with the experiment using rule #5. Two or three others said they had to shout to be heard, but guess what? Nobody else paid them the slightest bit of attention! *You* try New Rule #5, and the more you use it, the more comfortable it will become for you.

NEW RULE #6

The recovering person *will* be attentive to their companion! This should be a new twist for you, since most cocktail party behavior is bad, to say the least. By "bad," I mean the first order of business for so many couples is to play "ditch 'em" the minute they hit the door. That may have been your life-style before, but now, you will invoke New Rule #6 and pay a lot of attention to the person who has accompanied you to the party.

Again, you are trying here to break old habits and to reinforce the sober life. In your drinking days you thought that it was the thing to do to "circulate," and as a result many times both you and your companion had a terrible time. If you were the outgoing "life of the party" type then it was your companion who felt left out, ignored, and totally useless.

If you are female and you were the drinker, you may have drunk even *more* to combat the hostility you were feeling at having been "dumped."

If you are male and it was you who was the drinker, you probably don't remember most of what you said and did and yet had to end up the next morning making numerous apologies for what you were *told* you did! So New Rule #6 does a bit of intervening for you. It says, "I am proud to be seen here with you and will make *you* as much the object of my attention as I can!" Before, alcohol ruled the way you behaved and *mis*behaved; now you can further cement your sobriety by changing the *way in which you behave* at cocktail parties. What you are doing is setting up a perfectly logical formula that says: "Before, when drinking, I *needed* drink to be the relaxed, charming person I thought I was!" Now, "I no longer need drink; I am recovering and I *choose* to spend time with you. It is *you* who can help me be relaxed!" The "charming" part is up to you in the manner in which you conduct yourself.

The feedback from invoking New Rule #6 will be good; it will say things like, "This is the way I always wanted things to be," and "It was such a pleasure to be *with* you at the party — not just dragged there *by* you!" Use this New Rule and going to cocktail parties will not be a drudge that you may have decided they were destined to be. You will also find that you are the envy of many another person who wishes that *their* companion could find *them* stimulating just for themselves.

THE HOSTILITY METER

The more people drink the edgier they get; the more they drink, the more quarrelsome they can become. As a sober person you need to be aware of these changes in personality which you *will see* and about which you will be utterly amazed.

I call it the Hostility Meter. As you are engaged in cocktail party conversation you will notice that many things you say are being "picked up on." Points of view you thought you were able to express suddenly seem to be starting an argument. This is the escalation of the needle on the Hostility Meter. You need to watch out for it and extricate yourself from the situation as soon as you can. Why? Because people who are drinking can tend to reach your soft spots pretty quick and your new sobriety is still making you tender in the emotional spots!

As you see the Hostility Meter needle rise, you *know* there can be trouble brewing on the horizon. The conversation can be about most anything — sex, religion, politics, company policies. It doesn't matter. The more alcohol that is consumed by your companions the more the needle goes up.

Alcohol is loosening up emotions and, remember, "inhibitions." A lot of name-calling and bitter remarks can be exchanged in a big hurry as the Hostility Meter begins to show the "red line." For you, this is a direct threat to your sobriety. You begin to hear that small, always sleeping snake stir in your brain, ready to strike. That snake is saying, "If this sonofabitch keeps at me, I'm gonna take just one little drink so's I can handle him!" We already know that the "one little drink" can lead to the next drunk.

If you ignore the Hostility Meter it can mean disaster for your recovery. If you visualize that every person you are talking to at a cocktail party has this meter painted on their forehead, you can be safer. As they begin to take on that look of getting "bent out of shape," visualize the needle rising toward the red zone. When you hear positive clues that the person you are talking with is getting just a little hostile at either something you are saying or doing (such as *not* drinking) then start to "bail out" as quickly and politely as possible. Leave the conversation or group of people where the "action" is starting. Your sobriety depends on your taking evasive action before nerve endings get too exposed.

This Hostility Meter reading is another good reason to have your companion close by your side. He or she can learn to read the warnings on the Hostility Meter with you and together keep out of trouble.

By being able to read and interpret cocktail party hostility meters, you can count on not having to receive a series of apologizing phone calls the day after, or of having to make those calls yourself because you let some "red-line" situation get out of hand! But the real joy of being sober at a cocktail party is that you get to honestly *observe* people and their actions and reactions to the world around them; and you get to do it as one who is thinking and acting clearly.

This certainly doesn't mean that every cocktail party that's given is one big "lost weekend." It *does* mean that for you it can be a trying time unless you are willing to apply these new rules; turn them into working tools that will help make you feel comfortable around other people in drinking situations.

The cocktail party is still the great American pastime; you can enjoy the people, the action, the companionship, all for the very low price of knowing and using these few methods to help you keep your recovery intact without appearing to be either a great reformer-crusader or "holier than thou" person.

Just remember how great it's going to be for you to be waking up on "the morning after" and *knowing* what you said and did, *who* you were with, and probably the greatest joy of all, knowing *how* you got home!

*. . . And it was always said of him,
that he knew how to keep Christmas well, if any man alive possessed
the knowledge . . .*

Charles Dickens
A Christmas Carol

15
Holidays and How to Cope with Them

It is one of the rare events of my life; every time we trim the Christmas tree I think of a note hung on the tree the first year of my own recovery. It was written by one of my daughters. I don't remember which one. The note said, "Dear Daddy, it's so nice the only things *under* the tree this year, are the presents!"

It has a touch of class! Too many holidays have been spent in the past by recovering persons as just a blur on the landscape of their lives. Holidays were an excuse to increase the drinking time and find more reasons to drink earlier, heavier, and faster than at other times.

Well, we're going to help you change that. From now on your sobriety is going to *allow* you the opportunity to really enjoy, to really *find* the joy of the major and yes, even *minor* holidays, all without having to have one alcoholic drink!

It doesn't matter if you're a Christian or Jew because most of our national holiday celebrations overlap at the same periods of the year anyhow, so the same kinds of tools can be applied for coping with either religious persuasion. Notice the word "cope" both in the title of this chapter and the emphasis on the use of tools. "Coping" is very

149

hard during festive occasions because most everyone around you is really into the "spirits" of the holiday, and you are inclined to have your Grey Ghost Syndrome in full bore; your Pity Pot groweth larger as the holly and the mistletoe grow more abundant!

It isn't just at Christmas or Hanukkah either. Easter, Passover, your own birthday, even — people all make a big thing out of making alcohol an absolute *must;* some people think there *must* be drinks not only before and after an event, but *during* the celebration too. No wonder you get your hackles up; no wonder your jaws turn to steel mandibles when someone sloshes a glass of claret all over your gift of Irish linen napkins for sister Susie's birthday! It sure doesn't help your coping abilities!

So what we're going to do here is list a few of the "biggies" and some of the not-so-biggie holidays, and the pressure areas that can wreak havoc with your recovery plan, unless you face them squarely and make alternate plans. First the holidays and their "gremlins":

1. Christmas — Overbuying and overspending.
2. New Year's — Parties; staying up until midnight; "pressure kissing."
3. Thanksgiving — Family dinners and reunions.
4. Halloween — Kids in general.
5. Memorial Day — Sadness; the "must" visit to grave site.
6. Fourth of July — Beer busts; company picnics.
7. Labor Day — Last big-holiday-of-summer bash.
8. Easter — Overbuying; wardrobe pressure.
9. Your Birthday — Turning 30, 40, 50, whatever.
10. Kid's (yours) birthdays — They're "growing up and away" (Empty Nest Syndrome).

To begin with, remember that all of the tools you learned in Chapter 14 about the cocktail party still apply to these holiday coping methods. Now you strive to understand these additional pressure areas, and by understanding them, change certain things so there is *joy* in the holiday instead of heartache, hangover, and harsh words.

You can change the order of holiday importance to fit your own needs, religious beliefs, and traditions. I list them in the order that they caused my own pressures and in the order that I give them to clients in recovery who are having the same problems.

CHRISTMAS OR HANUKKAH

There is no question that we all get caught up in the buying and overspending of this greatest commercial holiday of the year. No matter how many vows you have taken to "stay within" your budget this year, no matter how you have sworn that you will use only the money that has been put in your Christmas Club account, you will overspend! Why? Because you're alcoholic! You will do everything to excess in keeping with your addictive nature and your grandiose ideas of what is important in life.

You will have been in the habit of completing your shopping list at least twice, and then the "perfect" gift for him or her or Uncle Harry or Aunt Meg or whomever, will show up on the shelves. You'll buy it! Your alcoholic behavior patterns will whip that old Visa or American Express or Floogle Department Store card right out of your pocketbook or wallet, and you'll buy, buy, buy!

Then, if old tapes are played to their accurate best, you would have engaged in an almost endless round of drinking, partying, drinking, partying; the bills and the financial obligations pushed farther and farther to the farthest back recesses of your mind. They stay there until later on Christmas Eve or Christmas morning, when the last package has been torn into; then reality hits and hits hard! "There is nothing more *over* than Christmas!" a friend of mine once said. How true! Suddenly, you may need to reach for a Bloody Mary or Screwdriver or Brandy Alexander or six pack, when the realization that all this stuff that was so important a few weeks and days ago, now has to be paid for!

Well, try something new. If you'll go back and consult your past bills you'll find that most of your *splurge* spending or "spur of the moment" gifting happened in the days just before the final day or evening of celebration. I started a little thing for some folks in recovery called pretty simply, "Twelve Days of Christmas." The rules are easy: if you are a family, each member puts his or her name in a bowl. Everyone draws a name but does not disclose whose name. Then the fun begins! You are limited to one dollar for spending for each of the Twelve Days of Christmas. Pretty obvious you won't be able to trot out any "Twelve Lords A' Leaping" or even "Partridges in a Pear Tree," unless you are really clever.

Each evening (or at whatever predetermined time) you and your exchangees gather and open these very simple, inexpensive gifts, still not divulging who is the benefactor.

You will be absolutely amazed at what you can still get, either buying or creating, for a dollar. People have reported finding cookie cutters in the shape of partridges; they make the cookies and then plant the cookie bird in a branch from a tree in the yard, sprinkle some glitter or *Ivory Flakes* on the thing, and have a really clever gift.

When I tried this, I had a lot of small kids to buy for, so things like colored pencils, packs of new colored chalk, rubber bands, file cards, hair bows, and balsa gliders were high on my list. The reason this little game works for you in your sobriety is it satisfies this craving you have for *buying* without breaking you.

You are not allowed to buy for more than one day of the twelve days. It will take you twelve separate little excursions to where you can savor the excitement, the hustle and bustle of the holiday and still not face an undue amount of debt. Does this replace your "major" gift or two on your list? Of course not. It *does* enable you to share more of what the *spirit* of giving is all about.

If you are a sober single with no particular member of the opposite sex to buy for, then pick a relative or friend and send twelve different Christmas (Hanukkah) cards. When one client tried this, she reported back that she had simply signed her card as "Your Angel." She drew a little angel on the card and put no return address (something I'm sure didn't please the post office, but it sure gave her some joy). She told me that she had heard from a bunch of old friends as a result of this, for some had deciphered the postmark of where the card was mailed and deduced it must be "her." It wasn't until after the holiday that she divulged her true identity to each of the folks she had selected for her Twelve Days giving. Now, two years later, four of them choose each other's names and play this simple game.

She has told me many times of the thrill and joy she gets from getting out of her apartment in the evenings and going to the various little card shops and art stores to select her inexpensive gifts for the "twelve days." One of her friends got so intrigued that he started making his cards and they are a delight to everyone who is lucky enough to receive them!

Another way to curb your overspending pressure is to wait until the last minute to shop. I didn't believe this when it was first suggested by another recovering friend. "Heck," he said, "If I wait until a day before Christmas, most of the really expensive things I would have bought are gone; I have to settle for something that turns out to be cheaper and just as much appreciated!" You would think that the opposite would be true, but it really *can* work that way! Try it yourself and see if you don't spend less than before in your drinking days.

Another new tool for Christmas pressure spending is to make a gift of yourself! The money you would spend on a lot of gifts might be better used to get yourself "Home for the Holidays." What nicer gift than to take yourself back home or better yet, bring someone to you! It's one cost that's fairly large, but one that will mean a great deal to you. If *you* are the present no one need expect anything else. If you decide on such a gift of travel, your travel agent or airline will help you work out prepaid trips that can coincide with your Christmas Club payments. Such a prepaid trip lets you ease your money pressure and allows you the freedom to enjoy your holiday without going as overboard as you did in your drinking days.

Finally, make it a point *never* to give liquor of any kind as a gift. You don't need even one trip into a liquor store, no matter how strong your sobriety is. Alcohol has no place in your list of priorities, and if you keep *giving* liquor you are not being honest with yourself as to the importance of alcohol in your sober life. Better a box of premium chocolates than that bottle of scotch in its tempting Christmas wrap!

There is so much that is *free* around Christmas that you simply can't believe it until you look around. There are concerts of sacred and traditional music, ballets, plays, and of course the real joy of attending children's Christmas pageants in a *sober* state can't be fully described until you try it yourself.

I have tried each year to investigate some new form of celebration of the meaning of the holiday; last time it was the discovery of a new brass group playing in the sanctuary of a local church. A "free will" offering was the only charge, but the evening was a memorable return to what sobriety in celebration of a holiday can really mean.

Be sure to include as many AA meetings as possible as you get nearer to Christmas itself. There is nothing like it for your ongoing support! No pressure to drink; no pressure to overspend. For many clients and for myself, I like to recommend attendance at a meeting before or after a Christmas church service or at least within one day of each other. It is a solid "bow" to put on anyone's Christmas package!

NEW YEAR'S EVE

You may think that you can handle all the New Year's late hours they can hand you, but you're wrong! Your energy level is still not what it might have been when you were pumping all that alcohol into your system, and you can get tired more easily than you think. So pick your party carefully; use all the other party tools you have learned, but add this one: Make sure you have an alternate way to get home from that New Year's Eve party.

As people drink, remember, their hostility meters get to running higher and higher, and you need to protect your means of retreat from whatever pressure situation may be building up. Your New Year's Eve companion might overdrink at this occasion when he or she might not at most other affairs; the pressure to overdrink is there for everyone, you see.

An additional element you need to be aware of is the somehow written-in-concrete concept that says you *must* stay at a New Year's Eve party until the stroke of midnight. Well, that's okay for people who are putting a lot of alcohol away for several hours, but it's damn tough on you! If the whole thrust of the party is to make sure you are there for "seeing in the New Year" instead of what socializing could be done *reasonably* in a shorter time, then I suggest to *arrive* at the party at around 10:30. That takes a lot of heat off of you to stay for hours and watch other folks hit the booze! You can get a lot more visits in to a lot of different gatherings if you invoke the 45-minute rule and make the last party the favorite one that you want to be at when it is time to salute the new year.

When the stroke of midnight arrives, you are inclined to meet up with another enemy of your sobriety and that's the pressure to kiss everyone and their brother! When you were drinking, your inhibitions were quite well blocked, and you may have very well even been the leader in this form of merrymaking. Now that you're sober it may be difficult or even somewhat embarrassing and awkward for you to exchange kisses with strangers, not to mention close friends. Your discomfort may be overwhelming.

If you've come to the party with someone special explain this little pressure to him or her and ask that you not be pushed into it. If you have come alone, you can pretty well give a quick smooch on the cheek to your host or hostess and split the scene, or you can always just extend your hand before you are forced into this "pressure kiss." Don't laugh! I've seen a couple of people who broke into crying just over this very real terror (for some). Fortunately, they worked through it with the aid of friends.

Again, if you are with sober people to start with, your own comfort level is going to be so much higher that even warm fuzzies of New Year's kisses will be okay, because you know that everyone, including yourself, is in total control!

Visit an AA meeting; visit a hospital ward. Both will remind you that you are ending a year that may have been partially in recovery and partially in sickness of alcoholism. Either way you will know for certain that this New Year will be one of joy, hope, and well-being as you continue your program of sobriety. If you have had your sobriety for the whole year then you already know the real meaning of "Happy New Year!"

THANKSGIVING

Here's the one holiday in the year that is so family-oriented that it's almost considered to be a crime against Norman Rockwell's view of American life not to have at least fourteen people gathered for dinner! If this has been one of the great chores in your past (preparing and hosting all those folks at your house) then you *know* what a little nip or two while you were preparing the dinner did for you. Well, you can't do that now and maybe you ought to look at some alternatives to that kind of pressure.

What's wrong with asking for a little help from other family members, if possible? How about a more buffet-style repast instead of a big sit-down-at-one-table bash? These two points are well taken for sobriety. Asking for help, *even if it hasn't been done before,* spreads out the pressure among a few, not just leaving it to you. Remember that almost all of your dear ones are inclined to give you more credit for your strength in recovery than you actually have. Big tasks take a lot out of you, tasks that were often masked with alcohol just to get through them. I'll never forget hearing Phylis Diller convulse her Palmer House audience by saying the only way she ever got her ironing done was to "put gin in the steam iron and invite in all the neighbors!" Passing along the pressure!

Call up your honesty forces and share with your sister or brother or whomever, that you need help to feed the whole gang. Remind them that there have to be new ground rules for celebrating such things as big family get-togethers. Don't shirk the task if your turn has come up in the rotation cycle among your family, but don't be dumb about asking for help! No one is going to think you are just "passing the buck" and your honesty about how *doing* these things increases your anxiety level will help them understand. The fact that you admit to yourself that doing a big family dinner or reunion is a pressure cooker will help *you* to keep a firmer grip on your sobriety. There isn't anyone who would expect all of these things of you if your arm was broken and in a cast; there is no shame in your reminding them that you are still recovering from a disease (even if it's been several months), and you need understanding and help.

Why try a buffet-style dinner? Because you need the freedom to not be confined at one spot at the table answering questions and getting more and more anxious, particularly if your sobriety is fairly new. If you are at a buffet dinner, then everyone kind of picks who they want to sit by or with. As the host or hostess you can be free to move around a little more and discharge what I call "anxiety adrenalin." When the initial panic strikes you and you think having a drink is the only way you might get through a big sit-down dinner, then you change the game plan. Don't *have* the big sit-down; go buffet. So *what* if it's Thanksgiving. The purpose of the holiday in the first place is to take time for expressions of gratitude for life's blessings. Chief among these is your sobriety and continued recovery.

The whole family can gather, holding hands in a circle if you like, and offer a word of thanks; then you can have the buffet-style dinner. You are much freer to spread yourself among all your family and friends and relieve the pressure and anxiety about not drinking as it *comes upon* you instead of letting it build up. That's important, and many times I have urged newly recovering people to *not* let the anxiety build up, but deal with it right then. The buffet dinner is a way you can deal effectively. How do I know? Because I did it, and it worked like a charm!

HALLOWEEN

A client told his therapy group that he had always "loved" Halloween because he could go "Trick or Treating" with his kids. He took them around the various blocks in their neighborhood. He carried a scotch glass and every few doors or so, he would holler "Trick or Treat" with his kids. They got the candy; he got his scotch glass refilled! No wonder he loved that holiday!

But now, in sobriety, you still deal with the pressures of this harmless little holiday, and those pressures are the kids themselves! You no longer have alcohol to insulate you from their doorbell ringing, their hounding you to get started on their rounds the minute you get home from work, etc. You may not have realized how irritable you've become when you can't have some booze to get you over these little annoyances.

When a group therapy session got to kicking this around, a really positive idea or two developed which I now gladly pass on to you. You are going to exhaust your energy level a lot quicker in the early days of your sobriety, making it harder for you to cope with little irritations as well as big ones. Use the family car to take the kids, and if both you and your spouse can go together, then you can trade off blocks. She stays curbside for a few houses and you walk your kids for their treating adventures. Then change places; you stay in the car and let your spouse handle the "watch over" chores. This trade-off procedure keeps you from getting absolutely crazy trying to cope with this whole kid's adventure! I know it's a lot of work getting in and out of the car and creating a lot of extra bother, but you'll find the whole thing will be more rewarding than you thought for both parents and children.

Here's another: Get a camera; a Polaroid or Kodak Instant is ideal. As kids come to your door, take a minute and invite them in! That's the fun of Halloween — to see how creative they've been with their costuming. Take their picture and begin to *enjoy* this event instead of just something you have to do to keep your windows from getting soaped. When you take the time to let the kids show off their costumes, you also get them to not just treat the night as a "grab-and-run" candy and cookie game. The strength for your sobriety around this little holiday is that you are able to *enjoy;* taking a few pictures also helps remind you that you are in control of yourself again. It's a positive reminder of sobriety that you're able to do a simple thing like take a few pictures. I've had many people say this was something they always "messed-up" when they were drinking. They wanted to take pictures of their kids in their costumes, of their *own* family, but were rarely able to do so because their drinking interfered with just the simple procedures of operating a camera. Now that you're sober you can reward yourself by doing this Halloween bit with the camera and saying "Hey look at this one! (picture) Pretty *good*, eh?"

If you're alone and have no children of your own, you may dread this night as a real bother. Don't avoid the night, however, by shutting off the lights and pretending you're not at home! Let the little buggers in and make their pure joy rub off on you! It will help keep you off the Pity Pot, even if the nerve ends get a little frayed! Getting them to stay just long enough for you to snap a picture will help remind you that you are *not alone,* even though you may think you are. If there is one underlying joy to being sober it is the one that builds on your need to share your own happiness with others. Taking an extra minute or two with the neighbor kids before giving them their treat will make *you* feel better at having rejoined the human race!

MEMORIAL DAY

It used to be called "Decoration Day" and for a reason. I can recall this as being the day when a visit to the cemetery was a dreaded must to "decorate" some loved one's grave. You probably went through the same thing. In recovery, death has been temporarily put "on hold" in your own life. Your decision to get alcohol out of your life meant that you were not going to drink yourself to death.

Visiting the grave site of *another* person is still traumatic; you may think that you can't handle it. If you can't, say so! Don't let the *unspoken* pressures turn into *real* pressures that might jeopardize your sobriety. One of the ways you can handle Memorial Day chores is to do the grave tending on the very first day of the holiday instead of on the *last*. Since it is now a three-day affair, this means you go to the cemetery the first thing on Saturday, or even better, on Friday evening before the start of the weekend.

This promises to put any trauma around the occasion at the front end of the holiday so you can make the days following ones of joy instead of sadness. You want to return to work in a good frame of mind and not one that shows stress and strain from having waited until the last minute to visit the grave or whatever place you pay homage to the departed.

When I had to bury my mother in a far-away state, my wife and I planted a new tree in her honor in our front yard. We did the same for the memory of a favorite aunt. Now, Memorial Day does not have to be a pressure-building scene. We can enjoy the memories of our loved ones every time we go out our front door. We named the two trees in honor of our dead relatives and can and *do* tend them much more frequently than if we were waiting for *one day* of the year.

I started giving small trees away to other friends who lost loved ones, in lieu of funeral flowers. The response from them is always so positive, but the real joy in it is what it does for *my* sobriety; it keeps a healthy picture before me that to drink was to die. To be always sober is to enjoy the living and the growing things of life!

Spreading your Memorial Day grief and sadness in the ways I've suggested may seem a little selfish to you until you give it a try. You'll find your own comfort level rising with every year's practice of this method of dealing with "Memorial Day Memories."

FOURTH OF JULY

Beer busts and company picnics are the big gremlins around this holiday, and once again the rule for you is to make all things meaningful. You should volunteer to be a part of the company picnic planning. Be one of the barbeque cooks or tend the watermelon table.

If sports is your thing, make sure you participate; play softball or volleyball, even if you're lousy (like I am!). It's the *joy* of being able to do things you never could before that helps make the coping easier on this holiday. You can laugh and play as hard *without* the beer! If you are worried that there will be no soft drinks, then bring your own cooler and plenty of pop. You'll be a big hit just *having* an alternative drink besides beer available! Others will welcome the chance *not* to have to bow to the social pressure at a "kegger." "Advertising" your sobriety by having your cooler of pop or jug of "sun tea" is a great way to meet other nondrinkers at big company parties and Fourth of July barbeques. Just stand around your own cooler and see who flocks over with a "Thank goodness! You brought something to drink besides beer!"

When you play the games, you are proving to yourself (and others) that this is a new you — one that may not be the greatest athlete, but one who has turned their life around! That makes you a winner!

Again, it will serve you well to make your appearances well within the time limits of your energy. Three hours for one of these picnics is probably the top end of that energy scale. If you are getting tired, that means you may also be starting to build some anxieties. Pack up and leave! It's okay!

LABOR DAY

Since this is the last big holiday of the summer, there is always pressure to make the weekend a long and enduring one. That's not okay for the newly sober. You will have a tendency to burn out very quickly if you have to cope with overcrowded beaches, mountain highways, or seaside resorts trying their best to cram the best of all summer into one three-day affair.

I find that Labor Day is a good time to adjust easily to the fact that the traditional summer is over. There's where you can be one up! Why accept that all the pretty weekends and all the bright times are suddenly put in mothballs just because the calendar says so? For the newly recovering person, you are probably better off to forego a long weekend that will put you in heavy return-home traffic, or will find you facing some services that have already begun to close because the tourist dollars are also heading home. This is pretty depressing stuff; avoid being depressed.

So don't think of Labor Day as the *end* of anything. Stay home that particular weekend, and pick the weekends right after to begin to wind down summer activities. This is the best time to go to some of the places "off the beaten path," places that are more open to serve you year-around instead of just during a tourist season. By extending the time that you bring activities from one lazy mode to another more frantic pace, you are giving yourself more time to adjust.

It has been my experience that changing *anything* rapidly is a mistake for your overall recovery. Think of how nice and joyful it will be for you to take a *series* of little summer "closer trips" instead of one gigantic and many times, depressing three-day "Goodbye to summer" foray.

When you were drinking, you did everything to excess. You don't have to do that now; no need for the abruptness of just suddenly forcing yourself to wind down from the sunning days of summer. I keep trying to wage a battle against swimming pools closing on the Labor Day weekend. What happens? Does the water suddenly become less appealing the day after? Of course not. It's a matter of not having the personnel available to keep the things open! So, I suggest making your last day or weekend at the pool *two* or *three* days before the Labor Day weekend, whenever it is really a wonderful day to just lie there and get good and hot, and all the sun you can handle! Then, you'll not have any "season-ending blues."

You see, you need to feel free to change the *ways* that you've been doing things, things that have caused emotional pressures on you; and again, don't worry about what other people think about how you do things. *You're* the one in recovery, and it's *your* comfort and coping levels that have to be kept high, no matter what anyone else thinks.

EASTER

Overbuying and "New Wardrobe *Wantitis*" are the pressures that seem to come into play for this holiday, much like the splurges of Christmas. For the recovering person, traditions sometimes have to give way to better judgement, and that's a hard pill to swallow; but swallow it you must. In the past, you *drank* to abandon and *spent* the same way. You've changed one; now it's time to change the other!

The way you can cope with the new clothes pressure is to start to buy whatever it is you need for your Easter finery well in advance of Easter. Pick up several small, inexpensive Easter cards or candy bunnies as soon as they appear on the grocery shelves. With each item you buy, attach a card or small bunny to the box as support that what you are planning for *now* is Easter later. It will be less painful on your pocketbook and will give you some instant reward-identification. Use a picture of the suit of clothes you want pinned on your bulletin board. Each $10 payment on the suit earns an Easter card pinned beneath the picture of the clothes. By the time the holiday arrives, you will have paid for the suit and you will have secured a variety of Easter cards to send to relatives and friends.

One other joy to Easter you may have forgotten. Get back to dyeing a dozen eggs! If you don't have any children to give them to, children in your local hospitals will love having a basket to help them enjoy a holiday they are spending confined to bed.

With each little gift like that you can pass on the message of what it means to *you* to be getting healthier each day of your sobriety. My only problem with egg dyeing is one dozen is never enough!

YOUR BIRTHDAY

The birthday celebration that should mean the most to you from here on out is the celebration of the years that you remain free from alcohol! Your natal birthday pales in comparison with the birthdays your family and your AA friends will share as being your most important birthdays.

When you put this amount of significance on your sobriety, then it doesn't really matter what the *chronological* years say; your *real* joy is to know that your first, fifth, fifteenth, or thirtieth birthday of *sobriety* has brought you more of a gift than could have ever been dreamed up by the most unique store!

So it becomes easy for you to gather family and friends for a celebration of your twenty-first, twenty-ninth, thirty-ninth, or (God forbid!) *forth-ninth* birthday. Your *real* birthday (you proudly exclaim) is the number of years or even just short *weeks* or *months* that you have had your sobriety.

How many times I have sat in a meeting and listened to a person proudly announce, "I'm celebrating my birthday today! I've been sober thirty days!" I last heard that message come from a woman who was chronologically fifty-eight years old. It didn't matter to her, not one bit! Her *real* birthday had been just one month ago when she began her sobriety! That's the joy of being able to celebrate your birthday, but in a different and more meaningful way than you ever have before. If you share this feeling of joy with your loved ones, with your friends, co-workers, whomever your life touches, then those old-fashioned "regular" birthdays will be a bore!

Plan your party around this important fact of your new life and the celebration of the "passing years" that we call "aging" will be a breeze; you will be able to cope with being whatever age you are, because you are always going to be *younger* in the years kept of your sobriety and recovery!

YOUR KIDS' BIRTHDAYS

This is the last of the so-called "troublesome" holidays that I think you need to be concerned about. As your children celebrate each new birthday, you may be inclined to be feeling very much alone, particularly if you have not resolved much of the guilt you had about all the times you spent drinking and wasting the good and sharing times with your children.

You are fearful of their growing up and leaving you and the protection of your house and your arms. Then what will you do when they are gone? This "Empty Nest Syndrome" is a very real source of depression and left unattended can cause you serious problems. What you don't want to happen is for the syndrome to rock your boat of sobriety.

Everyone has his special way to deal with kids growing up and moving out. A way for you to help yourself through this feeling of "They're getting older, soon they'll be gone!" is to *reverse* the feeling from dejection to *gladness* that they will soon be "out of the nest."

The gladness comes from knowing that in your sobriety you will be free to do and to be what you could never be in a state of alcoholic confusion. You can and will be a better parent, in-law, grandparent, traveling companion. Your children's birthday celebrations can be marked as days of happiness that your freedom from alcohol is going to *enable your children to leave you* and to live their own lives free from the worry that you are going to drink yourself to death! That's one hell of a present for you to give! It's a great cause for celebrating your kid's birthdays with sheer pleasure instead of depression. Your sadness at their growing older becomes *gladness* that they are witnessing another year of their life while you have your sobriety.

Let the guilt die; bury it and commit it to the soil. It will not bring back one day or minute of any shouting, harrassment, or general bad parenting that you did when you were actively alcoholic. Go on to the future *with* your children and celebrate their birthdays confident that you will see better years ahead for both them and you!

RELIGIOUS STRENGTH OF THE HOLIDAY

What I have been talking about in this chapter has to do with learning to deal with the social or man-made pressures of various holidays. It is necessary for the recovering person to press hard for the religious experience of what a Christmas, a Passover, or a Thanksgiving means to you. The search for the "God of your understanding" will be even more fruitful as you let the spiritual meanings of each of your holidays take a priority over the commercial aspects. For many, there never *was* a spiritual meaning to Christmas or Hanukkah. There was never any significance to Easter or to Passover. Maybe, now, in the new freshness of your sobriety, maybe *now* in the dawn of an era of understanding about yourself and the disease that has controlled your life, you will be free to explore the further joys of being sober on a special holiday. Those joys are in knowing that you *have* the *ability* to put spiritual meaning into your life. Pick up the tools as you come across them in your daily life of sobriety. You just may surprise yourself and find they have been there all along!

All nature is but art, unknown to thee; all chance, direction which thou cannot see.

Alexander Pope

16
The Joy of Risk-Taking

Take a chance! How often when we were children were we taunted by other friends to do just that. As we grew up in life, the chances we were willing to take seemed to be slimmer in priorities with how we wanted to live. The extra-fast sportscar of the years when you are in your twenties gives way to the more sedate models as a person takes on some family responsibility.

A friend of mine always talked about how badly he wanted a motorcycle. When he finally was able to afford the one he wanted, he discovered that the desire to have a high-powered machine had been replaced by more "mature judgement" as he put it. "Why," he intoned to me, "should I take a chance on breaking my fool neck at *this* age?"

I'm that way about skiing. You could drop my wife on the top of the highest mountain in Colorado, and she would ski down the thing! Not me! I'm a coward about skis, and happy to admit it. I won't take the risk! But *sobriety* and the disclosure of recovering from a disease, is quite another matter!

For you, it is a matter of wanting to get that all-important comfort level operating at peak efficiency. It isn't easy to stand up and say, "I'm an alcoholic!" On the other hand, as we have discussed in earlier chapters, it is essential to the solid base of your recovery that you are able to say just those words. It is an admission that you are, as AA teaches, "powerless over alcohol," and isn't that okay? Sure it is! You should also feel powerless over an atomic bomb, or over when the sun will shine. It's okay to admit to being an alcoholic, to saying for those you care to inform that your system is not capable of handling this drinking business. There is a joy in taking a risk of calling your disease what it is, instead of what you have been doing all the times you were drinking.

That's what being in recovery does for you; it enables you to look at past behaviors and make a *free choice* to do something different. If recovery and sobriety aren't going to make significant changes in your life, then you might ask, "What good are they?"

They *are* going to make things so different for you, if you make them! If you keep the joys of your life a big secret, what fun is there in having the joy? Would you be really happy to have saved and saved and finally found a way to purchase a diamond necklace you had always wanted, and then never *wear* it? You might be terrified of it getting ripped off your neck by a mugger, but you sure wouldn't want to just have it locked up somewhere with no opportunity to show it off, to share the joy of ownership. I've never met anyone who drove a new car home from the dealership and then just parked it in the garage and put it on wheel blocks! Collectors don't even do that for very long. Your sobriety is the same thing; it needs to be shared and by sharing, you are nurturing the very plant that has taken hold in your brain, the very hard realization that you *can't* and *won't* drink alcohol again, and live.

Who are you going to take the risk with? What are the benefits and the pitfalls? Here are the basic groups of people that form the core of your support in recovery, as I see it, anyway. Your particular situation may be quite different but it's pretty certain that you will fit at least two of these categories:

1. The "significant other" in your life
2. Your employer
3. Members of your family
4. Your banker
5. Your spiritual advisor

I have purposely not included AA members, because it is understood that you will be among friends like yourself whose very priority in their life of recovery is to admit, share freely, and with joy, "I am an alcoholic!" So let's look at the other categories of people that you can find joy with in risk-taking!

THE SIGNIFICANT OTHER

This can be someone other than your spouse who, we assume, is *very much* aware of your recovery. The person I'm concerned with here is the special girl or boyfriend, the roommate, the person with whom you have been keeping company and it looks like it could "be the start of something big!"

The concept of the Significant Other is that person who is most in contact with you on a social, personal basis. It is the someone in your life whose *own* wellness can depend to a great extent on *your* wellness.

Your Significant Other's life has been greatly affected or *will be* affected at disclosure of your disease of alcoholism. So you are in a dilemma, at least you think you are. There really *is* no choice, for your relationship with this person hinges on honesty, and there is no more honest disclosure you can make than that of your recovery process.

A young man who was a client of ours had wrestled for some time with the problem of whether to tell his lady friend about his alcoholism. He was feeling pressure for taking her to various places where liquor was a mainstay: the bars, dances, and private parties. As he was be-ginning to feel more and more anxiety about his disclosure he felt like he was "between a rock and a hard place." His lady friend was a social drinker. They had been dating more and more frequently, and the newly sober client was in a quandary. He took the risk of telling her about his alcoholism and about his recovery process. The romance was over! The lady dropped him because "she didn't want to change her life-style," he told me.

Where was the joy for him in taking this risk? At first there just plain wasn't any! He was disheartened and a little angry that perhaps I had urged his risk-taking when he thought he might "bring off" the charade a while longer. It was only a few days later though that this young man shared with me that "it was the best thing that could have happened" to him. He was feeling very free of his guilt for the first time in a long time. He was actually *glad* that he had taken the risk. "What makes you glad about this?" I asked him in a session. "Because I know now that I can be honest with *myself,* and that's the whole ball game for me!" he replied.

His risk-taking cost him a very special girlfriend who was unable or unwilling to cope with being involved with someone who could not or would not continue to make drinking the important event that it was to her. Your own Significant Other may only be aware that you "have had a drinking problem." That's not good enough, because it intimates that it is possible to "clear up" such a problem. That's not possible! The problem drinker and the alcoholic are not very far apart as it is, and if you have made the decision that you were and are powerless over alcohol and that indeed you are an alcoholic, your *problem* will be with you for the rest of your life!

"Oh what a tangled web we weave, / When first we practice to deceive!" wrote Sir Walter Scott. And it's true. The more you try to "fool" or put off your Significant Other, the deeper you will get into a morass of anxiety and guilt, from which it will be very hard to extricate either yourself or the relationship. So, 'fess up! You will probably do no more than confirm suspicions that the Significant Other has been feeling but was unable to approach as a subject for discussion. Once you have taken the risk, then evaluated whether your Significant Other is sticking with you or "splitting," your next shared joy is to *involve* that person in your recovery. Take him or her to group therapy if you are in a treatment program and such a group is available. Take him or her to an Open AA meeting and let them see for themselves that AA is more than whatever past stories they may have heard. By taking the risk of disclosure with your Significant Other, you are in a position to share the real *joy* of that risk-taking! You can plan activities together that were "borderline" in the past; you can breathe a lot easier in learning the true feelings of your special person and how he or she is willing to be a part of your "recovery team."

You may indeed suffer some temporary setbacks by risk-taking with a Significant Other. On the one hand, you may lose the relationship. On the other, you may learn that the relationship will grow even stronger by your trust, your sharing, your risk-taking. Again, I urge you to go for the gold on this one!

YOUR EMPLOYER

Federal law prohibits any employer from discharging you because you have the disease of alcoholism. They *can* fire you for being drunk on the job. They can fire you for all the other reasons like not showing up for work, being constantly tardy, embezzlement, etc. But just to be an alcoholic is a "No-No" in the firing department! What's to keep you, then, from sitting down with your employer, supervisor, or department head and telling him or her about your disease? Fear, that's what! The fear that if "anyone at work knows about me, I'll lose my job!" Well, we hear that a lot from people who have made the choice to enter treatment.

What you need to understand and be comfortable with is that your employer, nine out of ten times, will be one of the most supportive people on your team. Why? Because if you are a good employee you are *valuable*, that's why. It has been estimated that it can cost as much as $5,000 to replace just an average production-line employee. Companies *may* threaten to fire the employee who refuses to get help for his or her alcoholism, but that's a different matter. Your employer would far rather share the cost of your recovery in treatment than to pay the cost of firing and replacing you. That's why so many corporations are using the employee assistance program concept to help their people identify and do something about their drinking.

Your employer wants less tardiness, less absenteeism, fewer sick days, and improved productivity out of you. If his knowledge of your alcoholism and your treatment and recovery can help him have all those things, why wouldn't he want to know? Firestone Tire and Rubber reports saving about two million bucks a year through its employee assistance program, where about half the case load is alcohol related.

No one at your work is going to know about you unless *you* tell them. Insurance companies and other so-called "third party" payers are not going to disclose that they have been helping pay for your treatment. Your counselor or therapist isn't going to tell *anyone* because federal law protects your confidentiality. Unless you sign a specific release of information form, *nobody* can learn of your treatment for your disease. But you will have a strong-man in your corner in this battle if you confide in your immediate boss. If your company is one in which the lines of authority are very clearly established, then you will know the person to whom you should confide.

I know of many instances, almost on a daily basis, where the company EAP person is the only one that knows or has to know. He or she reports to the "big boss" that so-and-so has a problem and has been referred for treatment. And as long as "so-and-so" is doing their job and keeping their recovery program strong, that's an end to it!

So here you are applying for an important new position with a new company and the application form asks: "Have you ever been treated for alcoholism?" Do you lie? No. Unqualified No! If you want to live the rest of your life as *one big lie* then go ahead, but you will be the loser. Answer the question honestly, and then attach an explanatory letter of the details of your treatment program and the success of your sobriety. Ask for a personal, additional interview to elaborate on this point. You'll get your chance because an employer likes someone who will deal squarely with his company right from the start. You'll be pleased to know how many such administrators will disclose to you their own battles with the bottle; they will take the same risk with you as part of *their* program of recovery.

Employers want good people working for them. Your risk-taking in sharing the exact nature of your disease can only work for you in job security, advancement, and performance rewards. If you fail to get a job and you think that you have been discriminated against because of your disclosure of alcoholism, then report that company! If you had another "acceptable" disease you wouldn't be turned down, unless it was clearly indicated that having the job might prove risky to you and the company. Don't be bamboozled about the alcoholism! The American Medical Association recognized it as a disease in 1956, and you're entitled to the benefits of that recognition.

MEMBERS OF YOUR FAMILY

I don't know why this turns out to be the big problem that it appears to be. So many recovering people will say, "My wife knows, but my folks musn't *ever* know." That's downright ridiculous! You need the support and strength of those that have loved and cared about you no matter *what,* and to deprive *them* of the joy of your being sober is just not right and just. If you had counted on members of your family to bail you out of difficulties caused when you were drinking, then why in God's name wouldn't you want them to know of your recovery?

If you have been afraid to take this particular risk because of fear that family members will "disown" you, or because there hasn't been any such alcoholism in your family before, you may safely say, "nonsense." Logic should tell you that any family member who stood up for you in your alcohol-imbibing times will be only *too* glad to stand up with you in your sober, joyful days. *They* won't have to worry about you anymore!

As to the other point about family alcoholism, you may be doing a great disservice to those you love by failing to disclose your disease. There might be a brother or sister who is going through what you went through, who lives in another state or town and would welcome getting *their own* support around the problem. If you take the risk, then maybe they will come forward and seek the help they so badly need. Trying not to "rattle" any family skeletons is absurd. I subscribe to the genetic theory of alcoholism which tells us that there is a genetic tendency for the disease to be passed from generation to generation.

In the majority of cases the alcoholic in treatment will have at least one alcoholic family member that they can "put the finger on." Some are just stubborn to admit it, that's all!

Once, during a question and answer session following one of my lectures to hospital in-patients, I made the same point I've just told you. A lady patient blurted at me, "No, sir, you're wrong!" I pressed her, "What do you mean, I'm wrong?"

"I'm from a strong farm family and we didn't *have* any alcoholics in our family!" She was pretty righteous now, and I could tell she was fast winning some converts from the other patients. We began talking and I started getting her to share what life was like for her on her family farm. She told of hard work, little recreation except for big family dinners on Sundays when other relatives from neighboring farms would join her family. Suddenly, she turned almost white and let out a cry of amazement. "What is it?" I asked. "My Gawd," she wailed, "I almost forgot — ever' now and then we had to take Uncle Ed's head out of the mashed potatoes!" Well, the whole room broke up with laughter. This poor woman had forgotten about someone who obviously had an alcohol problem in her family tree! She had filed the incident away for a very good reason.

When I asked her why her Uncle Ed wasn't an alcoholic if his behavior at the dinner table was as she described, she replied with some great dignity I thought, "Because, my mother didn't *allow* any alcoholics in the family!" In long-term therapy this woman, now well on the road to recovery, has discovered several other family members who weren't "allowed" to be alcoholics, but sure have been clearly identified!

Share with those who make up your family, close or not. The risk you are taking will be minimal compared to the joy you will bring to an aunt, a sister, or a cousin who has, perhaps for longer than you know, been "praying for a miracle" to come into your life. The sharing of the joy of your being sober today can help answer those prayers.

YOUR BANKER

This is repeat business from Chapter 6, but it needs to be brought up again until it is clearly a decision that you can make in comfort. After all, what is the ultimate risk that can happen if your banker knows of your alcoholism? He can turn you down for a loan! Well, that's not all that bad. You may need the loan, and you'll have to shop around until you find someone, perhaps an AA member who doesn't have a prejudice against you because of alcoholism.

But your strength in financial recovery will be tenfold if you take the risk of disclosure to your banker. This doesn't mean that every teller in the place needs to know. It means you ask for an appointment with your own banker, the loan officer or "personal banker" who handles most of your special needs. You are confiding a trust to him or her that is very important to you, and he or she will not betray that trust. They will respect your risk-taking. You may still get refused your particular request, but you will at least know that it had nothing to do with your alcoholism. How do you know? Because you ask, that's how! You come right out and make certain that you are being treated solely on the basis of whether you meet the qualifications of the bank, not whether your past affliction has colored the bank's judgement. By taking this risk you will add another strong block to your sobriety foundation. A block that says, "I can be judged *now* on how I am *now* and not on how my behavior *was*."

Your banker controls not just your money. With him or her on your side you will have a staunch ally in many things that affect you and your standing in the community. Your banker will be beside you in many situations that you may never even know of at the time they happen, but will come to light in later years.

If you take the risk of disclosure with your banker, you will have increased your own personal worth far more than you may think. A banker looks at many elements of a balance sheet, not just the figures. The particular thing you may be denied by your bank today, may be possible tomorrow, and your honesty in disclosing your disease and in *sharing* the joy of your present sobriety will pay handsome dividends!

YOUR SPIRITUAL ADVISOR

If your priest, pastor, rabbi, or other spiritual advisor has been beside your through the tough times of your drinking, then he or others like him in similar positions already know of your alcoholism. But supposing this is a new church, a new congregation? Suppose you are anxious to involve yourself as part of your recovery (Chapter 10) but are unwilling to take the risk of sharing your disease? Are you uncomfortable as to how to do it? Rest easy! Invite the person to lunch! I love having lunch with my pastors whenever their schedule and mine permit. It's very open, low key, and full of joy, laughter, and warmth.

It's at lunch that disclosure can be made quite easily. When the cocktail person approaches your table for your order, you can indicate the friend to make his choice. When it's your turn, and you decline and choose something non-alcoholic, you have your natural opening to disclose in the most comfortable way you choose.

When my pastor and I had lunch at a favorite restaurant of mine at Christmas time, we were presented with a bottle of champagne with the compliments of the management for my "good customer" status with the place. Pastor Del and I had a warm laugh over that for many months. Our Christmas lunches are a tradition for just the two of us, for it was at such a lunch one time that I made my own disclosure, a fact that had been common knowledge to everyone but me!

Your spiritual advisor shares a very special place in your life for he represents a tie to your life from the past, the present, and into the future. Even if he is a new person in your life and you are new in his congregation, the quiet luncheon for the opportunity to lay your cards squarely on the table will bring you an element of rare peace and joy.

Many ministers and priests suffer the same affliction; many more deal with it on a daily basis, and their ease with the subject can very well be the turning point in your life for taking the risk of disclosure. Remember that anytime you make a disclosure it should be to *strengthen* your sobriety. Your spiritual advisor is part of your total recovery plan, and this makes him considerably different than just being your confessor, if that is your belief. Your spiritual advisor lends help in the ways you ask to keep your recovering strong. In the ways that he cannot help, he reverts to being first, your friend, and as such, a person who is willing to listen!

The joy of risk-taking is a real joy like the others that we've talked about. It is a way that the "boogie-man" can be brought out of your closet, and you can be unloaded of the years or months of guilt around your past alcoholic life. When you take a risk you are also casting a large line out into the world in which you live, love, work, play. The mere opportunity for you to snag *someone else* who has been hiding in darkness about their problem makes the risk-taking worthwhile!

As a member of the fellowship of Alcoholics Anonymous you can do just *that,* remain *totally* anonymous, and that's the protection it affords twenty-four hours a day. No one will quarrel with your decision.

If the spirit of adventure is in your soul, if your heart likes the feeling of lightness and guilt-free tranquility that your sobriety can bring, then you may want to do a little more risk-taking, and you have the freedom to do that, too. The joy will be in how you handle it, in how you learn that the ways and means of taking risks in sobriety are endless. You may lose a few rolls of the dice, but the odds are that you will come up a winner more often than you ever thought possible!

*Man therefore can, with a rigid sur-
face and a properly designed ap-
paratus, repeat the maneuvers of
ascension and direction performed
by the soaring birds. . . .*

Louis Mouillard
L'Empire de l'Air

17
Flying Without Drinking
(How to let the booze cart pass you by)

"No way! I gotta be six sheets to the wind just to get *near* the airport!"

"I'm a real white knuckler, and I don't want *anything* to make me feel any better about flying!"

"It's just pure goddam agony for me to go *anywhere* on a plane. I'd *never* make a trip without drinking!"

"If I have to fly, I drink! If I can't drink, I'm *not* flying!"

Well, well! Is this *you* we are quoting? Are *you* the newly sober person who just dreads the idea of your first flight where the booze cart is going to have to pass you by in order for you to remain in recovery? Probably. It's more common than you may think, particularly when you may have been skittish about flying in the first place. That little ole miniature bottle or two set on the fold-down tray at your seat certainly helped the flight go smoother, didn't it? I mean, there is no question in your mind that the turbulence was easier because *you* were politely getting sloshed, is there? It's amazing how all that electronic gear and massive machinery works in direct proportion to the amount of vodka you are helping run through your own engines!

175

What we'll attempt to do in this chapter is show you some ways you can actually feel okay about your flying and how you can let that booze cart sail right on down the aisle and stop only if you want a soft drink. So what I've done is go back and take some more of the basic fears that seem to crop up about flying, anxieties that come from lack of understanding about what's happening to you and the machine you're in. Together, we'll create a "checklist" for flying without the need to drink, before, during, or after the flight.

There is a basic premise here that needs to be your personal motto from now on: "There is absolutely *no* mechanical nor electrical, nor hydraulic link-up between your alcohol consumption and the operation of the aircraft!" There won't be any scientific prize for developing this axiom for you, but if you say it out loud enough, you'll understand the value of realizing that whatever happens, *including* the majority of really smooth, wonderful flights you make, happens from sources or circumstances beyond *your* control. Drinking in order to fly simply means that you have not come to grips with your life, nor with the joy of getting on a jet and going somewhere and really *enjoying* it.

So, let's look at the "Basic Checklist For Flying." The entire flight crew goes through checklists for every stage of your flight in preparation for all contingencies, all emergencies. They go through it step by step for *every* flight, no matter how many hours of experience they have logged. You can and should do the same thing. The checklist consists of:

1. Preflight preparation
2. Boarding procedures
3. Start-up and taxiing
4. Takeoff and "climb"
5. In flight
6. Descending
7. Landing
8. Leaving the aircraft

This Basic Checklist is not nearly as complex, obviously, as the manual you'll see the captain and crew using in their cockpit. By the way, I spent a number of hours refamiliarizing myself with this manual as used on a Boeing 727 aircraft. I would *like* to report that my cockpit simulation flights were as successful; they were not! I have been able to pilot an airplane since I was a young boy, spending all my lunch hours and job pay on flight lessons. Nothing helped! My jet flight instructor, my helicopter instructor, and many other pilot friends of mine keep hoping for better performance from me than I can return!

While I may have had trouble working that checklist, the Basic Flying-Without-Drinking Checklist is *very* workable; you just need to practice it, as if you were learning to pilot a modern aircraft. You use it *every time;* never vary from its basic principles unless you add to it for your own enjoyment. Ready? Here we go!

PREFLIGHT PREPARATION

Virtually every airline wants you to arrive at the airport at least "one hour before departure." Forget it. You don't need to sit around on some concourse watching a lot of other "happy" travelers make their steady and sometimes *unsteady* way into the many little cocktail bars that the airport provides. So you need some planning to prevent you from either getting tempted to break your sobriety or getting fouled up because you cut it *too* short and maybe missed your flight. I suggest that you try to arrive as close as possible to the half-hour before the aircraft is ready for boarding. If you are in the seat selection line, they are not going to leave without you! Seat selections can be done ahead of time by many airlines; the more you can do this, the better. What is ideal, is for you to arrive at the departure gate, spend no more than ten minutes there, and get on the aircraft.

But suppose it is impossible for you to use this technique? You may *have* to spend as much as one or more hours at the airport before boarding. You *sure* will have to if you are making a connecting flight, although the popular "hub and spoke" system of air connections used by most major airlines seems to cut that between-plane waiting time considerably. If you do have to wait, you can incorporate any of the techniques for meeting people that we talked about in other chapters, or you can read and listen to music. Now wait a minute! Don't get panicky! You *can too* meet people without going into the bar. There are hundreds of folks at airports who are flying and waiting to fly and like you, spending some hours in a concourse lounge.

You have part of your problem already whipped, because those you see waiting in some place *other than a bar* are obviously "okay" to do what you're going to do, fly, without being tanked! If you are a newly sober single female, you can just sit there and more people than you care to will want to start a conversation. You handle *that* any way that makes you comfortable. But let's say that you really just want to read and/or listen to music. About the music. Airlines won't let you play those AM/FM "personal portables" while in the plane, because they might interfere with the aircraft's own communications system, but you *can* use them in the concourse lounge.

Better are the personal cassette players that are so popular and are coming down in price every month. You can put in your favorite music, the kind that lends itself to reducing your personal anxiety about flying. Put those miniature earphones on; you're set! You can even take that kind of device into the plane with you and play it all during your flight if you wish.

Most of the larger airlines supply stereo headsets and programming right at your seat; we'll talk about that later. For now, here you are in the concourse waiting area, listening to your music. You want to read. Now, a basic mistake is made. You have probably brought along a choice of at least two new books or articles that you have been "meaning to get to." Your flight *seems* like the ideal time. But it isn't! Your anxiety level about flying without drinking is probably pretty high at this point, and your level of concentration is practically nil! You won't do anything with a new book but start over and over and over about three hundred times in between checking your watch, going to the bathroom, reshuffling your briefcase papers, or rummaging through your backpack, handbag, or "carry-on" luggage.

Nope! You want to read something that you're *already into,* something that you are so engrossed in that you can get right back into the story or the narrative, quickly. Save the new book or magazine for the "something" to read in your hotel room at your destination, or for lounging-around-the-pool reading. Your brain needs to be instantly occupied with something other than worry, nervousness, anxiety, and panic! Familiar characters, plots, dialogue, will help get you into a less frantic "head space" than trying to catalogue, sort, and digest new stuff. The one exception is for work materials. If there is a new report that must be read before you can attend the meeting you're flying to, then read it. But bear down on the concentration. You probably already carry a note pad or, like I do, a legal-size binder and pad. Use it! Make notes, even if they are lousy notes! The idea is to occupy your mind about the things in the report, not about what is about to happen when you have to "get on that damn plane!"

The brain, you know, is a marvelous organ. It has trouble concentrating on more than one thing at a time. If you are engrossed, if you are *forcing* yourself to concentrate on what you are reading and writing, you simply can't have space to worry about your flight! In recovery, more so than at other times in your life, you can't do two things at once, not do them well, for sure!

So concentrate on the work or reading material before you; don't pay attention to the activity of others around you in the lounge. Your personal music will sure help that. If you don't have one of these gadgets, then just bear down harder on what you are reading. Read at *least* one full page before allowing yourself to glance around at lounge activity. Reassure yourself that "everything seems to be okay" and go back to your reading (and making notes). *This* time, read at least *five* pages before looking up and around. Another five to ten minutes will have slipped by, depending on your reading speed.

As part of your preflight preparation, ease off on coffee and other high-caffeine drinks, if possible. Your state of agitation is going to be increased when you start pumping a lot of coffee into your bladder! Try and remember that it is *anxiety*, coupled with too much liquid that is making you have to leave your seat and get to the restroom every ten minutes. *Call* it "anxiety!" Tell yourself, or your traveling companion, "I'm nervous about flying. I'm nervous about flying *without* drinking!" The sharing of those pieces of information will help you in your preflight portion of the checklist. The mere verbalizing of your anxiety takes the major sting out of it. You can't be too scared of something you can talk about; remember that! You deal with your anxiety by *letting* it happen.

About ten minutes before you think boarding is to begin, close up your work or your reading. Put away or shut off your music. Get up and walk over to the nearest window where you can observe your aircraft in its final preparation stages. If this isn't possible, look at some *other* plane that is being readied. Look first into the cockpit. Most aircraft are parked "nose-in" to the jetway, and you can see the flight crew. They are going through *their* preflight checklist. Observe them being at ease. They may be laughing with one another or may be, having finished part of their preflight list, just be looking back in at you! Go ahead! Wave! You've always wanted to do that, now haven't you? They'll wave right back if they're not busy and if they know you're waving at them. It's a good feeling for you to know those folks are just like you. They love life just like you. They're going to *have a safe trip right along with you!* How about that?

I'll bet that you, now sober, never thought about that; these folks in your flight crew are *going with you* on your trip. They want to get there and back every bit as much or more than you do, in safety, comfort, and with ease. So why would they want to do something to make *you* uncomfortable when the same thing would make *them* uncomfortable?

Look at the other activities that are taking place around your plane — your food being loaded, the final "topping off" of jet fuel, the last carts of luggage being brought to the aircraft. Can you spot any of *your* luggage from where you are? Concentrate on the numbers of people who are all working to make sure that your aircraft is ready, for you. You might see a member of the flight crew walking around the outside of the plane shining a flashlight up into the wheel wells. "My God! What's wrong!" is the message that your nondrinking body receives. A moment of panic. If you were still in your active alcoholic days you could have cared less if anyone was even walking around the plane, much less shining a light into a wheel well!

Well, there's *nothing* wrong. That's the flight engineer or second officer; could be the first officer or the captain, however, making a *routine* checklist of his aircraft. It's as normal a part of his job as when you make a quick walk-around your family car. He's looking in the wheel wells to make certain there is nothing to interfere with gear retraction. He is checking, visibly, things that his cockpit instruments will also confirm; hatch doors are shutting and locking, wing-tip lights and underbelly strobe lights are operating, etc.

You will have more than used up any of those ten minutes that you were trying to use before boarding. But here's an important and final point about your preflight preparation. *Don't* try and make a last-minute dash for either the bathroom or the telephone! You will have already said your temporary goodbyes; no one needs to hear from you again. *Terminate* this link; you *are going to get on board;* you *will* call loved ones or business associates upon your arrival. What you are saying to yourself is, "I'm ready. Let's do it!"

BOARDING PROCEDURES

Item two on your Sober-Flying Checklist: you are now walking down the jetway or across the "apron" to arrive at your aircraft. Don't push or shove. Not only is it dangerous, but you will just keep your anxiety level high by rushing. When you arrive at the boarding door of the aircraft take *just a second* to look to your left, into the cockpit, if the door is still open. I make it a point to say, "Hello," even though I don't know the flight crew. But, hey, these folks are just like family, and I appreciate the job they are doing for me. You'll like seeing them going through their procedures. It won't block things up for the folks behind you either. Just a quick look in, seeing all the instrument lights on, the flight crew perhaps adjusting seat belts and harnesses. It's okay, do it!

Next, *thank your flight attendant* who greets you at the door. They are welcoming you into *their* home for the next couple of hours, and you are glad to be there! (Even if you are quaking with anxiety and wonder how you'll ever get through it without a drink or two or three.)

Use little mind tricks like "Thanks for having me!" Or, "I'm looking forward to this trip!" She or he may not have time to respond right away but these professionals will generally remember someone who took a moment to say something pleasant, and they'll remember you. It may be later in the flight, but many times I've had some flight attendant recall my "boarding comment" and take a moment or two to respond.

Get to your seat and buckle up right away. This helps you say to yourself, "I'm secure. I'm not going to 'fall,' either *out* or *down*." I hope that you will select a window seat when you get your boarding pass. It will be a greater help to your learning to fly without drinking than any other seat.

If you have selected or had no choice in a selection of seats, something other than a window seat, then, in order of preference are:

1. Any seat over the wing
2. Any aisle seat
3. Any seat directly behind the first-class bulkhead

If possible, seats to avoid are the ones in the very tail of the plane where turbulence may be felt more severely than elsewhere, and "middle" seats where you are somewhat cramped, and may tend to feel a little claustrophobic.

Next item in your boarding procedure is to look *up* and *around*, after you are seated. Notice how roomy this machine is. It's bigger than your bedroom, probably, and sure a lot more headroom than your recreation room. If you are at a window seat, see that your window shades will come up and down. Just like home—maybe better!

START UP AND TAXI

The door is shut and you are going to say to yourself, "I've done it! I actually am seated here on this plane and I'm going to make this trip *without* booze!" Now pay attention to the flight attendant giving you and everyone else the basic safety instructions. But here's the difference. Really *listen* and pay attention. By riveting yourself on what he or she is saying and demonstrating, you (once again) can't concentrate on anything else, like being anxious. So, in addition to paying attention to life-saving instructions you are helping yourself overcome an even more primary fear—the drinking and relapsing fear. This fear says, "I'll have just *one* when it's offered, to overcome my anxiety!" The fear part is thinking, even thinking that you might just *do* it, and hence undo all the time of your recovery and sobriety that you have worked so hard to build!

You will hear noises now and they are all accounted for. It's okay. The engines are being started and "spooled up" to taxi speed. In the cockpit, your flight crew is checking them for proper temperatures, performance, etc. Look out the window at the wing. You will see, at the same time you hear, the flaps coming down away from the wing. This is in preparation for your takeoff. You'll want to observe these flaps later, so watch them being lowered. When they are down in position, the whirring noise you have been hearing has stopped. What you have been hearing is the drive gear that raises and lowers the flaps. Get used to hearing, maybe for the first time in your sobriety, the chime that summons the flight attendant to the cockpit. There's a panic! Is something wrong up there already? Nope! Captain or other crew may want something from the galley or may need to relay some flight delay information to the senior flight attendant. No big deal. If it's important for you to hear it, you *will*, firsthand.

Now, look at and *reset* your watch. This is the first time that you should, in my opinion, reset your watch to reflect the time zone into which you are flying. The trick here is that you can see quite a lot of your elapsed trip has already been used up! "Hey! This is going to be shorter than I thought!" If you are East, coming West, you are moving your watch *back,* and you can say, "This is great! I'll have more daylight to spend than I thought!" Substitute whatever you like, but make yourself be aware of the time. You'll use it later on in flight to see what good progress you are making. If you are West, going East, the time has really marched along by more minutes than you thought. That's good! Use all these tricks and more to keep your anxiety level *down*. You are *not* going to have to drink!

As you are in your taxiing check, notice that a lot of folks have already closed their eyes and are even appearing to be asleep, even with their seatbacks still in an upright position. "Well!" you say to yourself, "They must feel okay about flying, and they're on the same plane I am!" See, what happens to you is you let your anxiety get to making you believe that it is only *you* involved in this activity. No one else on that plane is holding a drink in their hands, either, although many of them may have been drinking before they boarded. Doesn't matter; at this point, as you are taxiing, you are all, equally, *without alcohol* in your hands! Therefore, doesn't it stand to reason, the plane is moving without your help?

TAKEOFF AND CLIMB-OUT

Most generally, you will have had an announcement by some member of the flight crew telling you that your aircraft has been cleared for takeoff. You may *not* have and are simply feeling the acceleration and the push of gravity on you as the plane attains its lift-off speed. Look out the window; notice those flaps are still down. *Feel* the aircraft tilt or "rotate" its nose to the upward climb level. The jet engines are not increasing in noise level but are producing a steady, powerful whine. As you become airborne, it's time to unclutch your hands from the seat and observe two quick things that will contribute to your calming-down posture. (1) The "No-Smoking" sign is turned off. (2) Those flaps you saw go down are beginning to wind themselves back into the wing. You now *know* for a *positive fact* that everything is okay and that your crew has "trimmed" your aircraft for flight. Nothing's wrong! You now hear and feel the landing gear come bumping into its nest underneath the plane. Another good sign. You are okay, and just imagine, *still* no need to drink!

But just when you are feeling okay, you suddenly feel that plane go into a fairly sharp turn or "bank." "Oh-Oh" says newly sober and alert you. "What's happening?" Simple. No need for panic! Your captain has been told by "Departure Control" to clear the airspace above the runway so that planes behind yours can take off. Your aircraft has already been cleared to an assigned altitude, and the sharp veering away from the runway enables you to get where you're going and allows other planes to use "your" runway. You may also hear, shortly thereafter, all of the engine noise decrease; you believe that they are slowing down, and you're right! Again, the traffic controllers handling your flight have asked your captain to maintain a certain altitude while they clear traffic at the assigned level for your flight. The cutting back on the engine power is used to reduce speed and to maintain that altitude, usually for a brief period. Then, you'll hear the engines "spool-up" again, as your crew begins climbing to the assigned flight altitude.

So far, you are convinced that everything is okay, but the *real* test is starting. While you are asked to remain seated, your flight attendants have begun to ready that formidable monster the "booze cart," lurking there in the shadow of the galley! You *know* it's there; you sense it, and your anxiety may be at a still high enough point that you wonder how you're going to handle it. But you *will* handle it!

Don't look in the direction of the galley. Don't get up and go to the restroom if you can help it. If moving about is permitted at all, and you have to go, go toward the *rear* of the plane where any booze carts that are being prepared are likely not to be out in the aisle, yet. Most airlines prepare their first class, up-front service first, so going to the rear is a hedgier bet.

If you don't have to go, stay in your seat, use the convenient stereo provided by the airline, and crank that little puppy up as loud as you can handle! If it's your own cassette, do the same thing. The idea is to get you to a *state* of *irritation* (by the loud volume) as quickly as possible. When the music is so loud that it almost hurts, reach over or down and *slowly* reduce the volume until you're at a comfortable listening level and the noises of the aircraft cabin *seem welcome.* What you have done is show yourself that you are *capable* of *reducing anxiety* (symbolized by the manual reduction of the volume control). You are *in control,* therefore it will not be necessary to turn to a substitute (alcohol) to help you gain control of anxiety.

IN FLIGHT

So now here you are, level, sober, and feeling like you're going to make it after all when down the aisle comes that cocktail cart! You are staring at it and wondering if the new, recovering alcoholic person that you've become can let that thing get by you! Are you still frightened? Are you still digging your fingers into the arms of your seat? Have you hit a little clear air turbulence or has it been a little rough ever since you took off? Maybe the answers to all those questions are "Yes!" But once again you need to remind yourself that no matter how much alcohol anyone on that plane consumes, it will not affect the flight or the machine itself! So, go ahead and look at the booze cart! What do you see?

When you were drinking, you automatically saw that little cart just loaded with drinks on its top shelf, and it couldn't get to you quickly enough! Now, look again. *There is no alcohol in view.* The little miniatures of liquor, that is. You may very well see champagne or wine bottles, but the "hard stuff" is kept in a drawer underneath the cart. What you have conditioned yourself to seeing is all of the "set-ups"; the plastic cups with ice in them, surrounded by the lemon and lime wedges, olives, cherries, etc. that go into mixing a cocktail. You *think* they're filled with alcohol!

But you are *not* looking at endless glasses of cocktails! Now, pay close attention to how really *few* people on board a flight actually ordered alcoholic beverages. It's amazing! When several flight attendants who are in their own recovery were confronted about this observation, they reported back to group that they had never noticed it much before, but it was true! *Most* of the folks on the plane with you will have a soft drink, coffee, or tea. A *few* people will drink a lot. They are the ones you notice. Sure, a number of your fellow passengers will take wine or champagne, but remember those are not *quick-fix* beverages, so they must not *need* them to reduce anxiety! Neither do you! Make sense?

My own personal choice for taking something off the drink cart is orange juice and a diet *7-Up* or *Sprite* or *Fresca;* something bubbly that puts a little effervescence on top of the orange juice. You try it yourself and see if you don't like it. You get a "sugar boost" and a little "bubble-fallout." It's quite refreshing!

When the booze cart is past your row of seats, think of it as totally gone. You will not need it anymore, even if you want another juice or soft drink. You may find that your meal is coming right on top of the drink cart or perhaps just before it. Eat something! Even if you can't tolerate "airline" food, you need something in your stomach to counteract possible anxiety build-up. The blood that will have to be used to digest what food you eat is blood that will help drain your brain of being quite so "hyper."

Now, you can check your watch again. See how much time (flying) has elapsed and how well you've done. It's the same principle you have been practicing throughout your entire recovery period — the one that says you will live your life one day at a time, and if necessary one *hour* at a time! You can say, "Good for me! I've made it for (number of minutes or hours) flying, without a drink! You are now beginning to understand the basic premise we spoke of in the beginning of this chapter: alcohol intake by human beings on board an aircraft does not affect the flying capabilities of the machine.

One or more of the flight crew may do some walking and visiting in the cabin after meal service is completed. They expect to be asked some questions, and if you are still feeling anxious about something, stop the crew member and ask. It's what you *don't* know that is likely to cause you to create the "scaries." It's your own conjecture about what is happening as opposed to what actually is going on that can be your undoing.

If you are in some rough weather and you see the wing tips flapping, it's because they're supposed to; they're built to handle many more times the amount of stress than that to which the average flight is subjected. If you hear noise underneath the plane on take-offs and landings, it is because you *should* hear it; ninety-nine times out of a hundred everything that you hear or see is perfectly normal for your flight. It is safer to fly today than it is for you to drive on your own state's highways.

Go back to your book, the one you already have been reading. Keep your stereo on, and you might even (Saints forbid!) take a little snooze. Kick off your shoes. There's nothing quite as nice as flying in your stocking feet! It makes you feel right at home, in addition to being downright comfortable.

DESCENDING

As you start down in your flight you may have some more anxiety due to the "old tapes" you play about "needing a drink" to cover certain nervous situations. If there are clouds below you, you may be making your descent "blind," on instruments, as your flight crew skillfully threads their way down into the assigned landing pattern. Here are some things to remember. Many times, even though you can't see outside your window, your flight crew is seeing the various breaks in the clouds as they make the way down. Another thing—a good many people are all concentrating their efforts to bring your flight in safely.

Cut-backs in engine power do not automatically mean trouble; it means just what it did when you felt it while climbing. The captain has been asked to reduce speed; then he may pick up the speed a little; then cut back again. All of these things are quite normal in landing. Rest assured if there is something that is coming along that is not normal and requires your attention, you'll be told. You can have fun watching the flaps descend again. Even if you are in weather, you will see them and then, perhaps the sets of "slats" pull away from their in-line position on the wing and form a wind barrier in front of the wing. You'll hear the landing gear go down, and you can say to yourself, "The captain has just been told that the gear is down and we have green lights." The instrument panel in the cockpit has confirmed that the gear is down, locked, and ready by lighting a green light for each gear.

Look at your watch for the last time during your trip in the air. You can take pride in knowing that you spent "X" number of hours and minutes conquering a fear you've had, without using alcohol, without breaking your sobriety and your recovery process! That's great, isn't it? One more notch to add to your belt of whipping this disease of alcoholism. If you're still feeling nervous during the descent, use this trick. Crane your neck up and down the aisle. There is no booze cart in sight! There is *no alcohol* that can be called upon to interfere with your dealing with your anxieties or emotions. You will need your own pride in your recovery and your own inner strengths, the help you receive from the "God of Your Understanding," the calm assurances of your fellow passengers, and finally, the tool of communicating your nervousness to your companion or seat-mate.

Verbalizing such anxiety with, "Landings and coming down through weather always makes me nervous!" has an amazing effect. The minute you give voice to it, the less nervous you are. Try it sometime and see for yourself.

LANDINGS

An obvious continuation on your Basic Checklist is the landing. As the wheels touch the runway and just before the craft settles to the nose wheel, look out the window again and observe the wings and the engines (if you can see them). As the plane settles on its nose wheel, the pilot reverses the thrust of the engines to help brake the plane's speed. You will see vents and cowlings open up and appear to fly away from the engines. This is so the engine thrust can use those vents to push air against the plane, slowing it down.

Watch your flaps come up again as the plane slows, and listen for the cabin music to come on. Look around you at the happy faces of your traveling friends. Feel good about yourself and say to yourself, "I've done it!" Make it a point on your checklist to say, "That was a good trip!" even if there were some rough spots.

Look at the wing again. A new set of "spoilers" has been up; this set is on the back surface of the wing and acts as brakes that are used for landings. You didn't see them on the take-off as they weren't employed since you wanted to "go" then, and not "stop." Make everything as memorable in the way of an audio and visual effect as you can. Remember the sights and sounds of landings, and the next time you will come to expect those same happenings and will be more comfortable with them.

LEAVING THE AIRCRAFT

This is the last item on your sober Basic Checklist. You use this item to reinforce the fact that you *will be doing this* (flying) *again*. To do this, make it a point to thank your flight attendants. Tell them, "I'll see you next trip!" If the cockpit door is open when you leave, say goodbye and "Thanks" to your flight crew. They may still be busy going over their after-flight checklist, but mostly they will be completed enough with immediate detail to acknowledge your word of thanks.

You will be back in the air again! You have made a great step in overcoming the basic thoughts and actions that you have harbored for all the time of your active drinking—that basic premise again that the plane's performance and safety was all dependent upon the amount of alcohol *you* consumed! You'll arrive at your place of destination without a booze headache caused from drinking too much, too fast at high altitude. You will be able to *function,* and that's always one of the best joys of being sober. You will have mastered the booze cart and its dangers, its siren call. Best of all you will have learned that *it* didn't affect the flight of the plane either! You just *thought* it did all those other times!

18
Trying Different Work

It seems almost sinful to be talking about the possibility of changing jobs when we are seemingly in a period in our economy when just *having* a job is a real blessing. So let's begin by saying that the newly recovered person certainly shouldn't run right into the employment or personnel manager and turn in a resignation; that will only compli- cate your recovery and make it even more difficult for you to realize any joy at all in being sober.

What I am interested in having you do is consider the possibility of adding to your work with things that you may have always *thought* about doing but never had the right impetus for doing. Your sobriety and your new outlook on life may be just the ticket you have been looking for to urge you on. There is a little Walter Mitty in each of us, a little bit of the dreamer that imagines the "sky's the limit," and that's part of what contributed to our drinking behavior.

A recovering friend said only recently that "When I was drinking I felt ten feet tall!" Another recovering person said, "Now that I'm sober, I'm just trying to get back to being five-feet eleven-inches (his real height) tall!" When you were drinking there wasn't anything that you couldn't do, or so you thought. Now, in sobriety, there are many times when you wonder if there is anything you *can* do, and particularly do *right?*

But it's okay to let our Walter Mitty imagination lead us to the brink of discovery, to examine whether what we are doing for our life's work is really what we want to continue to do. There is no question but what stress and tensions are a part of any job. The alcoholic is inclined to justify their past drinking by laying all the blame for not "being able to drink" on job pressures. You realize, I'm sure, that was just the *excuse* you may have used; the *reason* you drank was that you have a disease and were unable to stop drinking without help. The job that you have gone back to is probably exactly the same one you had when alcoholism finally caught up with you; it still has pressures and tensions. There is one basic, large difference. You are now in a position to *handle* those pressures. You're sober, and what seemed like monumental problems at work before, now may still be problems, but there are solutions in sight, and your sobriety allows you to deal with those solutions.

Oftentimes people are inclined to worry about "climbing the highest ladder in the company," reaching the top echelon. What I suggest is that you don't worry about climbing to the top until you've learned how to not stumble on the stones in your path.

Changing jobs will not alleviate pressures; it might add to them and you might just find yourself under more stress and strain than you ever bargained for; worse, it could lead you down the path to a drinking episode and eventual breaking of your sobriety.

Instead, let's think about *adding* a job dimension to your life; trying different work means letting out the reins of your imagination and *experiencing* some different types of work as part of your recovery. For example, get a paper route! I took a sampling of jobs that turned out to be "fun" among people who wanted to add a new dimension to their lives while they worked their program of recovery. Having an adult paper route headed the list.

I'm not talking about beating some needy kid out of a job! There are generally loads of car routes for adults available in almost any size community. One couple I know started out with a small route to help her in recovery, getting needed exercise and earning a little extra money. Her husband agreed to help, and what started out as just a few-hundred-paper route ended up six months later as a district route of several thousand papers!

It helped this recovering lady get a new outlook on her life; she needed to know that she could tackle something new and make it work. You can do the same, if you're willing to make the extra effort. One of the best sources is to try retail selling, in local department stores, particularly for seasonal employment. You won't make a lot of money; you might be offered a courtesy discount which will help with your holiday shopping. What you *will* get is a sense of *confidence* that you can meet people, that you can actually carry on an intelligent sales routine and not need the booster of alcohol to make you pleasant. Alcohol has done funny things to you that way. It has had a tendency to make you very *un*pleasant and quarrelsome! Having to work in the public sector, having to learn to cope with the pressures of the day without the bottle is good for your recovery. You can do amazing things if you are willing to take the risk.

Finding additional work, something that is out of the ordinary from what you normally do, allows your fantasies to run the full gamut, too. A most refined lady in recovery had always wanted to try her hand at being a waitress. She really had not had to do much menial work of any kind before, having been born into a moneyed family. She wanted to learn what it was like to put in the hard hours, complaining customer encounters, and aching feet that go with food service jobs. She didn't need the money as much as some other people in her community, and she received some rather severe criticism for "taking food out of other's mouths." This lady told me in therapy sessions that she got quite tired of making up alibis to cover why she needed her waitress job. Finally she took the risk of disclosure to a few people; she was a recovering alcoholic. "I've never had to work hard in my life; just sat around and drank!" she confided to them. "It's important for me to know that I'm worth something as a person!"

She didn't keep the job long, maybe three or four months. But it gave her much needed confidence in herself as a *sober* person. She tried another position, this time as a receptionist in an automobile agency, a "greeter" who welcomed people into the showroom and put them together with whatever salesperson was due to work the prospect. This lady was quite good at this area of public relations. She moved up and asked for the opportunity to try auto sales herself. The agency gave her the job, and she is doing extremely well at it. Her sobriety is intact; her feelings about herself are in top-drawer condition, and she attributes this to her "getting off my duff" and trying different work!

A man in recovery told of his taking a job delivering telephone directories; it was menial work, and it was not what he was used to doing. His doctor had suggested that it would be good for him, that it would help clear "the cobwebs" of grandiose, alcoholic behavior out of his mind. When he completed treatment he took the directory job before going back to his profession in broadcasting. It did him a world of good!

I remember the client from another state who was so good at sewing that she was encouraged to try it as a business. Her recovery was secure, that is, she was in "good space" with her sobriety and was continuing an outpatient program of support. She started her sewing business in her home, actually just in the basement. She got more orders, starting with just simple alterations. She finally began to get requests for custom tailoring. This lady who had never done this kind of work as a profession, finally opened up a store in the community where she lived. Two of the shirts in my closet are from her skilled hands; her sobriety gave her the confidence to begin life anew with different work!

Changing job positions in the company where you currently work is another rewarding experience for the recovering person. Many times, you may have been considered for promotion only to either shoot yourself down with your own behavior, or to have your employer not "feel right about" you. No one was confronting you about the many absences or late arrivals to your work as a result of hangovers and general "stinkin' thinkin' " attitudes caused in large part by your drinking. But now, newly sober, why not try again? Approach the supervisor or the head honcho himself and make a stab for a promotion to a position that might be a step up for you. Be careful! You will not be able to handle giant strides all at once. Take it easy and feel your way slowly into areas that call for more responsibility. The best thing to do is employ your tools of honest disclosure to your supervisor or boss. Ask him or her how they feel about your taking on the new position. Try to get open discussion and honest evaluations of what will be expected of you, what the high anxiety and pressure areas could be, and what areas of help you can get if you feel overwhelmed.

A young man in recovery was confused about his chosen profession. He had been an elementary school teacher and was feeling that his recovery might allow him to expand his horizons. He did so, trying a number of rather menial positions until he discovered that he liked retail sales, working first as Christmas help when he was off of his school position. He applied for management training with the firm, took a leave of absence at the proper time (from teaching), and went on to work through a series of training and management seminars in the retail sales field. It was something that he had never mustered the courage to do until his sobriety. In recovery, he discovered that there was a new joy to doing something different. The Walter Mitty in him burst forth, and he is today still hard at work in management of retail sales. He is happy and feels that he is reaping the rewards of being sober in quite a different way than he had ever imagined!

Before you can determine whether you are interested in trying different work, it's a good idea to look, in sober fashion, at the work you are doing now. Ask yourself:

"Do I *like* what I'm doing, or is it just a means to earning a paycheck?"

"Do I *look forward* to going to work, or is every day 'Monday' for me?"

"Is there a chance to move up?"

"Do I find myself getting bored easily?"

"Are all of my potential talents really being used with this job?"

These are all questions that may not have even mattered when you were an active drinker. As long as the money arrived when it was supposed to, and as long as you were "getting by," that may have been good enough. In sobriety you begin to question a good many things about what your life is all about, where you are now, and where you want to be in the near future. So, take a little time and *be honest* about your present job. If it is not meeting some personal needs as well as just the basics of life that any employment provides, then you are going to find the winds of dissatisfaction blowing more steadily around you!

You can help yourself establish some criteria for your job satisfaction by making a list of what you think are your best qualities, those things that make an employer interested in you. It's equally important to your joy in being sober to make a list of the qualities that you think are *lacking*. Come on, now! Be open and honest with yourself! Many times in therapy sessions I will ask a client to bring in such a list. It is to be marked, "Ten things I *dislike* about myself." Easy enough. But when I say, "I also want you to bring in a list of ten things you *like* about yourself," then there is hesitation. A good many people won't have any trouble in lambasting themselves. I've had lists come back to me that numbered well into the fifteen, twenty, and even twenty-five item category. When I ask for the list of ten "likable" traits, I've been handed as few as three or four. That's fairly typical of the low self-esteem a recovering person can hold about themselves. There is so much guilt, anger, and shame around the alcohol issues that it comes through as a portrait of "poor, pitiful Pearl."

In sobriety, you have the ability to re-examine those lists. You can begin with job qualifications that are perhaps basic to your line of work. Typing speed, shorthand, drafting, accounting, writing abilities are some of the examples. Then go to other more personal skills you possess.

"Have good dress ability."

"I am punctual."

"I get along well with most people," are all items that could well be on your list. Don't forget to add to *every* list, "I don't drink!" That's something to be proud of, and one that should be a constant pleasure to see on anyone's list of job qualifications.

Examine the technical skills you have, but perhaps have not used just because your present job may not have called for them. How many times have you seen a particular piece of work come by your desk or pass through your hands and have found yourself muttering, "I could do a *better* job of that!" We tend to bury our talents to fit the needs of what we are doing at the present. This is particularly true when we are given a job that was not quite applied to the particular skills we possess.

Oftentimes we apply for a job, find that it is not available "at the moment" but discover "there is an opening" in another department. We take the second-best position in order to meet the needs of having work, salary, and a "foot in the door." However, as alcohol became a more dominant part of your life, you may have never moved out of the "temporary niche" you accepted. The particular job pressures and anxieties of a job you were not really interested in from the beginning became the *reasons* you used as *excuses* for your drinking.

Now, in sobriety you can take a new look at what happened to the job or position for which you *still* have those skills to offer. Your sickness with the disease of alcoholism didn't take your talents away from you; it simply put them on hold, or more correctly, "on ice" (with several ounces of alcohol poured over them!). You can begin the "big thaw" of these talents now that you have your sobriety. Listing all the extra skills you possess, even if they do not apply to an area of your company that you know exists, still gives you a personal and fresh inventory of what you have to offer.

The use of a skilled vocational counselor is very important to the recovering person. These special counselors can and do help you find the untapped reservoirs of your job and career potentials. You can remove many of the job pressures that you find are making you a "nervous wreck" with the aid of a vocational counselor who can help you analyze your skills and your potentials.

Even in your personal listing process, you can examine what skills you have and compare them with what skills are demanded by the job you are performing. Many times you will uncover a pressure area or two in just comparing those lists. A client of mine uncovered just such an area when she found, in making her lists, that more mathematical work was being required than she was capable of handling with comfort. "I could always get by in math," she told me, "but the more responsibility they gave me, the more complicated the damn time sheets, expense and budget records became!" The simple math that she had used wasn't good enough anymore for a job position that she was filling. It was causing an enormous pressure on her to just be able and keep up with the job demands. She attacked the problem with alcohol abuse instead of with honesty-dealing about the job.

In treatment she realized what was allowing her to use those job tensions as excuses for feeding her alcohol habit. In sobriety she was, and still is, able to confront her weaknesses in skills such as math, and exchange that weakness for her company's new use of her long-time talents to write, edit, and oversee the general publication of the company newsletter! This was a fine example, by the way, of an understanding employer who was very supportive of treatment for his employee, and then instrumental in finding better use of her talents in sobriety. He, the employer, knew he had a valuable employee. What he was unaware of was her alcohol abuse until it became painfully obvious. Instead of firing her, he gave her the opportunity to gain her recovery through treatment, saving and insuring his vested years in her as an employee.

The real joy of trying different work is that you are able to let your imaginations soar. You may not be able to pilot a jet plane, but by golly you *might* be able to go to flight school and get the private pilot's license you always wanted. Your sobriety will allow you the use of your faculties again, and you can be freer to look around for more challenging areas of life-work than may have mired you down during active drinking years, or even just months.

Volunteer work, while not adding one bit to the old coffers, is still an area where much of your new-found sobriety can be put to its better uses! The hospitals, fire departments, many civic organizations of your community that are always short-handed, can use the talents you have been keeping in mothballs for so long. If you are in a job position that seems to be okay with you, but is just a little dull, boring, and lacking in excitement, then volunteer work is a great stimulant and method to be used to put a little sparkle back into your life.

Most of our community theatres, dance troupes, and outlying fire departments are composed of people with a little or sometimes a lot of time to channel, in addition to their everyday work jobs, to better enrich their own lives. When you were drinking you scorned this kind of thing. Now that you have your sobriety, these kinds of different work can be a real big booster to you. I have recommended adult tutoring to many recovering alcoholics as a very rewarding method of enjoying and strengthening their own sobriety. There are so many people in your own community that do not possess the basic skills of reading, writing, or arithmetic that prevent them from getting a high school diploma or GED. You can use your own skills in these areas to do a little adult tutoring. It helps the people who are being held back because of the lack of these basics, and it helps you rediscover the joys of leading a sober life where care for others is on an equal footing with the selfish behavior patterns of the active alcoholic.

Many times, the newly sober will have the burst of energy that comes with sobriety to want to get into a new business or start a business for him or herself. There are basic rules to anyone who wants to go into business that certainly must be remembered. The same principles of sound business practices aren't any different for you, but you, the newly sober, need to have some special precautions. It is important that you don't bite off more than you can chew. Your new-found sobriety can be deceiving; you may not possess as much energy as you think you have, and the particular "bounce" you feel in your recovery can plummet to real tiredness and "burnout." Starting a new business requires enormous drains upon your personal energy. You must be able to budget your strength as well as your money!

Another important factor for the recovering person to keep in mind is the tension level that can be dangerously high over personal money. The rule of thumb that says you shouldn't start a business unless you can afford not to have a salary for at least six months and probably even a year, applies even more strongly to you. Money is always a problem in recovery, either from lack of it due to your alcoholic behavior and wild spending, or due to the lack of management of your resources both during your drinking days and during your recovery.

Starting your own business will take not only the usual "start-up" monies but many hidden extras you may not have considered. All of these drains on your money will lead to pressure, tension, and a lot of anxiety. Your recovery will not be immune to these pressures, and your sobriety can be threatened if you let the situation get out of hand. A good rule of thumb for the newly sober is, "Try to not make *any* major changes in career or other personal matters for at least six months of your sobriety." That's not going to work all the time, obviously. You may have lost a job, a marriage, a place to live. Changes will then have to be made. But if you can avoid things that will force you to jump "from the frying pan to the fire," it will be better insurance for your long-term recovery.

Starting a new business may appeal to your vanity; it may also be the lure of the siren, and could be the disaster that's just waiting for you! Much needed counsel from all your resources is highly recommended before you, in your recovery, jump in to those kinds of pressures that are natural heir to starting and operating a new business. Remember that in this area, as in all others we have talked about, your Number One Priority Every day ("NOPE" for short) is *your sobriety!* All else must pale and all else must be relegated to minor positions after that first and foremost endeavor, sobriety. A new business starting up can be the realization of all your many hopes and dreams for the future, dreams that were blocked for so long by alcohol abuse. But starting that new business can also dash you quickly against the rocks of financial and personal ruin and possibly back into the sea of despair where alcohol use and again, *abuse,* becomes the desperate driftwood you reach out to cling to, hoping against hope not to sink again to the bottom! Take it easy! Approach the idea of new work, new businesses, and new careers with the challenges they afford, but also with the knowledge that your strengths and weaknesses will *no longer be masked by alcohol,* nor will alcohol be able to enhance and build up what really isn't there! So move with caution. The finding of different work and the challenges of relocating your career and redefining your life's work are exciting! They can be the elixir of the new life that you are choosing to lead, one day at a time.

For the newly sober, the joys are all around you — at the desk where you spend your working days, at the drawing boards, the production lines, in the fields, or in the barracks. It doesn't matter what you do *now,* the joy of being sober can open the doors to endless possibilities for your future, if you are courageous and strong and honest in your risk-taking. Doing different work does not have to be radical surgery to what you are now doing. It can be the topping on your ice cream, or it can be the new main meals of your sober life. In recovery, all things are possible for you, where in the grips of your disease of alcoholism, very little was possible except existing. Mere existence is not good enough for you anymore! Look around you and explore the ways that your talents, abilities, and ambitions can be harnessed into the new energy of your sober life!

For Satan finds some mischief still /
For Idle hands to do

Isaac Watts

19
The New Importance
of Hobbies

You've got some idle time on your hands, now that you're sober. Now, wait; don't protest too much! If nothing else, you have time available that you used to spend sitting on a bar stool, or parked in front of the tube, "pigging out" on chips n' suds or whatever your particular drink happened to be.

You have idle time. The purpose of this chapter is to get you started on trying to take up a creative hobby of some kind that will do some important things for your recovery. What things? Well, for one, starting and *completing* a hobby project will be a positive reinforcement that you have begun the sobering process. When you were drinking, you may have started a half dozen or more projects. Oh, you *started* them all right, but how many of them every got finished? In sobriety, you will *want* to finish what you start! Another strong point for hobby-in-recovery therapy is the regaining of skills, or the finding of hidden talents and skills that have lain dormant because alcohol was the dominant thing for your leisure time activity.

Before, you probably were among those who scorned people who did things like work with stamp or coin collections, or rose gardens, workshops, or paint brushes and oils. You *need* those things now, as a stepping stone back to the world of the joyful recovering! So, here

198

are a few new tools that are designed to help you take another look at the new importance of hobbies in your life.

FRUSTRATION LEVELS

Perhaps one of the biggest stumbling blocks to the new hobbyist is frustration. It may have been just downright discouraging for you to try a particular hobby, because your frustration level got too high for you to cope with; so you tossed the work aside and snapped the cap on another can of beer. Your sobriety isn't going to increase your tolerance for frustration. As a matter of fact, you might be a little more on the "short fuse" side of things, because you no longer have alcohol to temporarily ease your anxiety and stress. So the kind of hobby you choose is going to be important.

To accommodate the fact that you might get easily discouraged, thus leading to frustration, I suggest you pick a hobby that does *not* have a seasonal time deadline. For example, if you have decided to try hooking or latching a rug, don't begin by saying, "This will be just perfect for Amy for Christmas!" Buying the materials and starting work on the project is okay, but forget pushing yourself into a corner around the deadline; it will become an unspoken frustration builder, and as the days get closer to the holiday, the more you will feel that every little mistake is setting you back from having the project completed in time for gifting.

So, avoid the time deadline, at least until you have done a few projects that contribute to your feeling okay about increasing the pressure on yourself a little. Another frustration builder is tackling something *much too complex* for your new sober self. I think of the many electronic projects that are on the market, enticing kits for stereo, television sets, and home computers. These, even in their most simplified "easy to follow" directions can be real frustration projects. You will invest a pretty sizable amount of money and then find yourself getting more uptight at the project than the good you are supposed to derive from the hobby.

Make your first project a simple one, maybe something that doesn't require constant attention, something you can put down for several days and then pick up where you left off without getting "bent out of shape" over where you're supposed to be in the project. To help you do this "put-down-and-pick-up" stroke, get in the habit of keeping a small note pad and pencil with your project. When you are ready to quit for the day, take a few minutes and write a simple note to yourself that says, "Begin with section two (whatever), on page seven (whatever)." *Attach* the note to the top of your work. It will help you get back in the mood of the project quickly, and will enable you to see that you have already made a good start.

This note writing will work with any hobby, even collecting. If it's gardening you're doing, put the note on your potting stand or tuck it in the cuff of your gloves. If you will keep the notes you write from day to day you will have *visible proof* that you are making progress in your project and that becomes a good road map for your recovery!

Another element to help you deal with frustration-level control is to try to share your work with a special person in your life. Whatever little progress you have made will be helped by him or her commending the steps you have already accomplished. I particularly think of my own work with oil painting. The work seemed to go so slowly that my own frustration levels built very high; a work in progress shown to a friend was helped considerably when he suggested switching from oil to acrylics. They would allow me to finish a section of a painting, go back over it, and make corrections if necessary, and still see some real progression in the painting. Struggling with the long-drying oils, and not being able to hurry the work was only contributing to my need to get something done that could not have been done in drinking days. My friend's comment and praise, and his suggestion to switch mediums, helped my frustration level to go lower.

I'm not dealing with the merits of "hurrying" through a project; for the person who is new in recovery, it's probably more important to start and *complete* something than it is to make a lasting contribution to the art world! Before you select a hobby to start, make careful consideration of how much frustration the project may impose on your still fragile temperament. With that in mind; here is the second tool:

PICK SOMETHING FAMILIAR

There is a very real foundation for your sobriety that can be built by picking up a hobby that you have tried to do before. In your active drinking days you may have completed many projects of a particular hobby, and thought they were as good as possible. Now, in sobriety, you've a chance to go back and do a thing *really well*; to show yourself that what you did before was not really your best effort at all. Many times I have looked through the "mistake box" in my workshop and wondered if many of the items I completed wouldn't have been better off staying in that box instead of being hustled out of the shop. In sobriety, my work is cleaner, more finished, more polished, and thus, shows more loving care and attention to detail than work done before. Your returning to a familiar hobby will give you the same or better satisfaction. There is no need for you to apologize for work you did before, it still was a good effort; what you will see in the *new work,* however, will be the result of an alcohol-free mind and body working in harmony to utilize your talents to their fullest.

A client of ours once shared with his group about going back to "paint-by-number" kits only to discover that about half of the time he had ignored the numbers called for in the painting; this was in his drinking days. He only discovered this because he decided to repeat a picture he had done before. He was convinced the kit manufacturer had made a mistake calling for the wrong numbers until he dug out the "old" painting and started comparing. This revelation of how his drinking had confused his brain was a graphic example of what his recovery was doing for him, and one that has continued to play an important role in this client's unwillingness to ever return to those "befuddled" days!

Another person, new in recovery, went back to her stamp collection to find that in the last few weeks of her active alcoholic days she had nearly ruined an entire book of stamps by placing her new acquisitions on the wrong pages! "They looked like the right spot when I did them!" she told me. "But when I hauled the books out again after starting my recovery, I found out all the places I had screwed up!" For her, and for you, returning to a familiar hobby will give you "on-site" inspection and comparisons of the "then" and "now" phases of your new life!

LEARNING SAFETY AGAIN

Here is a tool that applies to almost every hobby you start or pick up where power tools or mechanical devices of any kind are used in the project. When you were drinking, you became careless in the use of basic things like safety goggles, gloves, or proper electrical connections. I have seen so many people who, while drinking, became so overconfident in their supposed "mastery" of a particular tool that they abandoned all the precautions and almost lost fingers over it!

In your new sobriety, you need to start again just as if you were picking up the machinery or tools for the first time. You may feel a little "scary" about handling a large router or running stock through a jointer or table saw. You may be leery about handling even the smallest soldering pencil or sewing machine in the same free-wheeling manner that alcohol permitted you in the past. It may have been "free-wheeling," but it was also dangerous!

A good rule of thumb is to treat your hobby as if you didn't know very much about it and were trying to learn how to operate the particular tool for the first time. Another good method to help your safety reminder is to try to teach the use of the tool to someone else. In going over the basic things you want to show someone to protect *them,* you will reinforce their importance to your *own* safety.

You will not feel much joy in being sober if you seriously injure yourself by going back to the old habits you used when operating dangerous machinery while you were drinking. If you think your sewing machine is not dangerous, then think again! A lady told me that when she was an active drinker she got in the habit of making certain "high-speed long-run" stitches while watching her favorite television show. She would have her glass of vodka and the TV both close at hand. Once, during her operation of a fast row of sewing on her machine, she reached for her glass, did not take her foot off the treadle and sewed several painful stitches into the edge of her index finger.

"It seemed to me," she said, "as if I told myself to take my foot off the treadle, but thought at the time that I could do the job with one hand and still get my vodka with the other; so why stop the machine?" The lady was afraid to go back to her machine for awhile, even in recovery, because she was afraid she would "do something else stupid!" Alcohol affects the brain and the motor functions that are harnessed to your brain. Your sobriety puts you in control once again of what you do and how you do it; therefore, remember that safety first is more important than ever before. You need to *think* before you act, and then *act* with caution because you no longer have the crutch of alcohol to cover for your mistakes — mistakes that could cost you an eye or a limb. Your use of alcohol made you careless and befuddled the basic thinking that helps us protect ourselves from danger. You will need to reinstill the basic regard for safety that you ignored in the past!

SHARING CRAFT GIFTS

The new importance of hobbies for you is to be able to share with others the fruits of your new-found sobriety. One of the best ways to gain this foothold on a long-lasting recovery is to be able to put your hobby to good use, making gifts and giving them away to family and friends.

This may seem in direct contradiction to my earlier caution to let holiday deadlines go by the way to remove pressure, but it's not, really. The beauty of your making gifts is to build a little storehouse of things.

You don't have to wait for a special day. It's a lot better if you don't. I always like the Lewis Carroll concept of celebrating an "un-Birthday" better! So will you. The importance for your recovery is to make your gifts and then give them away as you see fit, regardless of whether it is a Christmas, birthday, or graduation gift. The receivers will be flattered that you will remember them at times not traditional, and you will get the benefits of receiving special attention at a time when gifts are not normally expected. While a Christmas gift you make is certainly appreciated, it may get lost in the pile of other lovely things under someone's tree. A gift that is specifically made and then delivered at *your time* schedule will do a lot for showing yourself that you are making continuing progress in your recovery, and not just getting involved in seasonal sobriety!

Many times I recommend to people that they make a series of gifts to use for their "Twelve Days of Christmas" or the Channuka gifts that we explored in Chapter 15. You have all year to work on these little gifts and then the added joy of giving them up one day at a time. Try it with things like knitting, wood carving, candle making, and lead and stained glass gifting. A recovering friend of mine dragged out his old toy soldier casting materials and spent many happy hours making new soldiers for giving away on the "Twelve Days." He was sober now and could spend the time necessary to do the intricate painting and hand finishing that he had let go by the boards for so many years of his active drinking. He told me of the great joy he had from hearing from nephews and other children he remembered with these handcrafted articles. His joy was twofold; he had weeks of fun making the gifts, and added days of fun giving them away!

Photographs that you have made, perhaps mounted on a piece of wood and then "decoupaged," can be worked on all year. Put them in your storehouse and when a particular "non-occasion" occurs to you, send the gift. Enclose a card that says, "My joy in being sober needed to be shared with you! Hope you like this remembrance of _____." You can think of more appropriate things you want to say, but the point is to *say* them! Let the gift you have made and then shared speak out loud and clear for your sobriety!

FINISHING YOUR PROJECT

Here is one of the biggest changes that you are going to have to work on yourself. In your alcoholic days you started many, many things, but the chances are, you didn't finish very many. I can't count the times I've heard people in group therapy tell about the projects that they always started and never finished! Of course the difference now is that you *can* and *will* finish what you start.

In order to help you over this hurdle, I suggest that you limit yourself to only one project at a time. Now this may be foolish to say if the project is, for example, "creative baking." Many women (and quite a few men) I know in recovery, like to bake bread and give it for special occasions. Well, it certainly doesn't make sense to make up just one loaf of bread. I know that! What I do suggest is that you confine the project to meeting the needs of just one person. If it means that you are going to bake two or three Christmas loaves and some cookies for one particular person or family, then do that; forget about trying to bake for six or seven! Six or seven different households, that is.

Limit what you do until you are back to establishing a solid "track record" for finishing what you start. Here, again, your frustration levels can be held in check; you can utilize your "one day at a time" philosophy into "one project, *completed,* at a time!"

It's perfectly natural to want to bite off more than you can chew. You feel so much better in recovery and you have more time to spend, that you fool yourself into thinking that you also have an unlimited energy bank from which to draw. That's not quite so; you will find yourself starting a bunch of craft or hobby projects and then "burnout" will strike, and you will end up with a lot of uncompleted half-done things sitting around making you angry!

Better to always put the reins on your activities and use the moderation in sobriety that you never experienced in your drinking days. A good tool for you to use to retrain yourself into finishing what you start is to *go back* and complete something you started when you were actively alcoholic. You may very well make the decision that the project is no longer worthy of completion. In that case, destroy it and clean out the memories that went with it, memories that were closely tied to your abuse of the chemical, alcohol.

A female client recently told me that she had gone back and totally torn out a large piece of crochet that she had never finished, but had started in her drinking heydays. Now, she is starting all over and finding great joy and satisfaction in "doing the thing right." The "mistake box" in my workshop is further evidence of the good therapeutic value of this line of thinking. More unfinished projects have found their way to the neighbors' fireplaces, so that new starts and more important, fresh *finishes* can be made!

Alcoholic thinking and behavior tend to make you believe that your judgement is invincible and therefore the alcoholic will continue to bite off much more than can be chewed. Better to start and finish one small project to build a new base of confidence in what your sober behavior patterns can be like, than to start another whole mass and *mess* of things that will go unfinished also!

A recovering friend has been working for months on building his own house, a job he freely admits would have been impossible during his drinking days. At first, however, he had the same old habits carried over from drinking to recovery; namely, hurry up and buy all the materials all at once and then let everything sit there because the project became overwhelming. He realized that he was back into the confetti thinking of his drinking days, so he began to stop buying, no matter how good the "bargains" were, and began finishing what he had started. "It's amazing," he told me recently, "that house is really coming along, now that I'm not trying to be Superman with it!"

It's kind of like the army phrase that appeared in so many mess tents worldwide during World War II (along with a lot of others not printable!). The slogan said, "*Take* all you want, but *eat* all you take!"

Do all the projects you want in your recovery, but do them one at a time, and complete *one* before starting another. That's the way of sobriety!

HAVING HOBBY SPACE

I don't care how small an apartment or even a room you have. It is essential that you have one little place where your hobby or project and crafting can be done that doesn't have to be picked up after every hour spent working at it! If you are in to model building, or puzzle working, then you know the frustration of having to stop and "clean up the mess." A lot of really great picture puzzles never get tackled because you haven't assigned a space where the thing can be left alone until you finish it.

Nothing is more discouraging than having to spend more time in picking up and putting away than in working on the hobby in the first place. This isn't always possible, of course, but wherever you can, assign yourself a working space that can remain undisturbed. The reasons for this are many, but I like the idea of being able to sit down for fifteen minutes or so and work at my project, maybe while I'm waiting to go somewhere, or before I have to leave for our treatment center. If there isn't a spot where I can sit down and draw a line or two, solder a part, drive a screw, or put a part into the wood clamps, I will soon lose interest in ever working on the project!

Look around your place and see where some unutilized corner or table top can be "commandeered" by you for a hobby spot. Of course you won't want to leave out valuable coins or stamps if that is your hobby, but you may want to have a spot where model building, ceramics, jewelry making, and other craft projects can basically be left undisturbed. Small children in the house will, of course, dictate different "security" measures, but if you put your mind to work, you will come up with something.

One woman I know found a very unusual spot to work on her knitting while insuring that she would be left alone and not have to do much "pick-up-put-away." Here's what Nancy did. She had several toddlers in her house and, of course, they had all used the playpen in their room. When her boys were able to crawl around and play more with each other than requiring her immediate attention, Nancy put the boys on the floor in the room with their various books, toys, and other amusements. Then *she* climbed into the playpen to knit! I thought it was the greatest thing I'd ever seen. She had her knitting in one easy-to-carry box, and all she had to do was haul that box in the playpen with her! It was her space to work on her hobby, and I have laughed about it every time I hear of some client who feels trapped by her small children and can't find "anyplace" to work on her hobby! I'd be afraid to take a count of how many times I've passed along this unique tool that Nancy first brought to my attention. Go to it! Find your own "playpen" and dare anyone to mess around with your hobby space!

HOW MUCH TO SPEND

If you are faced with the desire to want to start a new hobby but also have been trudging around from store to store or craft classes for days, you are perhaps feeling frightened by the cost of materials. The days of cheap leather, beads, balsa wood, lead, and glass are long gone, but here's one quick and easy way to help your spending. Go back as best you can and add up the amount of money you were spending on your drinking habit.

Be honest! Count the times you stopped in to the favorite bar and "set up" a round or two, left a tip, etc. Look in your checkbook (if you still have the old one) and see how many checks you wrote for liquor. Look back on credit card charges made at liquor stores or restaurants where the bar charges are "broken out" on the bill. *Then,* if you spend just *half* that amount on your new hobby, you will be in "fat city." It didn't seem like much when you were doing it, but you were probably spending an easy $20 dollars or more when you stopped at the bar or the liquor store. If you did this just twice a week, you can see how much money you can now afford to spend on a hobby; spend on something that can help your long-term recovery as opposed to contributing toward an early death.

Finally, make your hobbies the kinds of things that speak openly of your new wellness. Fine art work that requires steady hands and a sound mind shouts loudly that you are gaining control of your life in sobriety. A neatly organized stamp page or cleanly typed or cleverly decorated set of recipe cards and boxes show you and your immediate world that you are living a life of sober-satisfaction. Before, the idea of hobbies was just something that could possibly threaten your drinking time. Now, hobbies assume a new importance, not just as dreamed-up therapy, but as real, solid methods that can make you feel good about yourself again, and can demonstrate to all your new joy in being sober. Go forth and create!

Be sober, be vigilant; because your adversary the devil, as a roaring lion, walketh about seeking whom he may devour.

1 Peter (5:8) The Holy Bible

20
Staying Sober

So here we are, poised on the end of the diving board of your new recovery. Shall we take the plunge? For the past nineteen chapters I have been sharing tools, methods, and ways that help the newly sober person face and *enjoy* life without alcohol. This is the Joy Of Being Sober! To witness each day of your life as a new experience to be *lived*, not just tolerated. To know that you will be in control of yourself, what you say, what you do, and how you feel and react to what others do and say.

That's a new and wonderful experience. To *know* what's going on in this life and being a part of it instead of an observer, watching events through an alcoholic fog of unreality, uncaring, and unknowing behavior that are all facets of your past. That's behind you now, and the challenges ahead are those that will want to keep you sober, that will keep you making your sobriety the number one priority in your life.

To do this, here are the final set of tools that I lay before you. Like all of the others, these tools can sit within the pages of this book and never find their way into your daily living pattern. Or, they can be internalized and *used* as a regular part of your lifelong recovery program. I call them the Three "Rs" of Recovery:

208

1. Remember
2. Reinforce
3. Renew

That's easy enough, isn't it? As you go along in your recovery you will be able to add many more words that will trigger behavior modes to help you maintain and add to your sobriety. But for now, these are the basic three "Rs" that I have used with myself and with others in recovery.

REMEMBER

The first of the Three "Rs" is to Remember; remember how it *was* and by remembering, compare how it *is*. There will be many instances in your daily life where you will observe other people and their behavior when they are drinking. The key is to remember that persons not afflicted with the disease of alcoholism can do things with alcohol that you can't. For openers they can *quit*. When someone says, "Have another?" the non-alcoholic can comfortably say, "No, thanks. I've had enough!" Now, there's no way that you could respond like that; you are an alcoholic and you will drink as long as there is anything *to* drink. Not *now*, of course, because you are sober and in recovery, but you can *remember* and share with someone that you used to behave in such and such a way.

Remembering is not an effort to keep you nailed to the cross, which we spoke of in Chapter 5. It is a tool to make comparisons about how alcoholic behavior and sober behavior are different — how the two worlds that you have lived in are different and how you are *enjoying* the difference.

AA meetings are the best source of remember-sharing that you will be able to count on as long as you live. But you can also do this work with the significant other in your life, with the companion you may be with when a particular incident occurs that causes you to think back on your past life.

Using the past can also be painful, but growing is painful, and many times the very fact that you can remember an episode in which drinking was a particularly heavy disaster for you works to your advantage in recovery. The people around you who have cared about your recovery will oftentimes think of an episode and be afraid to share it, afraid that it might be too painful. You can encourage their telling you about the memory by saying, "It's okay. I'm strong enough to hear. I *need* to hear about my behavior so I can compare!"

The thing that will amaze you is that you have been totally unaware of much of your past behavior. The alcoholic amnesia, the "blackouts," may have wiped away many things that other people remember as clearly as if they just happened. Then you will be someplace and observe a particular behavior that will trigger a memory. Explore it! Make it work for you! It was a different person that acted how you did when alcohol was the master in life, and you the slave. That's all changed now, and it's part of the message of recovery to say, "It's *okay* to remember the past!"

Use the "R" of Remembering always in the context of a follow-up. If you are remembering a bad episode, ask for help from your companion who is remembering with you. Say something on the order of, "After *that,* what happened? What did I do?" When you have heard the entire memory, then follow through with citing a recent experience where circumstances (a party, for example) were the same, but your behavior was different. This retelling will counteract the bad memory and replace it with new, positive behavior.

Everyone knows that it's easier to forgive than to forget, but you, the newly sober, need to be willing to do both. You can first of all forgive your behavior because alcohol was calling your every move. You can then begin the process of *forgetting* the pain by *remembering* the incident, talking about it, and *sharing* it with another.

Most people will need encouragement from you to do the memory work with you. They may see something that reminds them of how you *were;* they start to chuckle, or say, "Do you . . ." then stop short, fearing that it will all be too painful. You need to encourage them to go ahead and say what's on their mind, that if it's about you and your past behavior you *need* to know, that it will strengthen your recovery.

The need for you to remember will also help tie together many missing links in your past life that were conveniently submerged in booze. Sure, there will be some pain, maybe even some tears at remembering. But the self-therapy provided will outweigh a raft of "stuffing" that you may have been in the habit of doing. Remembering just naturally leads us to the Second "R":

REINFORCE

Whenever a client tells me that they have had a particularly moving experience in their new life, I urge them to recount the details so they can fix things firmly in their mind — that *drinking* behavior prevented the good happenings that *sober* behavior provides.

To reinforce that sobriety, I then ask them how they would have acted when they were drinking in a similar circumstance, repeating the exact same set of details of the incident. Then, together, we explore how *sober* behavior far surpasses the old, alcoholic ways. You do the same every time you make comparisons. What you do is build in the good strokes, turn them into "Warm Fuzzies" for yourself, and then compare them to past behavior, thus *Reinforcing* your desire to remain alcohol-free for the rest of your life.

When a particular accomplishment is made, you need to say to yourself, "Could I have done this if I were drinking?" It's always better to share out loud, to verbalize. But if there is no one around and you are some time away from a meeting or group therapy session where you can share with others, then go ahead and ask yourself. This reinforcement has to work for you because the answers are most generally positive. I recall a recovering person who used to take great pride in telling people that "I never got so drunk that I'd fall down in public, like that guy!" What this person had conveniently filed away in his alcoholic memory bank was that he knew and remembered just *part* of the story. While it was true that he didn't make a "public spectacle" of himself, his wife started recalling incidents of his getting up in the middle of the night and taking horrendous falls! He would have great bruises on his arms and legs and not know where they came from.

Together, this couple began using the Second "R" to reinforce his new, sober behavior. It became a game for them, and one they openly shared with their friends. It went like this: he would see some poor fellow having to be helped up from the floor of a party or restaurant. Our recovering friend would start the process by saying, "Boy, that's *one* thing I never did when I was drinking!" Then his wife would pick up her cue by saying, "No, Charlie, you sure didn't, but tell (them) what you *did* do!" Charlie then began his reinforcement procedure by relating that he has been told that he would fall and stumble, hurting himself quite badly sometimes. His wife told me that "Charlie" would always add, "Thank God I don't have to do *that,* anymore!" And she would always add, "Nor explain where those awful bruises came from!"

The reinforcement tool was deftly used in its final form when the couple would tell that "Charlie's" disease wiped out the memories of those incidents, that seeing the person they were watching being helped from the floor only made their *dual* commitment to the new life of recovery and sobriety that much stronger. It's a good tool, this Second "R," and there are almost no limits to how it can be used. The person who could never drive himself home (thank God they didn't let him try!) or the person who could not handle a particular task because of alcohol impairment, can reinforce their new sobriety and their commitment to recovery every time they have the chance. Encourage others in your life to help you use the Second "R." Give them every opportunity to hand out the strokes that you need to hear, the positive results of your life without alcohol. Simple things like being able to thread a needle (you used to shake too badly to do it!), hitting a tennis ball *over* the net, riding a bicycle, or mowing the lawn in a *straight* path, all simple little everyday tasks that many people take for granted.

You should never take anything for granted. You have had the help of many people and the God of your understanding to bring you to this path of recovery. Everything that other people take for granted, you can take for all it's worth! Use everyday challenges as methods to reinforce the difference between the *good* life and the dismal, depressing, frantic life of the sick alcoholic.

Reinforce your own good behavior patterns by *repeating* them. Don't try a task just once and then, knowing you can perform it, give it up. Do it consistently so that it will become firmly implanted in your system that it is your sobriety and recovery that is enabling you to perform whatever the task may be.

You may drive people nuts for awhile, but keep telling them, "I *need* to hear that!" or, "Thanks for telling me that. It's very important that I hear the differences in my life!" Reinforce your program by visiting the hospitals and the de-tox wards on a more regular basis; see the other people who are just maybe beginning their painful steps toward recovery and *remember* where you *were;* then *reinforce* how far you have *come.*

When compliments are given you, accept them graciously but always tie it in to your recovery as added reinforcement for sobriety. You've "lost weight," says someone. You thank them and add, "That old booze was adding a lot of extra calories!" Be open and forthright. The person you are reinforcing is yourself, and you need all the help you can get. When other people seem embarrassed to mention some facet of your past behavior, you help them out and turn it into a reinforcement. "That's the way it was!" is more to you than just the familiar sign-off used by Walter Cronkite. You be the first to acknowledge that is how it was, and quickly follow it with how it is in your life, *now.* Don't let even one opportunity to reinforce yourself pass you by. Look at old photographs of yourself taken when you were drinking. Then either look at a recent photograph, take new ones, or just hold the old photo up beside a mirror and note the difference!

No more puffy eyes; no more yellow ones, but nice and clear and white. No excess jowels that made you look like "Miss Piggy" even when you were starving yourself with everything except alcohol. All of these positive reinforcements are necessary for you to maintain sobriety and continue to build your solid program of recovery.

RENEW

These last of my three "Rs" is my favorite for staying sober for all who are working at their personal program of recovery. Renew yourself in both spirit and body — every chance you get. We have already dwelled on the importance of spiritual activities for the recovering person. Your regular attendance at the church or temple of your choice, your willing participation in some form of worship can be a beacon in your new way of life. The regular attendance and active use of the fellowship of AA is a proven method of continued sobriety. It's there for you to use as a renewal tool for both mind and spirit. All you have to do is make the effort to get there; make the effort to *call* someone to get you to a meeting! The "R" of Renewal for your physical well-being is the most tangible evidence that you are beginning to be a new person. Your recovery is allowing you to *feel* again, to know the firm grip of a golf club in your hands, the pedals of a bike beneath your feet, the walks in the park, and the sting of snow on your lashes as you breathe in the fresh, clean air of a winter's day.

Every ounce of weight that comes off your body is another plus for the tool of renewal. You are being given the opportunity to *build* again and again the very thing (your body) that you spent so long in tearing down. You know the feeling of how food tastes differently in your sober state, how your energy levels build slowly but steadily until you actually get kind of paranoid if you can't *do* something!

Even if you are confined to wheelchair or crutches, your life is better without alcohol. You must never give up on the fact that you have taken certain steps to intervene in the process that was destroying you even more than whatever tragedy has already committed you to a less than active and mobile life.

For each of you, for every person who has made the steps toward a life of recovery, there is the spectre that it can all be wiped out with the return to the drinking arena that once was your life. It will require every support tool and every system of personal recovery that you can muster for the rest of your life to continue to enjoy the fruits of sobriety. You *can* and *will* do it! The tools we have examined together within this book are there for the taking every time. There are others, and you will learn them as you wend your way along the sober path.

The Joy Of Being Sober is a personal joy. It is a breath of a second life that requires your every effort to the maximum level to sustain you at times when you believe that there will be no hope, when the pressures of the disease that will always be with you become so strong that you believe you will cave in like swollen banks of a river!

But I believe you will not! If you are secure in the knowledge that to drink is to die, that to remain sober is to live, then you will have the very essence of life itself. No matter what befalls you in the way of personal trials and tribulations, return to alcohol is *not* the answer! Your personal program of recovery will gain strength with every shared moment with other recovering people, with every group and meeting in which you take an active part, with every hand you extend to the other unfortunates that are afflicted with this disease.

This is not the end but the start of your attempt to savor the *real* stuff of recovery. And it is more than ever up to you, personally, to pick up your life and carry on with the resolve that you will never again turn to alcohol as a method of attempting to cope with life. For you and for millions of others who have discovered it, there is a special Joy Of Being Sober. It is a joy I share gladly with you no matter who you are or where you may live. It is a force more positive than any "kick" received from champagne or any other alcoholic beverage. You know it's there; use it! Let it fly away from you with great abandon! You are earning it every day you draw breath. It is yours for the taking, this joy, this Joy Of Being Sober!